BUFFALO
MEMORIES

GONE BUT NOT FORGOTTEN

∾ stories by ∾
George Kunz
1923 – 1995

Canisius COLLEGE
Where leaders are made
Canisius College Press

For more information, contact:
Canisius College Press
2001 Main Street
Buffalo, NY 14208

Publisher: Joseph F. Bieron

Library of Congress
Catalog Card number pending

Layout Design: Anne-Marie Dobies
Copy Assistants: Stephanie Soehnlein
                 Andrew Campbell
Photos/Artwork: The Buffalo News/
                 Private Collection of George Kunz

ISBN 0-9671480-9-X
Printed in the United States of America

Photos and artwork are in large part from the Archives of the Buffalo News or scanned from the original newspaper articles that resulted in the less-defined reproduction.

TABLE OF
CONTENTS

Shelton Square Was Buffalo's Piccadilly Circus ... 1
Modern Bisons Stir Up Memories Of Those Of Half A Century Ago ... 3
The Year They Turned Off Niagara Falls ... 5
Those Coal Furnaces Did Strange Things To People ... 7
Preserving A Part Of Our Past ... 9
Trolley's Revenge Is Now Running On Main Street ... 11
A Game That Eased Great Depression ... 13
Good Old Days At 998 Broadway ... 15
Vaudeville Days Live Again In Mike Shea's Scrapbook ... 17
The Golden Years Of Buffalo Beers ... 21
Pierce Arrow Lives On In Legend ... 23
Buffalo Was Center Of The Universe the Day
    The Peace Bridge Was Dedicated ... 25
Spooning in a Canoe To The Crooning Of Crosby In Days Of Old ... 27
Al Smith, The Happy Warrior ... 29
FDR Inspired A Sense Of Hope ... 31
The Day That Beer Flowed Again ... 33
The Short Glorious Reign Of The Tomato ... 35
Festival '85 ... 37
Humble Music Hall Attracted The World's Top Entertainers ... 39
Reviving High School Diplomas ... 41
Old-Fashioned Fourth Sounded Like A Battlefield ... 43
The Priest Who Played Politics ... 49
The Old Days Of The Trolley Plows ... 51
Old Downtown Library Had Style ... 53
Days Of Downtown Movie Palaces ... 55
A Monster Living In The Basement ... 57
A Dimension Of Life Revolved Around The Icebox ... 59
Spidery Old Ferryboat Spun Warm Memories ... 61
Opener Conjures Memories ... 63
3rd Grader Learns A Lesson About Love On Valentine's Day ... 65
The Cyclone Was The Terror Of The Midway ... 67
Will Reagan Pull A Coolidge Stunt? ... 69
'36 St. Patrick's Day Storm Didn't Faze Irish Revelers ... 71
The DL&W Rail Terminal Was A Scene Of Classical Splendor ... 73
Legendary Days At Lewiston Hill ... 75
Life Before the Ball-Point Pen Was Often A Messy Business ... 77

I

The Card That Left Its Mark   79
The Day That Buffalonians Had A Darkness At Noon   81
When the City Ran On Horse Power   83
Transportation Goes Backward   85
Memories of A New Year's Eve In Buffalo At Turn Of Century   86
Even Castro Has Stopped Smoking   89
The Great Fire at Old St. Michael's   91
End Of Era Of The Great Dirigibles   93
Interurban Rapid Rail System Once A Reality On Frontier   95
At Gas Stations Of Yesteryear Pumps Had Personality   97
Life Cycle Of The Inner-Tube Tire   99
Back-To-School And The Radio Serials Cure   101
The Iceman Came And Went   103
Buffalo's Role In 100 Years Of Holmes   105
Palmer Method Dominated Age Of Beautiful Handwriting   109
The Legendary Telegraph Boys Often Bore Fateful Messages   111
The Old Lehigh Valley Terminal Was A Railroad Palace   113
Deco Eateries Had A Special Aura   115
The Old Post Office Came Alive Every Year For Christmas Season   117
Tickets Recall Glitter Of Erlanger Opening   119
Classy Columns Adorning UB Lake Came From Buffalo Bank   121
Buffalo Was Ravaged By Deadly Flu Epidemic of 1918   123
The Day the Spirit Of St. Louis Came To Buffalo   125
I'm Gonna Sit Write Down And Grammerize   127
In Days Gone By When Movies Were Innocent   129
The Day I Saved A Maiden From Distress   131
In the Days Of The Fruit Express   133
Wrong-Way Corrigan Was A Hero in Buffalo   135
Showbiz Greats Trod Boards Of The Old Teck   137
A Yankee Gets An Earful In Ottowa   139
Paradise For 10 cents: Shea's Matinees   141
He Just Missed Seeing Bridge Fall   143
When the Front Porch Was A Hive Of Summer Activities   144
On Sunday Evenings When Radio Ruled The Living Room   145
Lords Of The Sidewalks In Those Days Gone By   147
The Aging Of Peter Pan   149
In the Days Of The Itinerant Popcorn Man   151
When Milk Came In Bottles And Was Delivered To The Home   153
In the Days When Women Slaved Over A Flatiron   155
New Year's 1939– In A Different Buffalo   157
The Day A B-25 Hit The Empire State Building   159
Northerners Find Haven In Winter Haven   161
Blue Eagle Was Symbol Of Hope In Hard Times   163
They Don't Make Phone Booths Like They Used To   165
The Year That The Talkie Came To Buffalo   167
A Short But Colorful History Of The Trading Stamp War   169
Ice Skating On Cazenovia Pond In The Old Days Had A Matchless Charm   171

They Still Tell Of The Great Chase To Save A Niagara Gorge Trolley From Disaster 173
Buffalo Bubbled With Revelry on the Eve Of Prohibition 175
Grocery Shopping In The Days Before Supermarkets 177
Band Concerts In The Parks Helped Relieve Depression 179
Maybe The Stanley Steamer Should Have Won Auto Contest 181
The March Of Time Used To Be Measured With Grace And Dignity 183
An Institution Worth Remembering 185
"Scarlet Fever" Used To Get Your House Quarantined 187
Death Of Victrola Was Like Losing Family Member 189
Rudeness Was Just Part Of The Sattler's Shopping Experience 191
Niagara River Stopped Flowing For 30 Hours In 1848 193
Dying Art Of Tying A Parcel With A Piece Of String 195
It Takes More Than A Bullet To Kill A Bull Moose 197
That Old Gang That Used To Hang Out At The Neighborhood Ice Cream Parlor 199
The Day The Second Maid Of The Mist Got Caught In The Whirlpool 201
Dish Night At The Movies Had Shattering Impact 203
Legendary Trolleys That Rumbled Along Main Street 205
How The Ice Age Came To An End In South Buffalo 207
Old Downtown Stores With Winning Personalities 209
Popeye The Sailor Introduced Wealth Of Americana 211
In the Days When Buffalo Had Double-Deck Buses 213
On Blue Monday The Cellar Was A Woman's Dungeon 214
Old Wurlitzer Jukebox Has Lasting Influence 217
Radio Was Born In Buffalo In 1922 And It Burped, Screeched And Sputtered 219
The Proliferation Of 'Blue' Words 221
In Days When Canning Was A Home Industry 223
In Buffalo's Gilded Age, City's Transit Life Centered Around The Trolley Barn 225
When Every Phone Call Went Through Central 227
Home-Brewed Root Beer Was Powerful Stuff 229
Tin Lizzie Wasn't Perfect, But Everybody Loved Her 231
Horse-And-Buggy Rag Man Was The First Recycler 233
Story Behind The Scow Stuck Near Brink of Falls Since 1918 235
Smoke Gets In Your Eyes In Recalling The Big Bands On Radio 237
Back In The Old Days, Nearly Everything Had To Be Cranked 239
Old Downtown Library Seemed Haunted, Spooky – Like A Gothic Romance 241
Greatest of The Money – Grubbing Rail Barons 243
Chippewa Market Gave Flavor To Downtown Buffalo 245
A Sunday Afternoon Drive In The Days When The Auto Was A Gracious Novelty 247
In Remembrance Of Those Who Sat For The Family Photographer In Days Gone By 249
In The Days When The Drugstores Had Character 251
Nothing Like A Ride In Rumble Seat On A Warm Day 253
Fantastic Underwater Vessel That Robert Fulton Tries To Sell To Napolean 255
Can't Blot Out The Memory Of The Fountain Pen 257
Graveyard Of Departed Groceterias Getting Crowded 259
Hollywood Used Buffalo's Main Street To Test 3-D Weapon Against Television 261
The Wooden Matches That Brought Spark Into Our Lives In The Days Gone By 263
The Truth About Orphan Annie's Undercover Organization 265
All The Kids Used To Read Big-Little Books 267

III

There's No Business Like Show Business 268
Thrills, Chills, & Cinnamon Suckers 271
Diners Were The Fashionable Place To Go For 'Eats' During The Great Depression 279
Spring Cleaning In The Old-Fashioned Way 281
J.P. Morgan Tried In Vain To Escape From His Ridiculous Nose 283
The Spirit Of Christmas Presents 285
Dry Days & The Orleans 290
Remembering The Erlanger 293
Coal Dust Memories 297
Name That Town 303
"Number Plee-az" 305
My Private Central Terminal 310
The Shirt Menagerie Fights It Out 313
A German Named Quinn 317
Mary Jo, Sam Schuman And The Hotel Statler Ballroom 321
Splendor At The End Of The Line 328
The Trolley In The Gorge 333
Doo-Doo-Be-Doo In Buff-A-Loe 337
Chance Encounters 342

FOREWORD

*G*eorge Kunz was a sentimental man. I knew that from the time I was little, and so did my brothers and sisters. Dad loved Schubert, Keats, Mendelssohn's "Spring Song," Wagner's "Die Meistersinger," the Gershwin song "Our Love Is Here To Stay."

He also loved Buffalo history. I was a baby when Dad carried me into the old Buffalo and Erie County Public Library in Lafayette Square downtown. The place was doomed to be knocked down to make way for the dated '60s library that still stands on the site today, and Dad was griefstricken over the fate of the old, ornate building he loved. "You were there," he would tell me, years later. "I wanted you to be able to say you were there."

More field trips followed. When my sister Katie and I were tots, Dad walked us onto the Canadiana, better known as "the old Crystal Beach boat." It was due to be scrapped in a matter of days (a fate it was to escape, but we couldn't predict that). We'd heard family fables of Crystal Beach; our favorite was the story of how our grandmother, in the depths of the Depression, had lost her purse in the Old Mill and it had to be fished out by park workers. "You can say you were on the Crystal Beach boat," Dad would remind Katie and me. "I took you on board."

We grew up living and breathing this kind of nostalgia.

We loved to hear about Dad's school days at Holy Family parish in South Buffalo, and how his sister, our nonconformist Auntie Rose, used to fight a girl named Bull Montana at recess in the schoolyard. (Montana fought dirty, putting pen nibs between her fingers.)

We thrilled to an overwhelming tale of how Dad cut off his finger in a lawnmower accident, and it had to be reattached by Dr. Nash, who lived next door on McClellan Circle.

And colorful accounts concerned road trips the family used to take in the 1920s to Lewiston, their car groaning and stalling on the Lewiston Hill.

On it went. All over Western New York, Dad found things worth remembering and recounting. And recount them he did. After he retired from his job as an English and Latin teacher at Williamsville South High School, he found a new career in telling his stories, on the editorial pages of The Buffalo News, occasionally in the Wall Street Journal and in various nostalgic magazines.

Dad loved the newspaper business, and he was good at it. A born chronicler, he had a passionate and hilarious eye for detail. People who read his stories responded with fascination, as we had, to his tales of the dog-eat-dog sales at Sattler's or the bum used car he bought as a teen-ager "out Bailey." (I still laugh, reading about how the radiator exploded with a giant sneeze.)

More serious stories, such as the one that dealt with the collapse of the Honeymoon Bridge, would be followed by a protest over the change in the formula for Wheaties or a nutty exploration of what it was like to be pretty much the only German in South Buffalo. Dad's topics were unpredictable.

Losing him suddenly, eight years ago, was the saddest thing our family has ever been through. I still feel the loss acutely at work; he was thrilled when I stumbled into a career at The Buffalo News, and it seems funny to be going on without him. Dad was a big presence in our lives, and it seems not a day passes that my mother, my brothers and sisters and I don't remind each other of something he said.

It has cheered us up, though, to receive the outpouring of condolence from strangers who had read Dad's stories, loved them (collected them, in some cases) and felt as if they knew him. For years, we've had the idea of collecting his writings, putting them together so we and other people could revel in them all over again. Of course, it took years. But if there's one thing Dad taught us, it's that it's never too late to remember.

Here they are, then, everything we could find, from the rattling old streetcars to the squawking Sattler's sales. I still can't read many of them without laughing. God bless Dad and his marvelous observations. The old days live. And he does, too.

∞ Mary Kunz ∞
November 2002

SHELTON SQUARE WAS
BUFFALO'S PICCADILLY CIRCUS

FIRST PRINTED ☜ 04 – 07 – 85

ew York has Times Square; Paris has its Place de la Concorde. London has Piccadilly Circus, and Buffalo used to have Shelton Square. It was the focus at which many principal streets joined: Shelton Square was the city's epicenter.

Located at the junction where Niagara, Church and Erie streets met Main, Shelton Square was Buffalo's busy hub for many years. In days of the trolley, the area was an intricate web of tracks.

Important buildings were located at the intersection points. Occupying the angle formed by Church and Niagara was the old Erie County Savings Bank Building, a towering bastion of financial security.

On the bank's one side, across Church Street was St. Paul's Cathedral, balancing, stone for stone, a religious citadel with a financial one. On the other side of the red stone Erie Bank was the central Buffalo store of the Harvey and Carey drugstore chain.

Contributing to the bustle of Shelton Square was the proximity of two other buildings of architectural as well as commercial interest; the Ellicott Square and the Prudential-Guaranty Buildings.

However, the most famous Shelton Square landmark was none of these.

Rather, on Main's east side stood a raucous theatrical establishment whose performances to a large, balconied house are part of local lore. It was the last of Buffalo's burlesque houses, the Palace.

Whenever you needed any downtown logistical information — how to get to the telephone company, for example — directions usually began: "Do you know where the Palace is?" In nine times out of ten, the questioner did, and having established this fact of mutual agreement, the directioner could proceed.

The Palace Burlesque had an animated, flashing marquee with high-kicking chorus girls. Inverted V-signs always stood in front: there were the naughty girls with fans and feathers smiling out archly from their picture frames, across to Shelton Square.

Two doors down from the Palace was another institution — Foody's Bar, highly revered especially by the city's Irish. Its pink, neon sign gleamed through the snow on many a winter night.

To accommodate travelers, there was a small shelter in Shelton Square, made part of brick, part of glass blocks. Here, trolley and bus passengers would stand and shiver, waiting for one of the many lines that operated out of the square.

This small edifice had restrooms downstairs, but except in abject crisis, you stayed away. Anybody who remembers Shelton Square will agree that its comfort station was the coldest and most redolent in town.

With construction of Main Place Mall, Shelton Square gradually disappeared during the 1960s and '70s. Transit lines were rerouted, and new buildings sprang up where Niagara Street used to be. The original Erie County Bank Building was replaced, part of its location occupied by its successor, the Empire of America Savings.

Another part of the Shelton Square area holds Cathedral Park, attractively adjoining St. Paul's Church. The entire section is so drastically altered now that only St. Paul's remains as a guide to where the square was once situated.

Vanished, therefore, is the Shelton Square of yore, and perhaps it's as well. Certainly the new look is more cosmetic, more functional. Yet it is difficult to realize that the noisy commotion, along with the blaring music of the Palace, are silenced forever. ∞

MODERN BISONS STIR UP MEMORIES OF THOSE OF HALF A CENTURY AGO

FIRST PRINTED 04 – 19 – 86

*M*y Uncle Bill, who lived in the upper flat at our house, was an engineer on the New York Central. Except for his regular run to Corning, the only place Uncle Bill ever went was Offermann Stadium.

Fifty years ago, as did half of Buffalo, my uncle caught pennant fever. For several years, the Bisons had been strong International League contenders, but 1936 was the year they put their act together. At nearly every night game that summer, Uncle Bill took his son and me to see the Bisons play.

To get the most for our Depression money, we arrived early to watch the teams warm up. Once inside the stadium, senses fuse: the smell of hot dogs, cigar smoke and beer blend with the bat's crack, the crowd's cheer, to conjure up memories of an unforgettable team.

On the 1936 Bisons, every player was a star. The infield was manned by Butch Meyers, Greg Mulleavy, Marv Olsen and Elbie Fletcher — only names now, but in 1936, they inspired awe in the International League.

Before the game, cousin Billy and I would wander through the stands, eluding the ushers, to sneak down to the railing near the dugouts. There, if we were lucky and the ushers did not chase us, we pleaded with ballplayers to sign our scorecards.

In 1936, kids treated anyone older with deference. I can recall addressing the players as "Mister" and using the permissive subjunctive in my speech: "Mr. Kline, may I have your autograph?"

The big, friendly pitcher, Bob Kline, ambled over, leaking chewing tobacco, and scrawled a signature. Bob was a member of a fearsome pitching staff: Carl Fisher, Ken Ash, Bill Harris, Rip Sewell, relievers Art Jacobs and Steamer Lucas. Their battery mates were catchers Bucky Crouse and Eddie Phillips.

The real showmen at the Bison warm-ups were the outfielders. This 1936 group was made up of Beauty McGowan, Johnny Dickshot and beloved Bison Ollie Carnegie.

They stand up yet, tall and straight, at the home plate of my memory. During batting practice, the outfielders would swat some sharp grounders; then to mollify the kids, whack a few balls over the fence.

One night, left fielder Eddie Boland, who had a peculiar way of teetering on one foot at the plate, smashed a foul ball at us. Uncle Bill knocked the ball down with his big, callused paw, and I scampered to retrieve it. I have that ball still.

Manager Ray Schalk brought all these stars together that year, and pennant fever swept Buffalo. At every game, the stadium rocked with excitement, swelled with huge crowds.

When the team was on the road, I listened to Roger Baker's imaginative radio descriptions, hanging on every tap of the ticker tape. With intensity, I studied the Bison newspaper write-ups of reporters W.S. Coughlin in the Courier, Bob Stedler in The News.

All summer, the 1936 Bisons were nip-and-tuck for first place: the International League held some fine, evenly matched clubs that season. Finally, in late August, Buffalo pulled inexorably into the lead.

Those 1936 Bisons were the heroes of my boyhood, but half a century later, I'm hoping for another pennant. I'm ready to accept a new set of heroes for my mature years. ∽

GREEN GRASS & BASEBALL

George Kunz wrote a heartwarming article in the sports pages about the 1936 championship Buffalo Bisons and the huge crowds in Offerman Stadium, with all the aromas of the hot dogs, fresh peanuts, green grass and even the cigar smoke.

I was born and raised for most of my life in Buffalo, and now live in Niagara Falls and remember those days very well. After many a game, I would walk with the players back to the Hotel Markeen, at Main and Utica streets, where many of them stayed. I know many things have changed downtown and, am sorry to say, for the worse. However I hope and pray that Bob Rich Jr. and Mayor Jimmy Griffin, who seem to care for the people, will build a stadium as much as possible like Offerman Stadium, with real grass and no dome so that baseball will be played the way it should be.

JOHN T. DiNUNZIO Niagara Falls

THE YEAR THEY TURNED OFF NIAGARA FALLS

FIRST PRINTED ⚬⚬ 05 – 11 – 86

Since the ice age, tons of water have tumbled over the brink at Niagara Falls. To interrupt the torrent, like interfering with any great force of Nature, was unthinkable: the sun rises, earth revolves, the Niagara falls.

Until 1969. For nearly six months that year, the American Falls went dry, and visitors were faced with the eerie spectacle of a parched river bed where the rapids had roared for centuries.

The American Falls, over which about 15 percent of the Niagara River's water passes, had accumulated huge formations of rock at its base. The rock, called talus, was the result of erosion from the backward movement of the falls toward Lake Erie.

In some sections, talus was piled half-way to the brink, resulting in a water drop that was more cascade than falls. Disturbed by this altered appearance, the U.S. Congress in 1965 authorized the Army Corps of Engineers to study measures necessary to preserve the beauty of the American Falls.

The engineers were enjoined to remove talus, retard future erosion, investigate public safety at the Goat Island observation flanks — especially after the major rockfalls of July, 1954, and December, 1959.

To accomplish these objectives, the apparently impossible had to be done: the American Falls at Niagara must be turned off.

A coffer dam was fitted into place at the upper end of Goat Island, stretching from the island to the opposite shore. Piece by piece, coffers gradually slowed the rapids, shrank their size, muffled their roar. The final pieces were put into place on June 12, 1969, and the American Falls became a ghostly skeleton.

That summer, to walk along the familiar pathways by moonlight was to see not the rushing, silvery waters; instead, rocks lying on the river bed resembled the dried, gray bones of cattle, dead of thirst. The scene might have been the Rio Grande and not the Niagara.

During their investigation, engineers scrupulously respected the great river's integrity, determined that every aspect of the Niagara should be returned to its pristine condition. The four small islands near the falls' brink — now temporarily islands no longer — were protected and irrigated so that their vegetation should not be damaged.

In all, 46 core borings were taken, talus was photographed, analyzed; boulders were measured; geological studies were made to establish the safety of viewing positions. These data later resulted in a realignment of the railings and observation areas at Prospect Point, Goat Island and Terrapin Point.

Niagara Falls, of course, belongs to the world, and the phenomenon of its partial shut-off stimulated international concern. Pictures and accounts of the dewatered falls appeared throughout the world; over 50 magazines in the United States alone ran stories about the unusual situation.

By autumn, researches were finished; all statistics had been completed by engineers for presentation to an international commission for their future action.

In late November, removal of the coffer dam began. As each piece was taken away, water from the Niagara main stream spurted back into the familiar channel.

Little by little, like turning on a great water faucet, the flow increased from a spurt to a stream to a torrent. The rapids swept back over their accustomed bed. The islands became islands again.

The American Falls, which had looked like a forsaken gulch, soon was a massive waterway once more. Again it resumed that dramatic grandeur which earned the river its Indian name "Thunderer of Waters." ∽

THOSE COAL FURNACES DID STRANGE THINGS TO PEOPLE

FIRST PRINTED ∾ 01 – 13 – 91

All the long, winter night, I could hear howling winds. Toward morning, I saw steam coming from my breath. I knew at once what had happened: The coal furnace had gone out.

From the next bedroom I caught my mother's voice, tense and worried. "Dad, did you take care of the furnace last night?"

My father squawked out a stark reply. "Oh, my gosh!" he exclaimed as he always did on such occasions "I forgot."

In the era of coal home heating, the furnace demanded stoking at least twice a day. Poor Dad, often careless of this chore, had neglected to bank the coal fire. He was about to pay for his omission.

Soon from the frigid heat registers, I could hear him working in the cold cellar. Because as a boy I had watched my father start many fires, I vividly imagined the activities.

First, he shook out the ashes, stirring up swarms of dust. Next, he searched for odd pieces of wood. Taking crumpled newspapers, he laid a bed for the wood. After lighting, he studied the crackling, snapping timbers for the moment at which the flames were hot enough to ignite coal.

When that precise moment came. Dad would place in pockets of coal, fervently hoping that they might burn. This was the climax of the basement drama.

Meanwhile, upstairs, Mother bustled about with makeshift emergency heating measures; the stove oven: a primitive, electric coil device for the bathroom.

We kids shivered into our icy school clothes in a house smoky with Dad's fire-providing efforts. In the kitchen, we scraped the skin off a cup of cocoa Mother had prepared to warm us.

I can still see my father as he emerged from the cellar after a morning bout with the coal furnace. His hands were grimy, sometimes bleeding. Dust powdered his bald head but a look of hope transfixed his face.

"I think the coal is taking fire," he whispered, and his voice was reverent, as though in prayer.

Those coal furnaces did strange things to people. ∾

7

PERSERVING A
PART OF OUR PAST

FIRST PRINTED ☞ 08 – 30 – 84

*T*he Canadiana is the stuff that dreams are made of.

As a boy, I ran along the ship's decks clutching my Buffalo Evening News Amusement Coupons. I watched the mighty engines as they churned up the rancid waters of Buffalo Harbor for another trip to Crystal Beach. My head was teeming with visions of the Caterpillar, HeyDey, Tumblebug, and Hall's cinnamon suckers.

When I was a young man, I escorted summer girl friends across the Canadiana's gangway. Now my dreams focused on the Cyclone, the dance hall and naturally the long, late boat ride home. The Canadiana meant romance.

One chilly summer afternoon in 1965, I thought that I had paid the good ship my final farewell. I had read of the ship's hapless adventures after it had left Buffalo, how it had been transferred to Toledo, had suffered a smashed nose in an accident, been towed back to Buffalo, and all but given up for dead. Moored at the foot of Amherst Street for years, the Canadiana slowly sank into ignominious decline.

Then I read with sorrow that the ship was to be pulled to Cleveland for a final disposition, and I knew that it was time for my last melancholy goodbye to an old friend. Leaving my wife in charge of Child III, I took the two older children with me to see the Canadiana.

The old ship seemed ashamed to see me. Like a once-proud lady fallen on bad times, the Canadiana listed. Its paint was blistered, windows were broken, posts were rusting. My two-year-old daughter began to cry.

I tried to explain to my children that this was authentic Buffalo history. Holding my son by the hand, I carried Mary, still howling, along the decks, through the paneled sitting room, across the dance floor, up the ladder to the third deck.

That afternoon, there was broken glass everywhere; abandonment and decay hung in the air. It took real imagination to think of this as the Canadiana, the stuff of dreams. Haunted by ghosts of happier times, I paid my final farewell.

Final farewell? Maybe not. A courageous group, called the Friends of the Canadiana, is trying to bring the old legend back home to Buffalo — where it belongs. The hope is to tow the ship back from its present berth in Ashtabula, and then gradually to restore it.

What a terrific idea! The Canadiana, like Shea's Buffalo or the Wilcox Mansion, is a window to yesterday. Future generations can clasp hands with the past on its decks. The high point of summer for children of my Depression era was the ride to Crystal Beach on the Canadiana, and I'll bet half the married couples in Western New York shared that late boat trip together on Saturday nights.

Such a dream of restoring the Crystal Beach boat is costly, and there is a fund-raising party at the Hyatt Regency tonight to help the dream get afloat. I will be there with my whole family, hoping to meet old girl friends of fondly remembered moonlight cruises. One of these girl friends is coming along, because if she didn't, I'd divorce her. ∞

'TROLLEY'S REVENGE' IS NOW RUNNING ON MAIN STREET

FIRST PRINTED ⚬ 09 – 03 – 84

*C*oming toward me on shiny steel tracks was a sleek, new yellow trolley. Strung out into the distance were taut overhead wires.

The motorman saw me wave, the car stopped and I stepped on board. Silently, effortlessly, the electric car accelerated. I was on a journey into yesterday and tomorrow on Buffalo's new light-rail rapid transit line.

Vividly I remembered a summer evening in 1950. Electric streetcars, or trolleys, were making their final trips through the streets of Buffalo.

Crowds lined Main Street, and a Dixieland band was playing. The mayor, the police commissioner, the president of the transit workers' union all were on hand, laughing, exultant, because this day, July 1, 1950, would mark the end of electric railway service.

Only a few electric lines were left in Buffalo that summer night: Broadway, Fillmore, Main Street, Parkside Zoo, Kensington. Trolleys on these surviving lines were all poised for their final runs at 7 p.m.

Forlorn the trolleys were that evening. They bore mock funeral bunting: "23 Skidoo" read signs on the Fillmore 23 line. "RIP" was posted on Broadway cars. "End of the Trail" sneered Parkside. "Who is there to Mourn for Logan?" was the old Indian's lament affixed to 8 Main.

When the time came, balloons were released and the last electric street cars began their final journeys along Buffalo's streets. On these routes, generations of Buffalonians had ridden trolleys to work, to the vaudeville houses, to the Pan American Exposition, to the Crystal Beach boat dock.

There was no joy in my heart that evening as I rode on the last run out Main Street. Trolleys had been part of my life. They had carried me to school, to my first job. I could remember as a boy charcoal or wood fires on some of the older cars during raw weather. Many are the girlfriends whose hands I held on winter rides coming home from downtown movies.

The band was playing on that July evening, and behind the streetcars came buses bearing signs "Welcome Buses." That was the way of progress, we were told in 1950.

Within weeks, the overhead wires were cut down, tracks were torn from their street beds and trolleys clattered off into oblivion forever — or so they said then.

Thirty-four years have passed, and in a way, Main Street has begun to look much as it did long ago. Gleaming, silvery tracks stretch out proudly; new overhead wires line the skies, and like a phoenix, shiny new streetcars (they are called subways now) glide smoothly along.

Sometimes we make progress by going backward, an old maxim says. I prefer to think of the new Buffalo transit system as the trolley's revenge — the emergence of reason in the form of a quiet, smooth, odorless, economic medium.

In this case, what was good enough for my father is good enough for me. ∽

A GAME THAT EASED
GREAT DEPRESSION

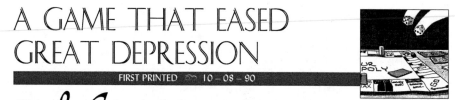

FIRST PRINTED ∽ 10 – 08 – 90

*M*onopoly was a Parker Brothers game devised in 1936 by an unemployed engineer. It was about money, at a discouraging time when people didn't have any.

I first played the game of a friend's house; and I was so captivated by the fantasy of finance that I couldn't wait to introduce it at my home. I raved about the fun to my parents, but alas, the family budget was too austere to lay out $3.95 for the wonder game.

I ask any survivor of the Great Depression: What did we do when we lacked the price of a luxury? Of course, we devised a substitute.

I collected materials: a firm box cover for the game matrix; I cut up other boxes to form little squares of varying sizes for property deeds and Chance cards.

Quickly, I discovered that making my own Monopoly was a game in itself. I mixed odd paints in the basement to decorate the master board. I tried to duplicate the standard colors: purple for Baltic-Mediterranean, yellow for the Marvin Gardens, bright red for Kentucky, etc.

I made many trips to W.T. Grant store at Seneca Street and Cazenovia to study a Monopoly game on display. Gradually, I copied all the names and sketched the graphics.

When it came to fashioning hotels and houses, I learned that a piece of scrap pinewood was soft enough to whittle. Construction took shape.

Play money presented a problem, especially because my sister took to counterfeiting. I discovered that my Uncle Bill, who worked for the New York Central, had some pads for railroad freight shipment records. The paper was distinctive in color and texture — ideal for money.

I don't remember how many times I remade my game, each effort to remedy some fault. Nor can I estimate how many times we passed "Go," collected $200, went to jail or donated to the Community Chest.

My homemade version of Monopoly was typical of some good things that came out of life in the Depression. We learned to improvise and find fun in our own inventiveness.

Even if life brought few chances in our favor or hotels on the Boardwalk, there was joy in pretending. ∽

GOOD OLD DAYS AT '998 BROADWAY'

FIRST PRINTED 12 – 23 – 85

At Christmas time, my thoughts go back to Sattler's famous department store, Buffalo's Bargain Center, the One-Stop Wonder Store. Such were only a couple of the titles which proclaimed Sattler's glory in newspaper advertisements.

The location? You wouldn't ask that question if you were around during the store's golden years of the 1940s and '50s because everybody knew Sattler's singing commercials from the radio. They all closed with the refrain:

"Shop and Save at Sattler's *9-9-8 Broadway.*"

Anytime, but especially at Christmas, the mood at Sattler's store was near hysteria.

Although the basement sold food, the real challenge was upstairs. Sattler's bargain frenzy there ran in a weekly cycle. Monday and Tuesday at the big store were just normally insane, but on Wednesday, weekly newspaper ads came out. Then the real madness erupted.

Sattler's routinely ran at least six full pages of newspaper ads which read something like this in scream headlines: "Atlanta Clothing Store Burns; Sattler's Buys Up Entire Stock!"

Then would follow a listing of some famous labels on the clothes Sattler's had acquired. Ads would warn that certain merchandise was smoke or water damaged, but the prices were frantically low. Ads always closed with a clincher like: "Their Burn Is Your Bargain! Hurry!"

After shoppers had been stirred to frenzy by such ads, crowds would descend on old 998 Broadway. There was no parking lot so customers often had to leave their cars on narrow streets blocks away.

Shopping bags with handles were de rigueur for Sattler's customers, and everybody arrived ready for combat. Counters groaned under the fire-damaged merchandise, and the whole store would smell of smoke from the Atlanta fire, which had been shipped with the clothes.

Once inside Sattler's, panic took over. Whether you needed anything or not, you pushed your way through crowds fighting for bargains.

Arguments on the sales floor were common. "That's the last size 9 and you took it out of my shopping bag!" a customer would snarl. "I did like hell!" came a returning snap. At Christmas time, the fabric of Peace on Earth and Goodwill Among Men wore thin at Sattler's bargain tables.

To encourage holiday spirit, carols would crackle over the public address system: you'd hear "Silent Night" blasting above the chaos. Then, frequently in mid-stanza, a loud clunk would interrupt the carol.

"Attention, Shoppers!" a voice would bark. "We have a lost girl in the Customer Service Office. She's looking for her mother. Her name is..." And then, off mike, you'd catch, "what's your name, kid?" There would be a loud howl from the lost child.

Sattler's did not have only fire-sale goods: they seemed to have a finger on the pulse of retail operations all over the country. Many are the stores that lost their leases, fell victim to changing times and went out of business, updated inventories. Their surplus found its way to 998 Broadway.

Flush with its success on Buffalo's East Side, Sattler's later tried to expand to several suburban plazas. However, such ventures were never successful because, as the big store used to say in its own ads: "There's Only One Sattler's!" The spirit of 998 was unique, untranslatable.

As years passed, altered retail and lifestyles finally caught up with the big one-stop wonder store too. After years of decline, Sattler's closed two years ago. This Christmas, the doors are locked, the lights are dark, the corridors are empty and cold. Yet, many Buffalonians will always feel a warm glow when they remember wild shopping sprees at "9-9-8 Broadway in Buffalo"! ∾

VAUDEVILLE DAYS LIVE AGAIN IN MIKE SHEA'S SCRAPBOOK

FIRST PRINTED ⌒ 08 – 17 – 86

*W*hat an assortment of acts tumble out of Mike Shea's scrapbooks — jugglers, Irish tenors, whistlers, dog trainers, pretenders to European thrones, magicians, blackface comics, aerialists; German, Jewish, Russian and Irish mimics; violin and trumpet virtuosos.

The scrapbooks, donated to the library at Buffalo State College by the showman's daughter, the recently deceased Mary Shea Giffoniello, are a compendium of letters to Mike Shea. Hundreds of performers wrote to seek bookings at the Shea-managed theaters.

In time, the letters embrace about five years at the turn of this century. There is, for instance, an offer from Toronto dated Dec. 7, 1901, asking Shea "to manage a theater since this city of 80,000 population does not have one."

Shea accepted this invitation, and his scrapbooks contain transactions to arrange vaudeville programs for the stage of Toronto's Shea Theater alongside those for Buffalo's Court Street Theater.

In those days, most vaudeville performers had no agents: they did their own negotiating on their own stationery, designed like advertisements with color and graphics to catch the eye.

There is, for example, a note from Laura Comstock in 1901. Her name is printed in inch-high blue characters on the white paper. Underneath in red is the caption "18 Minutes of Hurrah Stuff." Since the lady is pictured carrying an American flag, her note required little text.

"Dear Friend Shea," Miss Comstock wrote, "I am available weeks of June 7 and 14. Will really stir up the crowd. $150 per week."

Uniformly, vaudeville performers had neat, bold handwriting, and some script possesses a beauty of precision, the ink deftly shaded across paper of many colors and textures.

On March 8, 1902, Mike Shea's mail brought him this note: "Mr. M. Shea. Dear Sir; Would be pleased to play for you any week after May 5th. Salary $200 per week. Respond to the Duquesne Theater, Pittsburgh."

This note was signed "Bill" and is written under the letterhead "W. C. Fields — the Eccentric Juggler: Original, Unique, and Eccentric."

Next to Houdini, Howard Thurston was perhaps the world's best known magician. He sent an impressive communication to Shea on Jan. 29, 1902.

"World's Master Magician," proclaims the engraving on the letter from Breslau, Germany. Then riding the crest of his career, Thurston included newspaper reviews of his recent command performance in Budapest before Austrian Emperor Franz Joseph.

He referred to a six-month booking in London, but said he would be available to Buffalo audiences after July 15. Two years later, in June of 1904, Thurston wrote again and described "4 big new, original illusions — 7 people in the company including several beautiful girls. Cost for company: $500 per week."

The Four Cohans, including George M., wrote signifying their willingness to perform for their "old friend Mike" on April 1, 1899.

Sad-faced comedian Buster Keaton of silent-movie fame was only a child in 1900, so his parents took care of business. "Joe, Myra and Buster Keaton" is printed on their stationery. "Comedians, Introducing Singing, Dancing, Grotesque, Acrobatic and Eccentric Comedy."

The father, Joe Keaton, wrote a personal message: "Dear Michael — We have an added attraction now — little Buster, the tiny comedian. We were recently booked in Elmira, Scranton, Pastor's in New York City. $150 per week."

There is certain frustration in poring over the Shea scrapbooks because only the performer's side is there. What Shea replied, how he behaved to his correspondents, is largely conjecture. But occasionally a glimpse of the Buffalo showman peeks through.

Shea must have given the letters of application to a secretary for handling. On some of the performers' messages there is a firm, penciled note, evidently Shea's. "Offer him $100," one specifies. Another says "Say we're full. He's a drunk."

Drinks used to be served in the theaters during shows. A 1901 wine list from the Court Street Theater advertises: Booth's Gin — $2 per quart, 15 cents per glass; Whiskey Sour — 15 cents per glass; Rum — 15 cents per glass.

However, theater drinking was for the audience. Woe to the vaudevillian who indulged. Worse than any peril on stage, drinking was a traditional pitfall for the stage performer. Long hours to fill between shows, interesting old pals to converse with, the common bond of show biz, all helped to create a powerful thirst for a friendly drink. Many a performer was found hopelessly inebriated when his showtime arrived.

The drinking problem is a repetitious undercurrent in the applications to Mike Shea.

In June of 1902 a forgotten pair, Berry and Hughes, wrote: "Don't you think we have done penance enough? You have kept us out for two years. We are absolutely sober now." Mike Shea's heart must have been touched. The pencil note says: "Book August 4. $100."

Another performer sheepishly alluded to an occasion he hoped was forgotten when he had been "a little the worse for a few drops between shows."

The Shea scrapbooks include several contracts signed by performers. These standard vaudeville contracts specify that the player "agrees to faithfully perform all duties required. . . intoxication or failure to comply with necessary rules shall be the cause for instant dismissal."

Paging through the Mike Shea correspondence is like taking a walk through

American theater. The modern observer finds himself wishing he could have been there to see so many of those exotically skilled acts:

Adolph Adams - The Absolute Master of Memory
Charles Goheen with Automo, the Mechanical Doll
Captain Weber's Educated Seals and Sea Lions
Ventriloquist Ed Reynard
Sa-Van's Clown Mishaps
The Hawaiian Glee Club

Rio Brothers - Novelty Act on Flying Rings
Sansone and Delila - World's Greatest Bicycle Act
Creatore and his Italian Band
Two Jacks - Black Faced Comedy
William Cahill - the Man from Ireland
Dooley and Kent - Singing Comedians
Almont and Dumont - Instrumental Hussars
Sherman Mandolin Quartette
McCann Family with Baby Geraldine
Master Carron - Wonderful Boy Dancer
Bickett Family - Aerialists Supreme
Ollie Young and Brother Rolling Return Hoops
Gracie Emmett in "Mrs. Murphy's Second Husband"
Eckert and Bert - Operatic Stars
May Evans - Superb Whistling and Bird Imitations
Ben Welch - Natural Hebrew Character
Sisters Roppo - Siberian Dancers
Lew Bloom and Jane Cooper One Continuous Laugh for 20 Minutes
Imperial Japanese Troop
Gastor and Jermos - German Dialect Comedian and Singing Comedienne
The Dancing Dawsons assisted by Baby Mac Dawson
Madame Emmy's Little Pets
Howard's Comic Ponies
Rawson and June Boomerang Throwing
Charles Maclay - Revival of Shakespeare's Othello
DeOnzo Brothers - Trick Barrel Jumpers.

The list seems endless and the ideas are endlessly inventive. Too bad there were no videocassettes to preserve these long-forgotten artists of Michael Shea's Theaters. ∞

THE GOLDEN YEARS
OF BUFFALO BEERS

FIRST PRINTED ☞ 08 – 10 – 86

*T*hey are all gone now, those wonderful Buffalo beers, but their names sing back like familiar songs heard on a warm, summer night: Beck's and Lang's, Simon Pure Beer and Old Abbey Ale, Schreiber's Manru; Mohawk, Germania, Iroquois Indian Head Ale.

Before the Civil War, 35 breweries bubbled away in Buffalo with an annual output of 10,000 barrels. During the following half century, the number of local breweries shrank to 18, but their output foamed up to 1.3 million barrels. Then came Prohibition, which parched local brewing.

To ride out this unpopular law, several Buffalo breweries tried to protect their workers' jobs by changing products. Lang's became a bakery; Schreiber's turned to another beverage, marketing Manru Coffee. Other former breweries attempted to make candy, soft drinks, non-alcoholic near-beer. It was all very sad.

When the 14 years of Prohibition ended in 1933, the country rejoiced, but only seven Buffalo breweries were in a position to reopen. The rest had withered away during the long drought.

The surviving seven are probably the best remembered of local breweries. Oldest was the big Gerhard Lang Brewery, just across Jefferson Avenue from War Memorial Stadium.

Second in seniority was the Magnus Beck Brewery at 467 North Division St., whose products were advertised as "naturally smooth." Another survivor was Schreiber's, 662 Fillmore, makers of "thoroughly delicious Manru beer."

Using a chorus from Romberg's operetta "The Student Prince," Stein's Brewery at 797 Broadway used to sing: "With Stein's on the table" on radio promotions of its beverages. Moffat's Ale was marketed from the Phoenix plant on Emslie Street.

The Iroquois Brewing Co. was situated on Pratt Street near Broadway. An aggressive advertiser, they spread their Indian Head logo throughout Western New York. Smallest of the Buffalo breweries was the William Simon plant on Clinton Street, which outlived most local breweries. In 1973, the final bottles and cans of Simon Pure were pumped off assemblies.

Shutdown of Western New York breweries was simply part of a national trend. With the rise of the non-returnable bottle and can, big breweries were able to operate on a huge, countrywide basis. In price wars, they gulped down hundreds of regional beer companies. Today, 70 percent of American beer is supplied by the five giant breweries.

There are plenty of souvenirs of the golden years of Buffalo beers. You can hardly walk around a flea market without spotting those heavy, high-rimmed trays, once used to carry beer through saloons. In the tray's center, boldly embossed, is the brewery name.

Bottle openers, coaster pads, neon tavern signs — all such memorabilia are still in abundance on the collectible circuits. These artifacts preserve the legendary names of familiar Buffalo beers, which dried up during Prohibition or were swallowed by greedy national brewers. ∞

PIERCE ARROW
LIVES ON IN LEGEND

FIRST PRINTED ⌾ 07 – 14 – 85

W henever my cousin Eddie came to visit us in South Buffalo, there was a neighborhood sensation. Eddie had become a successful businessman, and the token of his prosperity was the Pierce Arrow automobile that he drove.

Local kids would swarm around to gawk at the long, swank coupe parked in our driveway. There were the spare wheels mounted jauntily into the front fenders, but the unmistakable Pierce hallmark was the famous headlights, staring boldly out of the fenders.

In an age when most luxury cars were manufactured in Europe, the Pierce Arrow became distinguished as a foremost American rival. It was an automobile of excellence, and it was made in Buffalo.

The Pierce Company dates back to 1878, when a factory near lower Main Street cranked out children's tricycles. Ten years later, when the bicycle's reign began, the company switched focus from the trike to the bike.

George N. Pierce, president of the cycle company, insisted that his products should be characterized by excellence. The words "tried and true" often occurred in advertisements.

In transportation history, the early automobile sputtered along shortly after the bike, and again Pierce changed with the times. In l896, the Pierce Motor Company, was formed to make automobiles.

First came the two-passenger Pierce Motorette in 1900; then, the Pierce Stanhope, with a small passenger seat in front of the driver. 1n 1903, a new line called the Pierce Arrow rolled out of the former bicycle factory, and an era had begun.

Pierce Arrows were entered in many competitions, and they regularly outperformed the European cars. Their reputation for quality and durability quickly caught on so that demand for Pierce Arrows required more factory space.

In 1907, a huge, new building was opened at 1685 Elmwood Ave. By this time, Pierce Arrow was the biggest employer in Buffalo, making not only luxury cars but also trucks, many of which were shipped abroad for use by the War.

The Pierce story is one of standard success. Production grew; in 1927, 6,032 elegant cars purred out of the Elmwood Avenue factory. Added to 749 sturdy trucks, the Pierce operation had become prestigious and profitable. A large budget for slick magazine advertising carried the Pierce Arrow message of opulence to all sections of the country.

Graphics on these ads often pointed up the unique Pierce fender headlights. Often, under the picture was the snobbish observation: "The Pierce owner is never embarrassed by having his car mistaken for any other make."

American presidents from Woodrow Wilson to Franklin Roosevelt selected the Pierce Arrow for official functions and parades. Prices rose from about $5,000 to $7,300, until a new model — a V-12 — was introduced in 1931. This super car sold for $10,000.

At the 1933 Chicago World's Fair, the innovative Pierce Silver Arrow was spectacularly presented. With running boards and rear trunk blended as one unit into the auto's body, the Silver Arrow anticipated modern design.

Along with such successes came misfortune. During the Depression, the market for luxury cars shrank. Also, the big American motor cartels were squeezing all small competitors. General Motors' Cadillac was an especially hot rival for the Pierce Arrow.

The venerable Pierce-Arrow Motor Company was liquidated in March 1938, but the legend lives on. Hundreds of Pierce Arrows are stars of classic auto shows everywhere. They carry the words "Made in Buffalo" throughout the world. Owners are members of an exclusive club, the Pierce Arrow Society.

The mighty factory on Elmwood Avenue still stands, used now mainly for department store warehousing and occasional sales. No one has ever had the bad taste to remove the famous Pierce name from the building's main arch.

The familiar facade on Elmwood looks as indestructible as that shiny, stylish, sturdy coupe that my cousin Eddie parked in our driveway years ago. ∞

BUFFALO WAS 'CENTER OF THE UNIVERSE' THE DAY THE PEACE BRIDGE WAS DEDICATED

FIRST PRINTED ∞ 08 – 02 –87

"Buffalo is News Center of Universe."

This local newspaper headline was a forgivable hyperbole because rarely in American history had such a galaxy of world luminaries been assembled in one city.

The occasion was a dramatic one: formal dedication of the Peace Bridge, that triumph of engineering that provided an international crossing of the storied Niagara River.

The date was Aug. 7, 1927. For practical purposes, the Peace Bridge had opened two months earlier when, on June 1, 25,000 cars drove

over the Niagara. Formal dedication, however, was deferred until August.

Even now, 60 years later, the list of visitors for the dedication is dazzling: Edward, Prince of Wales, his brother Prince George, British Prime Minister Stanley Baldwin, Premier W. L. Mackenzie King of Canada, American Vice President Charles Dawes, Secretary of State Frank Kellogg, New York Gov. Alfred Smith. Ambassadors, ministers, corporation executives, governors general of Canada followed by dozens.

Indisputably the most famous personality was the romantic bachelor Prince of Wales. Like his grandfather, King Edward VII, the prince was world renowned, not only as heir apparent to the British throne, but also as a charming bon vivant whose interests climaxed in polo and pretty women.

Although rain had been predicted for the Sunday ceremonies, the weather turned out to be hot and humid under a merciless midsummer sun. The

25

Prince of Wales had spent Saturday night in Toronto and was traveling down for a 3:30 afternoon reception at Fort Erie.

Upon arrival he complained incessantly about the heat. For the ceremonies at the Peace Bridge, he was clad in striped trousers, cutaway coat and top hat. No wonder he grumbled about the heat.

At either end of the Peace Bridge, enormous crowds of about a quarter of a million people gathered. The famous broadcaster, Graham McNamee, was in Buffalo describing the formalities to a world radio audience, estimated at 50 million.

Newsreel cameras rolled as Vice President Dawes led the American delegation to a midpoint on the Peace Bridge. Simultaneously, the Prince of Wales set out with the Canadian-British group to meet them. At the midpoint, the ceremonial ribbon was to be severed.

The Prince of Wales interrupted his complaints about the heat to deliver a short speech celebrating over a century of peace between Britain and the United States. That duty done, while the ribbon was being cut he tapped Secretary of State Kellogg on the shoulder and was overheard to ask, "I say, how is your golf game lately?"

After ribbon cutting, all dignitaries walked to Front Park in Buffalo for speeches. Along the way the Prince of Wales greeted individual Buffalonians with handshakes and a routine "very happy to see you." He was followed by his brother Prince George.

A Buffalo reporter described a warmth and cordiality in the prince's manner with admirers; even though he seemed "a nervous young man." On the speakers' platform, he sat between his brother and Prime Minister Baldwin.

Nine years after his Buffalo visit, the Prince of Wales became King Edward VIII. However, his reign was brief and troubled, ending in abdication so that he could marry "the woman he loved" — unfortunately a divorced American commoner. Edward was succeeded by his younger brother, who ruled as King George VI.

Little did Buffalonians know on that steamy dedication day, as they craned for a look at the future King of England, that they were seeing not one, but two future kings. ∞

SPOONING IN A CANOE TO THE CROONING OF CROSBY IN DAYS OF OLD

FIRST PRINTED 04 – 16 – 89

elaware and Cazenovia parks both had them: canoes to rent and lakes to sail on.

It was an early sign of spring in an age that was slower moving and easier going. Out into the hesitant sunshine of April would come old canoes for new painting.

As boys, we would watch the rite of spring. Parks employees unloaded the dusty canoes from storage racks and laid them atop two sawhorses. When they had dried from a hosing, bright coats of paint were carefully applied.

Like Tom Sawyer's friends, we would gladly have done the work for the park workers. It looked such fun: smugly they drew the brush over a smooth surface and gleaming reds and yellows, greens and blues glowed at the sunny afternoon.

If spring was early canoes were available for rent in May. For deposit ranging from $5 to a secondhand watch, clients over 16 could rent a canoe: cost, 75 cents an hour.

What better setting for romance than a park background, a slick canoe and the gentle currents of Cazenovia or Delaware Park lakes? What else could young lovers need?

Only music: and in an age of technological miracles, even music was available. The inventive secured portable record players: wind-up, of course, with those heavy, scratchy 78 rpm platters, but it was music.

Over placid park waters in those far-off years, you could hear the gentle crooning of Bing Crosby: "When the b-b-blue of the night/Meets the g-gold of the day…" Or the sophisticated Rudy Vallee: "My time is your time…"

In spring, to be sure, a young man's fancy turns to thoughts of love. Even though I was only 10 or 12 years old in days of romantic canoeing, I confess now that my thoughts were already those of a young man.

Although I didn't have either a girlfriend or 75 cents to spend for an hour's use of a city canoe, my heart lay with those who did. I would not have admitted it to my best friend, but my deepest desires bobbed in the boats which floated alluringly along the lake.

The park lake at Cazenovia has long since been filled in, seeded and is even sprouting with trees, but there's talk of reviving rental canoes for the refurbished lake at Delaware.

Should the day come when shiny, sleek canoes are again available for rental, I'll be standing in line. I now can afford the 75 cents, and watch out wife, in spring, even an older man's fancy turns. ∞

AL SMITH,
THE 'HAPPY WARRIOR'

FIRST PRINTED 10 - 24 - 82

"Let's look at the record," he was fond of saying in his campaign speeches. That man of generosity and heart, that man of sad face and compassionate eyes, was New York's governor through most of the 1920s. Perhaps, as New Yorkers prepare to elect a new chief executive, it is fitting to look at the record of the happy warrior, the man in the brown derby, Alfred E. Smith.

He referred to the area around the Brooklyn Bridge as "the old neighborhood" because he was born there in 1873. He never received much education beyond his Catholic Church school training on Manhattan's Lower East Side. "Anyone desiring to have a proper understanding of the necessity for an education need only talk to the man who was denied it," he said to the state Legislature in 1923. Such wistful regret prompted him to improve state schools more than any previous governor in New York.

Smith guided the Legislature to increase spending for teacher salaries and for local school systems. Standards of rural schools, notoriously inadequate, were improved, and the first moves were made toward centralizing small districts.

Smith's conservation program extended to the establishment of a Water Power Commission, forerunner of the New York State Power Authority. This was a big step into modern times.

At the age of 12, Al Smith had sold papers to help his widowed mother. He worked later as a laborer at the Fulton Fish Market. He knew the abuses against labor when he acted as governor to correct them. "In canneries, women and children work sixteen hours a day, seven days a week," he said. "I've read the commandment Remember the Sabbath Day — to keep it holy. Nowhere does it say — except in the canneries."

Look at the labor record. A 48-hour workweek became law. Workmen's Compensation benefits were revised liberally.

Smith never forgot his modest roots. When he steered the state to purchase land for the Jones Beach Park on Long Island, a wealthy member of the sugar-rich Havemeyer family asked him, "Where are we going to find a place to live with all this rabble coming in?"

"What rabble?" Smith exclaimed. "I'm the rabble."

Look at the record on state parks. Al Smith initiated the Council of Parks to enlarge and coordinate the historic and natural-beauty lands of the state. It was he who envisioned the string of state parks which now spans New York.

Smith's years as governor saw vast building programs. State highways, office buildings, hospitals, bridges were undertaken. He initiated many of these projects; he supported them all.

"Law, in a democracy, means the protection of the rights of the minority." In 1920, the state assembly voted to exclude five duly-elected Socialist members. Unsympathetic himself to socialism, the governor spoke forcefully in defense of the Socialists' rights. "It is a confession of the weakness of our own faith when we attempt to suppress those who do not agree with us." The five socialists were excluded, but Al had made his position clear.

Smith's morals were not universally popular: he was against Prohibition, and he said so; he was against the Ku Klux Klan, and he told the members so to their faces. He was a Catholic all his life but denied that loyalty to his church influenced his political stands.

At the state convention in 1926, when Gov. Smith was nominated for a fourth term, Jimmy Walker, carried away in his enthusiasm, introduced the governor as "the next president of the United States," When the noise had subsided Al quipped, "One nomination at a time — please." Later: "Not so much applause. You waste time on the radd-io."

Perhaps it is best to forget Al Smith's presidential campaign in 1928, filled as it was with prejudice, bigotry and outlandish lies.

Instead, let's be content with looking at the record of a distinguished governor of New York State. Whoever his successor will be in 1983 can look back respectfully to Al Smith for examples of grace, courage and character. ∞

FDR INSPIRED A
SENSE OF HOPE

FIRST PRINTED ∽ 03 – 04 – 83

America has watched exciting presidential inaugurations. It has heard many inaugural speeches, filled, as most beginnings are, with hope. Yet, it is hard to match the expectation that Americans felt 50 years ago, on March 4, 1933.

That Saturday morning was windy and raw in Washington, like the rough economic weather the new president would face. When he walked slowly from the Capitol Rotunda to the inaugural stand, the president-elect was supported on the arm of his oldest son. But there was no weakness or need of support when he repeated the oath of office. "I, Franklin Delano Roosevelt," he said firmly, "do solemnly swear…"

Half a century ago, presidents took office in March, instead of January. For Franklin Roosevelt, that winter morning was the climax of a spectacular life. He had served as a secretary of the Navy, had been a vice-presidential candidate before calamity struck. This man, loaded with talent and energy, fell victim to the deadly disease of poliomyelitis. He barely survived with his life, his legs permanently paralyzed. Roosevelt was able to walk only with help and with heavy, steel braces fitted to his legs.

Over the years, Franklin Roosevelt made many enemies but the quality that his bitterest foe would concede to him was courage. He never gave up hope for his future. He fought

31
∽

back to become governor of New York, then, in 1932, to win the Democratic nomination for president.

In the 1930s, America was starved for hope. Incredibly, the great country, the land of dreams and promise, wallowed in financial misery. Everywhere, there was mass unemployment, failing businesses, bread lines and soup kitchens for the destitute. Mobs lived in shacks made of packing cases and scrap lumber. These dwellings were called "Hoovervilles," a sneering reference to an ineffectual president.

Enter Franklin Roosevelt on the national stage. So handsome, so debonair, so anxious to assume the nation's cares was he that many Americans never knew that he was a cripple, unable to walk or stand without assistance.

In a spectacular campaign, Roosevelt had made Herbert Hoover seem callous, careless, naive. Hoover, a sincere humanitarian but altogether deprived of personal magnetism, was a classic example of a man placed on the world stage at the wrong time of history. He was humiliatingly rejected by the American voters in 1932.

On inauguration morning, Roosevelt had invited his newly appointed cabinet to join him and his family for prayers at St. John's Church. All of us who remember that morning joined in spirit praying with the new president — for him and the stricken nation. There was a sense of standing together in crisis.

Secretary of Labor Frances Perkins years later wrote about the church services: "In St. John's we were Catholics, Protestants, and Jews, but I doubt that anyone remembered the difference." After church, there followed the chilling ride in an open car; Roosevelt and Hoover, two men forced to share a back seat, but otherwise with nothing in common except mutual dislike and resentment.

When the new president stepped onto the inaugural platform, the Marine Band played "Hail to the Chief," and President Roosevelt flashed the stunning smile that was to become as familiar as his initials.

The whole country wanted FDR to succeed because people were confused and discouraged. His words that March day were full of reassurance and confidence: "The only thing we have to fear is fear itself," he said, savoring the paradox in the inimitable Roosevelt style.

While FDR was speaking, sunlight broke hesitantly through the troubled winter sky. Happy days are here again? Not yet, but despite the biting cold, there was a sense of hope that March morning 50 years ago. ∞

THE DAY THAT BEER FLOWED AGAIN

FIRST PRINTED ∞ 04 – 03 – 83

*F*oaming with good spirit, brimming with renewed life, bubbling with triumph, beer flowed back 50 years ago, on April 7, 1933. It poured through the first hole in the Prohibition wall, and for most Americans, beer's return was a reunion with an old friend who had been rudely treated.

Beer's enemies sneered that the country was trying to drink itself out of the Depression. True, there was some of that sentiment. Prohibition, which had been the law of the land for 13 years (however many the violations), did seem a relative of the Great Depression. In cheerless dejection, the two walked hand in hand.

During bleak Prohibition years, Americans had tried unsuccessfully to replace a favorite beverage. There was "near beer," a purchasable, non-alcoholic substitute, but for the beer drinker, it was like an unlighted cigarette to a smoker.

Many Americans tried their hand at making "home brew." For this concoction, the amateur brewer needed large crocks to ferment yeast and malt; he needed large kettles for simmering hops; above all, he required practice and patience. Many, a beer drinker spat out in disgust samplings of his home brew, a product born of toil and devotion, but lacking expertise.

A location near the Canadian border was fortunate for Buffalonians, who frequently rode the ferries across the Niagara River to nearby Fort Erie, where beer still was abundant and cool.

National disenchantment with Prohibition had grown gradually from rumblings to roars. Bootleggers and speakeasies, instead of sobriety, seemed the result of the 18th Amendment. Jokes abounded, all of which centered on a scorn and disregard for the Prohibition law.

In his campaign of 1932, Franklin Roosevelt had made repeal of the unpopular 18th Amendment one of his election objectives. There was little doubt that people agreed with him. Early in 1933, even before repeal, congressional action enabled the return of beer with a 3.2 percent alcoholic content. Only the president's signature was necessary to make beer legal again, and on March 27, the new president performed that ceremony.

Now a brief waiting period began before beer's official return on April 7. Overjoyed, America's breweries prepared to market their favorite product. In sympathetic anticipation, pretzel makers began working three shifts twisting out tons of beer's traditional companion.

In Buffalo, breweries like Lang's and Manru, which had survived Prohibition as bakeries or coffee distributors, began bottling again. Soon, well-known, fondly remembered brewery names like Schreiber's, Beck's, Phoenix and Iroquois would reappear.

At 12:01 a.m., on the big day, April 7, 1933, the Anheuser Busch clock in Times Square chimed out "Happy Days Are Here Again!" to all Manhattan. In Milwaukee, Miller's Brewery offered free samples to anyone who brought an empty container; drinkers lined up with galvanized pails, tin cans, milk bottles, earthen jugs. In St. Louis, crowds paraded through downtown streets singing "Sweet Adeline."

In Washington, a beer truck barreled up Pennsylvania Avenue, draped with bright bunting and the sign, "President Roosevelt, the first beer is for you." (With accustomed style, FDR donated his samples to the National Press Club.)

Baltimore's terrible-tempered H.L. Mencken, fierce in writing of politicians but poetic in his praise of the glories of beer, stopped by the Rennert Hotel bar. After downing a first glass appreciatively, he smacked his lips, gave a wry smile and understated, "Not bad at all. Fill it again."

The Women's Christian Temperance Union remained sober. A bulletin was issued: "No nation ever drank itself out of a depression. If women take to the beer habit, they have only to look at some of the beer drinkers in the London slums to see what is ahead of them: Beer Makes Fat."

However one felt about beer's comeback, there was a statistic that nearly everyone cheered. In less than a month, from April 7 to May 1, while beer was being sold in only 35 states, the U.S. Treasury netted more than $9 million in taxes. Even in depressed times experts projected a revenue of well over $120 million per year from beer sales tax. There was little question that Americans were glad to have beer back.

At our house, April 7 carried additional significance because it was my younger brother's birthday. Thereafter, my father often referred to him proudly as "the beer baby" and accepted the coincidence as an omen of good fortune that would favor his new son. ∞

THE SHORT, GLORIOUS REIGN
FIRST PRINTED ∞ 09 – 23 – 84 OF THE TOMATO

'Tis the season to celebrate the tomato.

For but a short time, it is with us to grace our tables. In that brief sojourn, the tomato bursts into our lives, teeming with color, size, fullness and taste.

Even the most bumbling gardener can be successful with the tomato. Start a few plants in almost any kind of soil, and with a reasonable amount of sunshine, the vines will be heavy with blossoms that become yellow, green and finally an exultant, exuberant red.

Oddly enough, in America this brilliantly scarlet fruit once was thought to be poisonous — probably because it is derived from the same family as the deadly nightshade. It was well into the 20th century until tomatoes were cultivated in the new world as food and later still that they were discovered to be rich in potassium and in vitamins A and C, although low in calories.

The Italians were first to develop wide use of the tomato and demonstrated a tangy imagination for injecting it into many recipes. In fact, it was Italians in New York City, showing the same appreciation of feminine beauty as of cooking, who called a stunning girl a "tomato."

Man has dreamed of extending the tomato's short season. In my youth, housewives ceased all other chores in September and devoted their energies to preserving the tomato. Family excursions to farms had resulted in bushels of tomatoes being stored in the house.

For weeks, huge kettles of tomatoes bubbled and frothed on the stove. The house — the whole neighborhood — was deliciously redolent of cooking tomatoes: to walk down the street was to bask in their heady scents. Tops were snapped on hundreds of Ball canning jars enclosing chili sauce, stewed tomato, ketchup and the like.

Scientists, too, regretting the bare two-month season of the tomato, have tried to improve the situation. In laboratories, they have mutated a tomato that not only survives all seasons but also is impervious to rough handling.

Yet no one ever could confuse the tomato of September with the scrawny, pink variety you find in restaurant salad bars in January. Those puny, pink, pathetic midwinter tomatoes issue from some scientific and forlorn hothouse or from parched southern fields. To bite into them is like biting into a golf ball — hard, rubbery, tasteless. Whoever enjoys them could enjoy a meal of sawdust.

So with resignation, let us accept the short tenure of the tomato and enjoy it in its season. It is a proof of Nature's bounty that God is in his heaven and at least one thing is right with his world. ∞

FESTIVAL '85

I know the whole story about fund-raisers like Festival '85 on Channel 17. I know that public stations are non-commercial, nonprofit, that they depend substantially on viewers for their support. I have been battered with complaints about diminished government subsidies. And yet, I wonder whether the capitalist principle does not assert itself even in public media.

Although public TV likes to boast that its viewers never see commercials, annoyances abound. There are constant blurbs about upcoming programs which begin to cloy, just as any other oft-repeated message. However, all distractions, commercial or public, pale before the regular membership fund-raising drives, which are cynically called "Festivals."

It would be difficult to conjure up a method better-designed to alienate any audience than these tiresome weeks. Frenzied, bleary-eyed, the representatives of public radio-TV often lash out at their viewers. They hope by smiles and surface affability to allay their abrasiveness, but the tone is aggressive, bellicose, patronizing, proprietary. The image of public TV during these weeks is not an attractive one.

Were one to tally up air time spent on future-program promotional spots, on the prolonged membership campaigns during which the station is tantalizingly unwatchable, on benefit auctions: then actual program hours might be just about the same as those on bad, old, capitalist, commercial media.

I am not unappreciative of the contribution of public broadcasting. Indeed, the term used by a former FCC chairman comes to mind: without public broadcasting, radio and television would be a "wasteland."

Nor do I intend to demean the efforts of the management of public media. During those agonizing membership campaigns, it must require a measure of courage, as well as physical stamina, to stand before a camera berating an unseen audience, repeating endlessly. I have seen barkers at the Erie County Fair tire more quickly.

Is there an alternative? I believe that there is. I suggest an espousal of the capitalist principle: allow PBS to support itself by accepting advertising. Commercials on public radio-TV could be inoffensive; they could be informative and helpful.

While the audience on public media is relatively small, it is also discriminating and affluent. Commercials directed at such viewers would have to be discerning, discreet. Given such an approach, I'd wager that these commercials would bear rich fruit for the advertiser. I am certain that they would save wear-and-tear on the rest of us during Channel 17's "Festivals." ∽

HUMBLE MUSIC HALL ATTRACTED THE WORLD'S TOP ENTERTAINERS

FIRST PRINTED ∞ 11 – 14 – 82

f I mention the famous name Enrico Caruso, of course you think of operatic music. If I say Franklin Roosevelt, you think: politics, New York State governor, later U.S. president. But let me drop the name John L. Sullivan: your response changes to prize-fighting. Let me say Strangler Lewis, and if you know anything of the steamy sport of wrestling, you will recognize that name.

Yehudi Menuhin

What do the thuds and cheers of boxing or the groans and grunts of wrestling have to do with the velvet sounds of Caruso and the practiced speech-cadences of Franklin Roosevelt? Answer: they were all heard in Buffalo's Elmwood Music Hall.

In the Gay Nineties, Buffalo had some of the flavor of a frontier town, bustling terminus that it was between the Erie Canal and the Great Lakes. The busy young city could not afford separate buildings for music, sports, parties, commencements, dog shows, organ recitals. One building had to hold them all, and that place was called The Music Hall.

In fact, it was not even built with music in mind. In 1885, at the northeast corner of Elmwood and Virginia, the state dedicated an armory and drill hall for the 74th Infantry. Late in 1899, the 74th transferred its military functions to a new fortress-like armory on Connecticut Street. (It is this building that was severely damaged in a fire last July.)

At the turn of the century, with the huge Pan-American Exposition in prospect, the city acquired the vacated armory on Elmwood Avenue. First, it was named Convention Hall, later The Music Hall; finally in 1912, the City Council officially designated the building as the Elmwood Music Hall.

From outside, the Music Hall was a piece of nondescript Victoriana, blending several styles of architecture without distinction. Within, it was plain and bare. There were no claims for acoustical perfection. In, fact, violinist Yehudi Menuhin once vowed to give no recital unless the Elmwood Avenue trolleys were stopped during his program. (It was a hollow threat: Menuhin played while the trolleys continued to creak and screech.)

The hall saw some great days. The New York State Democratic Convention was held there in 1906 when publisher William Randolph Hearst won nomination for governor (although he was defeated in the general election by Charles Evans Hughes). Governors Al Smith and Franklin Roosevelt spoke there frequently. Charity balls were held annually on New Year's Night, the first one in 1900 with Ansley Wilcox as general chairman.

Since it was a music hall, it is for music that the building is primarily remembered. Victor Herbert and his orchestra presented a series of summer concerts in 1904. Some of the nation's outstanding orchestras performed there; the New York, Pittsburgh, Detroit Symphonies, and, of course, a fledgling Buffalo Philharmonic.

John Philip Sousa directed his band in several stirring programs. Some veteran Buffalonians still recall these Sousa appearances: Mrs. Elizabeth Nash Gormley of South Buffalo remembers buying an inexpensive ticket for a Sousa concert. To her chagrin, Mrs. Gormley was seated in the center of the hall's very front row.

As she took her seat, Mrs. Gormley thought that through some lucky chance, she had been sold a choice seat at a bargain price. There was the great band leader entering only a few feet away from her!

But when Sousa lowered his baton, Mrs. Gormley realized that there had been no mistake: in the front row, she was overwhelmed by the Sousa sound!

Elizabeth Gormley remembers hearing Irish tenor John McCormick, pianist-composer Serge Rachmaninoff, portly British author-lecturer Gilbert K. Chesterton. She recollects with pleasure the kindly smile and courtly manner of Polish pianist Ignaz Paderewski.

Many musicians of legend performed at Buffalo's Elmwood Music Hall: singers Mary Garden, Madame Schumann-Heink, Geraldine Ferrar, Anelita Galli-Curci, Lily Pons, Nellie Melba, Rose Bampton; composer-pianists Camille Saint-Saens, Richard Strauss, Percy Grainger; violinists Jascha Heifetz, Mischa Elman, Fritz Kreisler.

The largest crowd in the history of the Elmwood Music Hall turned out to hear Enrico Caruso singing arias from *Aida* and *Pagliacci*. Nearly as big was the audience that assembled on Feb. 25, 1938, for baritone Nelson Eddy. This was the last event at the Elmwood because two days later, the building was declared unsafe and condemned for future use. Before the year's end, it was demolished.

There were no efforts to save the Elmwood Music Hall from destruction because the wooden roof supports had been groaning threateningly for years.

CONTINUED ON PAGE 42

REVIVING HIGH SCHOOL DIPLOMAS

PUBLISHED IN THE WALL STREET JOURNAL ∞ 06 – 11 – 84

*T*he poor high school diploma — more's the pity — has fallen on bad days. For too long, it has been conferred indiscriminately on all who pursue a high school program, however haphazard that program may be. The standard diploma is a blanket that covers the competent and the conscientious as well as the lazy and indifferent. Because all students receive the same document, it has ceased to attest to much knowledge or skill.

Some who despaired at the turn of events made the observation that the diploma resembled a good-conduct recommendation instead of a certificate of academic mastery. After all, graduates walked down aisles carrying their high school's credential, although they were, alas, unable functionally to read and write.

But the diploma was hardly awarded for good conduct either. Some frightful miscreants, who outraged teachers and school authority, have walked across stages and shaken hands with principals who heaved deep sighs of relief at their departures.

The diploma was not even an attendance certificate since recipients had often been extremely irregular and undependable in their school appearances.

So what does the diploma from high school mean? Requirements stipulate a number of non-sequential units in English — four; in social studies, but not necessarily history — two; in mathematics and science — one each. A grand total of 16 units, about four per year, is the modest minimum for graduation.

The program permits "electives" so that, instead of studying basic English skills and usage, a student may elect, say, a unit in rock music lyrics. "Parenting" is a popular social studies elective useful, perhaps, but scarcely academic.

New York State has an alternate diploma — the so-called Regents Certificate. Candidates for this testimonial must submit to standardized tests to establish competence in given areas. However, few people were aware of the difference between a Regents diploma and an ordinary school diploma. And so, regardless of the courses taken or the level of their difficulty, nearly everyone got the same high school diploma of dubious value.

Happily, however slowly, times seem to be changing. With the general and

41

justifiable cry for improvement in education (really it should not yet be called excellence), New York State has taken firm steps to restore meaning to the high school diploma.

In 1978, New York instituted basic competency tests in mathematics, reading and writing. Without successfully passing these state prepared, state-supervised tests, no student can now attain a diploma.

This year, basic diploma requirements have been raised. Effective with the class that enters 9th grade next September, each high school candidate for a Regents diploma must complete four units in social studies, as well as English, and two units each in mathematics and science. In addition to this, a brave new stipulation mandates three years of foreign language study.

Furthermore, new teachers beginning assignments after September "must demonstrate proficiency in English, social studies, mathematics, science and arts and pedagogical practices as part of an entry-level examination."

Pending legislative approval, in June 1985, schools will receive additional state financial aid for net increases in the number of students passing Regents examinations in subjects like foreign language study.

Such steps have been a long time coming; they are sound and wise. It is planned to extend the upgradings to the school-diploma program also. Given time, the battered high school diploma may once again earn a status that it deserves. ∞

— ∞ —

HUMBLE MUSIC HALL ATTRACTED...

CONTINUED FROM PAGE 40

Anyway, Buffalo had attained an age when it could afford separate show-places for sports and music. Already in 1938, there were proposals for a new sports auditorium and a different music hall.

In its half century of service, no one ever said seriously that the Elmwood Music Hall was a beautiful building — nor with its folding chairs was it a comfortable one. At its departure from the local scene, musical functions moved to the Buffalo Consistory (now Canisius High School), then, within two years, to a completely new Kleinhans Music Hall.

What its predecessor had lacked in comfort and charm, this new hall possessed. Happily, Kleinhans Music Hall, a structure of grace and acoustical excellence, continues to maintain Buffalo's musical traditions, once embodied in the bare and bleak Elmwood Music Hall. ∞

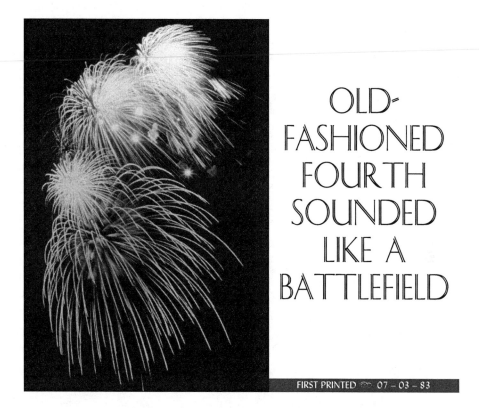

OLD-FASHIONED FOURTH SOUNDED LIKE A BATTLEFIELD

FIRST PRINTED ⌀ 07 – 03 – 83

"When in the course of human events, it becomes necessary for one people to dissolve the political bands..."

The stirring phrases of Thomas Jefferson's Declaration were not often in my thoughts on the Fourth of July; and yet he was in a measure responsible for; the mad, wild, dangerous doings that I remember from my boyhood. For excitement and love of life, nothing compared to the "Fourth" of the years in the early 1930s, a time when I was about ten years old.

Fireworks were completely legal then and could be purchased freely at any corner store. Every boy would save his money to buy several packages of fireworks, and even though the money quite literally went up in smoke, the shooting was a moment of glorious climax — a shot heard round our little world.

At that period in American history, more than a century since Jefferson had breathed his last, the Great Depression was a discouraging fact of life. To save money for firecrackers, boys had to forego many pleasures, but the

Depression never interfered with my family's lavish observance of Independence Day. I can explain simply why it did not.

My father had worked for the S.O. Barnum Co. on Main Street before he opened his own business, and for the rest of Barnum's business tenure, Dad maintained a close connection with his former employer and fellow employees. This connection was especially exciting for me at Fourth of July because Barnum's sold fireworks in wholesale quantities, and fireworks obviously could not be stored from one year until the next.

So, every year, late in the afternoon of July 3, Dad would drive uptown to buy assorted unsold fireworks. The boxes, the variety, the sheer amount that Dad brought home for us to explode was staggering. We could have supplied the American insurgents for an additional skirmish against the British.

Dad loved fireworks. With a danger-be-damned attitude, he would-dismiss any objections of my faint-hearted mother. "They've got to learn to use fireworks," he would say about us children. The weight of such logic overwhelmed all argument, as though he were saying, "The boys have to learn arithmetic." I was totally convinced and ready to devote myself whole-heartedly to the mastery of fireworks.

The supply of explosives had transformed our house into an arsenal, and on the morning of July 4, my brother and I could not wait to start shooting off the seemingly endless supply. Dad was never home until later in the morning, and I suspect that he was making another trip to Barnum's to get more leftovers.

In Dad's absence, we would run to my mother, whose job it was to parcel out firecrackers. Mother's lack of enthusiasm always conflicted with our expectation, and now I can realize why. The poor woman was understandably terrified for our safety. After all, she was giving us explosives which, carelessly used, were more than adequate to cost the loss of a finger or an eye or the use of an ear.

Her face would contort. So, I suppose, many a mother in Colonial America kissed off her son as he went to join Washington's tattered army. "Hold out your hands," she would say, forcing a kind of smile.

My brother Joe and I would extend our fingers, twitching to begin the compelling activities associated with our nation's birthday.

"How many fingers do you have?" Mother asked.

Patiently, Joe and I answered the strange question.

"You want to have your ten fingers left tonight, don't you?" There followed a stern lecture on safety, and I suppose it did make some impression on us because I can recall it so vividly. Poor Mother was a very conservative woman, married to my father, whose devotion to fireworks was fanatical. Finally, she issued us our first round.

We received a pack of "Attaboy" firecrackers. Attaboys came in several sizes, and Mother would start us on the medium range. A two-inch Attaboy would be about the diameter of a pencil; a wick protruded from each cracker and these wicks were neatly braided so the firecrackers formed a flat, compact package, wrapped in shiny, pink paper. On the top was a picture of an emotionless Oriental youth, sitting in Buddha-like position. The letters A-T-T-A-B-O-Y were spelled out in yellow over his head.

To light these firecrackers, Mother gave us a piece of punk. "Punk" was a brownish stick; lighted, it would glow with a red tip, emitting a stale, heavy smell. One touch of the punk's glowing tip to the firecracker's wick, and the wick would begin to hiss and spark.

We would start Fourth of July morning gingerly, heeding Mother's admonitions. A firecracker lighted in the sandbox would blow sand about in all directions; another under an empty coffee can would produce a hollow noise, and the can would jump several feet into the air.

In no time, we would be back to Mother, asking for a new supply. Ruefully, she gave us from her bounty. There were lady-fingers, tiny, pin-sized firecrackers which were intended to be shot off in series with one pop after another. Or torpedoes: a torpedo looked like a Hershey Bud of chocolate except that the wrapping was of brown paper instead of tin-foil. Inside, there was a powder charge surrounded by countless granular stones.

A torpedo was thrown, and on impact, the tiny stones smashing together detonated the explosive. There followed a bang, and the bits of paper and stone flew about. (I shudder now to imagine how many accidents torpedoes may have caused. My older brother once filled his trouser pocket with torpedoes and promptly fell down the stairs. Resultant explosions burned his pants and drove bits of the stone and shrapnel into his leg.)

Late in the morning, Dad came home, surreptitiously carrying several large boxes more of Barnum's leftovers. He couldn't wait to change his clothes and get out in the yard with us. Ignoring my mother's solicitations that he have lunch, Dad would appear with his own piece of punk and a package of the large-size Attaboys. Each large Attaboy was about the size of a normal forefinger. Dad was dealing with powerful explosives now, and naturally, we kids loved it.

Out would come more empty coffee cans, and under them, Dad would set a giant Attaboy. Poised in an athletic stance, ready to run, Dad would light the wick. Pow! The can went flying 15 feet into the air. We would look on with dismay while Dad, transfixed with glee, planned his next shot.

Every year, our father made us a cannon. For some reason, this rustic device was not saved from year to year. Instead, we would go to the cellar with Dad while he fashioned a triangular frame out of 2 by 4's. The hypotenuse of this frame was about three feet in length, and to this piece, Dad would fasten a length of lead pipe. He would drive in 3-inch nails half way and bend them over to grasp the pipe.

We bore our crude cannon outside and into its mouth would go Attaboy firecrackers. I can recall the nervous excitement when the glowing end of punk was touched to the firecracker's fuse.

We would crouch behind the primitive cannon like Revolutionary artillerymen at Yorktown. With a huge noise, the Attaboys would explode in the lead pipe, and the cannon's frame would shake with the shock. As I reconstruct the scene now, I wonder that we were not seriously hurt, but always there was my father, supremely confident, enjoying the spectacle and the noise no end.

I can't remember any lunch on the Fourth of July, probably because we were all so preoccupied that we forgot hunger. Pack after pack of Attaboys was consumed. An endless supply of tin cans was blown into the air; cardboard boxes were blasted apart; our cannons roared.

As the day drew on, we became more careless. Having shot off so many firecrackers, we lost our fear and began to ignore Mother's specific interdict. Holding the punk in our left hand and the firecracker in our right, we would touch one to the other. Watching the lighted wick begin to sizzle, we would throw the firecracker into the air. There was a special attraction to seeing the firecracker burst with a flash.

Or woe to the unwary cat who tried to slink by us on the Fourth. In our careless phase, we would throw a lighted firecracker at the hapless animal and it would scurry for safety.

Somehow, the Fourth would slow toward evening, and our firecrackers and torpedoes proved not to be limitless. Aside from a few minor burns, we had escaped injury, and Mother began to breathe easier. Now we waited eagerly for nightfall because Dad had several boxes filled with evening attractions.

Neighbors would come to our house at twilight because every year, Dad's display was worth seeing. The neighbors would sit on rockers on the front porch or on the steps; they would draw the awnings to get a fuller view. Some little old women like Mrs. Clifford would jump at the slightest bang.

Dad was just as impatient as we were to get the evening display started. Before it was really dark enough for best effect, he nailed the first pinwheel to a telegraph pole; it would whiz round and round sending off white, green and red sparks.

Roman candles were flaming, varicolored balls, propelled from a cardboard tube about 18 inches in length. They afforded a striking spectacle, propelled about 15 feet through the darkness. If the operator was intrepid, like my impresario father, he waved the wand in a circle, launching the fiery balls into various orbits.

Once, a flaming ball backfired through the end of the tube and shot into and burned through Dad's shirtsleeve. He was undaunted, although several old neighbors gasped.

Then, there was the "House on Fire." This structure was made of cardboard and as a chimney, the house had a round, red cartridge filled with surprises. When lighted, this chimney first shot brilliant silver sparks at the night; after a moment, it belched a fiery, green torrent; finally, there would be an explosion followed by a general conflagration which would consume the ill-fated house.

The "House on Fire" sometimes assumed the Identity of the "Little Red School House." The very same display occurred, but the frame of the doomed structure was now that of a school. Perhaps the manufacturers were giving children a chance to vent their simmering resentments after a recently completed school year.

The summer evening had burned itself down, even as the "House on Fire." Piece by piece, all Dad's stock had been consumed, but one thing remained.

Sparklers! We had boxes of sparklers, enough for everybody, and enough to last for a long time. By now, it was totally dark, and when the silvery sparks jabbed into the blackness, they brought a quiet, almost hypnotic peace.

We children got our sparklers first; then, each neighbor was given one to hold. Mrs. Nash took the sparkler's wire handle and held it timidly at a distance, smiling appreciatively.

Over sparklers, there was always neighborhood conversation among the "old folks," while we children held our sparklers aloft in the stance of the Statue of Liberty. Or we waved our arms and made patterns of sparks in the night around us.

We were fast approaching the concluding phase of Fourth of July. When the final sparkler had coughed its dying flicker, when the neighbors had said their good-byes and complimented Dad on his show, there was left only cleanup.

We took push brooms and swept together the forsaken relics of our Independence Day celebration. All the battered wrappings of Attaboy crackers and packages, the dented blackened tin cans, a few charred walls of the disaster-prone House on Fire, tubes that had held the Roman Candles — all were swept into the debris of Fourth of July.

"And for the support of this declaration," concluded Jefferson's Declaration of Independence, "we mutually pledge to each other our lives, our fortunes and our sacred honor."

Such noble words deserved a more dignified and respectful anniversary celebration than we accorded them. Yet, Thomas Jefferson had a capacity for gadgets and novelty; I am sure he would have smiled tolerantly at our observance because he also had a sense of fun. ∞

THE PRIEST WHO PLAYED POLITICS

FIRST PRINTED ⌒ 09 – 30 – 84

In the middle of a Sunday afternoon 50 years ago, an eerie but habitual stillness brooded over our house. Dad sat expectantly in his shirt sleeves while we children perched gingerly on overstuffed chairs.

Focus of attention was the table-model radio, shaped like a Gothic cathedral window. Dad was working the dials, and gradually through the crackling, a rich, deep, prophet-like voice filled the room. It was time to listen to Father Coughlin.

For us survivors of the Great Depression, Father Coughlin's name, like his voice, was magic. He commanded an immense radio following, as he struggled at first to create the New Deal, later to destroy it.

Talk about religion in politics. "The New Deal is Christ's deal," proclaimed the radio priest to 20 million faithful. Mesmerized listeners responded with about 50,000 letters each week, most of them containing a scarce Depression commodity, the dollar bill.

The Rev. Charles E. Coughlin was a big, handsome man. Irish Canadian by birth, he had been educated in Canada and always retained a trace of brogue in his speech. He was pastor of a small, frame Catholic church, "The Shrine of the Little Flower" in Royal Oak, Mich., where he began his radio career.

In the mid-1920s, Father Coughlin ministered to a children's audience on WJR in Detroit. Early in his talks to kiddies about saints and catechism, he made asides to parents, warning against: "money changers" and "subversive socialism." When hard times struck Detroit, Father Coughlin gradually changed his radio audience from children to adults, and his sermons became increasingly political. In Depression time, Herbert Hoover was an easy and obvious target.

Father Coughlin loved alliteration. He damned Hoover for his affiliation with bankers: "Morgan, Mellon, Mills and Meyer." He urged the president's defeat in 1932, championing the Democratic candidate with the ringing phrase "Roosevelt or Ruin!"

49

However, Father Coughlin's alliance with President Roosevelt was short-lived. By 1934, he was denouncing the new president as a liar; that year, Coughlin's power reached its apogee when he founded his own political party, the Union Party. To complement the political movement, Father Coughlin launched a newspaper called Social Justice.

What the new party was "for" was more difficult to assess than what it was "against." It was for social justice (a difficult concept to oppose), nationalizing banks, utilities and natural resources. More dynamically stated was what Coughlin and his party opposed: Roosevelt, communism, labor unions, "godless capitalism," "international bankers and plutocrats."

Donations poured in to the shrine at Royal Oak. In place of the frame church, Father Coughlin built a new stone edifice, topped by a seven-story tower. Here, Coughlin composed his fiery sermons. Chain-smoking cigarettes, his only companion was a huge, Great Dane dog.

In 1934, more than 5 million Americans affiliated with the Union Party. In 1936, to oppose Roosevelt's reelection, the party nominated Conservative North Dakota Rep. William Lemke for president. Coughlin's rhetoric against Roosevelt was reminiscent of Cicero's against Catiline in ancient Rome. Coughlin called the president "Franklin Double-Crossing Roosevelt" and "the great betrayer and liar."

As a third-party candidate, Lemke polled fewer than 900,000 votes, partially because the Union Party was disallowed from the ballot in many big states. With this rebuke, Father Coughlin withdrew temporarily from politics, only to return in 1938, as head of a new group of more militant followers. By now, threats of World War II were apparent, and Father Coughlin placed himself firmly on the side of American isolation.

His newspaper Social Justice assumed an anti-Semitic flavor, flailing at Jewish bankers. Week after week in his newspaper and on the radio, Father Coughlin's charges became more fanatical. Then, in 1941, Cardinal Mooney ordered the priest to stop broadcasting.

Shortly after, America entered the war, and Social Justice was banned from the mails. Father Coughlin, deprived of his weapons and under further pressure from church authorities, accepted obscurity with unexpected composure.

Devoting himself only to pastoral duties, Father Coughlin served his congregation quietly until his retirement in 1966. When he died on Oct. 27, 1979, few Americans noticed.

We, who knew the Depression, remember that Sunday afternoon hush when it was time for Father Coughlin, part mystic, part demagogue, to pass on his message to millions. ∞

THE OLD DAYS OF
THE TROLLEY PLOWS

FIRST PRINTED ☞ 02 – 03 – 85

*W*hen streetcars rumbled over Buffalo streets, the transit company, then called the International Railway Company (IRC), used to share snow removal chores with the city. Different from city equipment, the IRC plows moved on tracks, never got stuck, and never had crippling visibility problems. Sleet, snow, blizzard — plows cleared the tracks, and streetcars kept running.

It is curious to remember storm cleanup back then in contrast to that of recent experience. Fifty years ago, as soon as a storm struck, out came the trolley sweepers; huge, revolving brushes scraped tracks bare. Then the plows followed, fitted with immense blades which could be lowered into position on both sides. Since tracks lay in midstreet, plows could effectively clear the entire street in one sweep.

I can still see these mighty vehicles, grinding through deep and heavy drifts. Like a Cyclops, their single front light pierced the darkness of night or storm. Snow would fly frantically in every direction, as rail-plows moved with the ponderous inexorability of a Sherman tank. For years, they kept the city open when ordinary plows faltered.

Not all rail-plows had the push of the double-blade vehicles I describe. The IRC, never notable for modern equipment, had installed plow blades to the front of some of its old Niagara Gorge Route trolley cars. Awaiting a call to winter action, they stood along one siding in the Cold Spring Yard at Main and Michigan Streets. Even these veterans of a defunct line pushed the snow with stubborn authority.

In the wake of such snowfighting engines came the streetcars, now able to pass safely through city streets. The whole snow attack proceeded with the efficiency of a well-planned military maneuver.

I do not remember any protracted urban paralysis following those storms of half a century ago. The reason lies partially in the fact that transit ridership was high, and streets were free of disabled cars. Plows were unhampered.

Today, most workers rely on their private motor cars for commuting to jobs. Many live outside the reach of mass transit in the country or in the suburbs. Many others shun public transit, seized by a jejune reliance on the personal car.

Given these facts, modern storm paralysis is understandable. Workers drive cars, cars get stuck and are abandoned; snowplows cannot get through to do their job. Result: traffic bans, closing of businesses and ultimately loss of future commercial contracts. The city bleeds.

Regrettably, the urban street railway will never again reclaim its former status. However, perhaps we can learn a lesson from days of the trolley. A reliable and steady mass transit system might lure passengers away from their own cars, especially in a time of storm threat. The fewer cars on city streets, the quicker any storm cleanup can proceed.

Ask anyone who remembers the Buffalo trolley era. ∞

OLD DOWNTOWN LIBRARY
HAD STYLE

FIRST PRINTED ☞ 12 – 02 – 84

Even in a time of financial crisis, talk of curtailing Buffalo's library system ought to be unspeakable. There's always been a library, and unless we return to a civilization of cave dwellers, there always will be.

True, libraries were not always as comfortable and convenient as the county's central building is now. There was, for example, the Downtown Public Library of my youth, an edifice once situated on Washington Street on the very site of its replacement.

Drafty, rambling, illogical, the old library had nonetheless a mighty charm. Built in 1874, the old library building was a geometer's dream. There were triangles and hexagons and parabolas. Romanesque arches were everywhere, popping out from gables and towers. It was an indescribable building, but it was our central library until 1960.

People waiting for the Broadway streetcar used to duck into the vaulted foyer in bad weather and stand huddled in its gloom waiting for the sparks and clanging that meant that the No. 4 trolley was on its way along Washington Street.

To enter the big hall, where most of the library's business was transacted, you walked past a ponderous elevator, encased in a mesh of iron work. This elevator, when it operated, was nearly as noisy as the trolleys outside.

The great hall with huge semicircular windows held the card catalogs, request counter, book return desk; it was a hum of activity, and from it opened all sorts of smaller rooms.

If you wanted to kill a few spare hours (of which I had plenty back then), you could amble along to a reading room toward Washington Street. This room formed a corner — or as much of a corner as a hexagonal front provided. It had large, single-pane windows.

Since the library was not far from the Seamen's Home down Main Street, retired sailors often battened into the BPL reading room. Many are the times

53

that I sat in one of the big Windsor chairs and shared a table with a veteran seaman from the Great Lakes.

The sailors were voracious readers, swimming through books like "Before the Mast on the Pacific" or "With Camera and Compass in the Caribbean." Whenever a Broadway streetcar rounded the bend just outside on Washington Street, the huge windows would tremble and the floors would shake. Noise built to a feverish crescendo until the trolley executed its turn and rattled away out Broadway. Regular readers had been conditioned to ignore this temporary eruption.

On rainy days, the trickle of water was everywhere, and not all of it was outside. Leaks were common around the windows, and in fact, to remedy some minor drainage problem, a formidable downspout ran horizontally through about 50 feet of the fiction open shelf. Wires embraced this pipe and held it uncertainly to the ceiling. In a heavy downpour, rainwater gargled wildly right over the Cs and Ds. Thus, if you happened to be searching out a Joseph Conrad novel like "Typhoon," the mood would be complete.

Air conditioning? Of course in winter, the air conditioning was so efficient that without any imagination, you could feel bursts of cold air fresh off the lake. Naturally in summer, the heating system was likewise efficient, especially in the two upper floors.

Upper floors remind me of those stairs. Reluctant to entrust one's safety to the elevator or unable to afford the considerable wait, most researchers made their way to the second floor up the narrow stone steps.

Having attained the second floor, there were archways leading into connecting rooms. Wooden floors groaned underfoot as you went to one of the massive tables. Most research books were on the second floor.

The truly dedicated school might even ascend to the third floor, where old newspapers and magazines were stored. (It was an age long before microfilm.) The going here was increasingly precarious, with steep wood stairs and floors that creaked threateningly.

Before the old main library was demolished, there was a sale of the building's artifacts. I bought several Windsor chairs of the kind that used to furnish the first floor reading room. One of them survives in my basement room. Sitting in that chair, I can brood dire thoughts about any legislator who wants to hamper the county libraries.

Or, in a benign mood, I can close my eyes and dream that I am in the reading room, seated across the table from an old sailor. If a noisy airplane, flying very low, passes overhead, I can even imagine a Broadway streetcar rounding the turn from Washington Street heading out toward Sattler's. ∞

DAYS OF DOWNTOWN MOVIE PALACES

FIRST PRINTED ☞ 01 – 20 – 85

$\mathcal{G}$ reat Lakes, Hippodrome, Century, Lafayette: those were the names of giant theaters which once winked and glittered along Main Street. They formed Buffalo's moving picture district in the era of Garbo and Gable, of Betty Grable and Errol Flynn. At closing time on a busy weekend night, these theaters spilled about 10,000 people into downtown streets.

Every large city had its central moving picture houses: huge, cavernous, palatial. Buffalo's movie section began with the Lafayette Theater, the only big, downtown showplace located off Main Street. Flagship of the Basil theater chain, the Lafayette had a circular marquee wrapped around its corner on Washington Street, just opposite the Rand Building.

The next theater out Main Street was the Century. Originally called Loew's State, the Century changed its name when it became the first-run outlet for film of the 20th Century Hollywood studio.

Two blocks farther out Main began Shea Country. The Hippodrome and the Great Lakes (later, under Paramount ownership, renamed the Center and the Paramount) were massive theaters which had originally been designed for vaudeville.

The real glory of the Shea theater empire, however, was unquestionably the Buffalo. Planned and built by Mike Shea, the Buffalo opened in 1926. Spectacularly ornate, Shea's Buffalo was the colossus of local theaters. It seated 3,000 people, had a mighty organ and boasted a majestic dome capable of many spectacular lighting effects.

Shea's Buffalo even had its own theater orchestra, which was hoisted out of a pit to accompany vaudeville acts and performers. For years, D'Artega conducted and Gertrude Lutzi sang. Such live entertainment was coupled with a feature movie.

All downtown theaters were manned by an elite cadre of ushers. Their uniforms were dignified, subdued, impeccable: wing-tipped collars, bow tie, cutaway vest, side-striped trousers. Colors varied: ushers at the Hippodrome wore dark blue; at the Lafayette, maroon; at the Buffalo, black. At one period, Shea's Buffalo ushers even wore white gloves to emphasize their formality.

In those days, you didn't have to go to London's Buckingham Palace to see the changing of the guard. Three times a day, at downtown theaters, ushers marched with military precision to take their positions or to relieve a retiring corps.

Overflow crowds were common. After all seats were filled, ushers stretched velvet ropes across aisles to hold standees in place. Meanwhile, they patrolled the aisles, searching out empty seats, piercing the darkness with their indispensable flashlights. Sometimes for very popular attractions, crowds trailed out into long lines stretching along Main Street.

All the big downtown theaters had balconies which were the scenes of countless off-screen romances. Maybe it was the influence of Gary Cooper and Joan Crawford setting an example in front of them, maybe it was just the altitude, but love bloomed freely among couples in the balconies.

Not much is left today of those great downtown movie shows. The Lafayette and the Hippodrome are obliterated. The Main Street facades of the Century and the Great Lakes still stand, patiently awaiting demolition. If anyone should feel sentimental about the Century, he can drop into the Macaroni Company restaurant on Pearl Street. Imaginatively mounted there are some of the old theater's signs and seats as part of Macaroni's decor.

Only Shea's Buffalo survives from the golden days of the silver screen. Its organ, its paintings, its elegant foyer are preserved almost intact.

Actually Shea's Buffalo has a double sense of purpose. It offers a vivid look at the bygone glamour of the movie era, and it fills a key position in the city's hopes for a new, vibrant theater section of the future. ∞

A MONSTER LIVING IN THE BASEMENT

FIRST PRINTED ∞ 01 – 20 – 85

All of us who remember the era of the coal furnace will agree on one thing: from November until April, it dominated our lives. Any plans we made had to include the coal furnace because to forget it could mean disaster.

It was like having an animal — a monster — living in the basement. The furnace had to be fed, emptied, cleaned, put to sleep at night. It had a mind of its own and usually disregarded orders from its master.

Fat, burly, squat, arrogant, the coal furnace had big, asbestos-covered pipes growing out of its top. Through these pipes rose the air that kept us warm — well, fairly warm during the long Buffalo winter.

Rube Goldberg must have grown up next to a coal furnace because it had a series of devices that he might have thought up. The furnace's cast-iron front had two principal doors: the firebox door and the ash-box door.

However, there were doors on doors. The firebox door had a tiny door that slid open to give a peek on what was going on within. The ash pit had a smaller door called the draft which was pulled up to make the fire burn more hotly.

The furnace's back had a sort of horizontal chimney with still another door called the damper. When opened, this door cooled a raging fire. All former furnace tenders will remember what I am describing.

Now, Rube Goldberg would have loved this next part. From the control doors, draft and damper, issued a ganglia of chains. Through dark walls and under floors, these chains stretched over a network of rings and pulleys so that they could regulate the house's temperature.

Bah, humbug! The fire in our house was always sinking in cold spells, but during a thaw, the firebox was an inferno.

Then, remember that pathetic water tank in the rear of the furnace? It

57
∞

looked like a gaping, stretched back pocket on a cheap pair of pants. Pouring in water, so said tradition, humidified the house atmosphere. Maybe, but I can recall jolts of static electricity that sent me dancing.

Anybody who ever undertook the care and feeding of the furnace will remember that stark feeling of waking up at 2 a.m. with an anxiety attack: Did I take care of the furnace last night? You'd get up then and trudge to the cellar because if you didn't...

If you didn't, if you skipped a furnace feeding, there was a fearful consequence. In the dawn's early light, you'd see steam coming from your mouth. When you got out of bed, the whole house would feel like a deserted barn because the furnace had gone out. Misery was to open the door and look into the chilly blackness of a fire that had been starved to death.

To relight the furnace was formidable. The firemaker had to plan carefully to get a wood fire blazing hot and persistently enough to ignite the coal. Then the new fire had to be watched closely for several hours because fresh fires had a way of soaring out of control.

A word about another aspect of coal-furnace care. Just as we heaved in shovels of hard, black coal, so in the normal cycle, we removed coarse, white ashes. Shaking out the ashes required special equipment — overalls. The ashes sent clouds of fine, white dust into the cellar. Woe to that furnace tender who had plastered down his hair with Wildroot Cream Oil because he could turn gray in seconds.

Nostalgia, a sentimental view of the past, can often do strange tricks. But it can never make me regret the passing out of my life of the old coal furnace. ∞

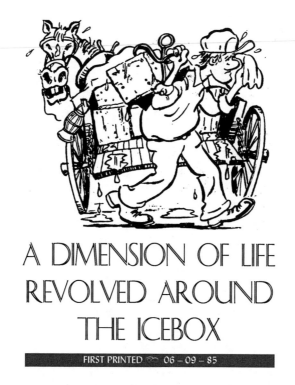

A DIMENSION OF LIFE
REVOLVED AROUND
THE ICEBOX

FIRST PRINTED ∽ 06 – 09 – 85

*T*he sleek, enameled refrigerators of the 1980s are a haughty breed. Proud and erect, they stand loaded with snob appeal — frost freedom, automatic ice-maker; top, bottom or side freezers.

In their splendor, they may try to forget their poor relations, especially that primitive oaf, the icebox.

The icebox! This harsh name derived from an exactness of description. Unused food was kept for storage in a wooden chest of stained oak. Such chests were used effectively in winter, but a large part of their advantage was lost when the cold weather yielded to summer sunshine.

Then someone had the idea of putting a cake of ice inside the box, and thereby imparting a measure of coolness even in hot weather. A dimension of life revolved around this system.

Community businesses sprang up: the local icehouse, a squat, brick or stone edifice stored tons of ice, and of course, the icehouse supplied the iceman.

A word about this dexterous tradesman. Frequently, the iceman of summer became the coalman of winter.

Thus, a common neighborhood business, "Coal and Ice," provided year-round employment. (In South Buffalo, our coal and iceman was named Joe E. Brown, a name we easily remembered because it was the same as that of a favorite movie comedian).

A burly fellow was the iceman. Tools of his trade were a gaping pair of tongs with which to wrestle the ice; his other tool was a heavy piece of leather, which padded the shoulder. His familiar figure was bent under the weight of a silver block of ice, balanced tenuously on his shoulder.

As children, we followed the ice truck, pleading for a piece of ice to suckle on a scorching July day. Sometimes, Mr. Brown would be indulgent and throw back the black, canvas tarpaulin covering the dripping ice. With a pick, he chipped off a wedge and bestowed it with kingly largess.

It was a soggy job, and no iceman wanted to lug a 25-pound of ice into a house only to discover that the housewife didn't want it. So a signal emerged.

Every ice company provided a square card, and it was the customer's task to hang this card conspicuously in the front window. The card would be suspended diamond-fashion, by its angle with one corner pointing upward. On each corner was a number 5, 10, 20, 25: these numbers referred to the size by weight of the ice cake to be delivered.

With his sharp eyes, the iceman would spot the card's top angle. "A hot day," he would ruminate. "No wonder Mrs. Lee needs 25 pounds." The tongs would snap into the ice block, and he was on his way.

A problem for the owner of the icebox lay in this: the icebox was incontinent. What was to become of the water as the big ice cakes melted?

Several solutions were presented. Some iceboxes had a catcher-pan underneath, but this required regular emptying. Other models accommodated a hose connection, and the hose might be strung down steps and out a lower window to drip freely.

However, if you lived in a beautiful house, there was the latest futuristic luxury. Designers had provided a pipe, which protruded through the floor. This pipe burrowed inside walls, under steps, finally spilling into a basement drain. A hose connected icebox channels to this marvel. Ah, the convenience of technology!

The icebox, like Cinderella, was usually kept in a back hall or a cluttered back porch. Its era is nearly forgotten today. Only now and then, a few oldsters make a slip: they mean the refrigerator, but they slip and say, "Put this away in the icebox!"

Their children wonder then, and the shiny, modern refrigerator, if it could, might wince at this reminder of its uncouth ancestor. ∞

SPIDERY OLD
FERRYBOAT SPUN
WARM MEMORIES

FIRST PRINTED ∞ 02 – 03 – 85

*L*ike crocus or robins, ships are a sign of spring. When the ferryboats leans and City of Toledo came out of winter hibernation to resume their Niagara River crossings, you could be sure that spring had come to Buffalo.

Before the Peace Bridge opened, ferries provided the only access to Canada this side of Niagara Falls for both cars and pedestrians. Until 1951, there were immigration stations at the foot of Ferry Street in Buffalo and across the river in Fort Erie.

The ferryboats Orleans and City of Toledo each had a capacity of 15 to 20 cars and up to 350 pedestrians. They accommodated international commuters year-round until the Peace Bridge opened but the traffic was especially brisk during the racing season at Fort Erie — and during the bleak American Prohibition years, when drinkers sought refuge in Canada.

The opening of the Peace Bridge in 1927 drastically cut into the ferryboats' business; nevertheless, the two ships kept operating during the summers until 1948. Then, in the face of diminishing revenues, the City of Toledo retired, leaving only the Orleans.

The Orleans was lopsided, blunt-nosed, tipsy; it sounded asthmatic, clanky, hollow. Maybe most of all, the Orleans was an arachneologist's dream.

What, you may wonder, is an arachneologist? Why, a spider expert, and he could have filled a book by studying specimens on the Orleans.

Spiders were everywhere: among the life preservers, on the windows, under stairways, in the second deck cabin, but especially lining the open, square windows on the automobile deck.

Each trip of the Orleans began with high drama — horns would blare, bells shrieked, steel platforms would crash, waters gurgled and swished. Amid such turmoil, the spidery old tub would set off on its 10 minute voyage across the Niagara River.

On the opposite side, the routine was repeated. Bangs, thuds, crashes, wheezes. The passengers, even the spiders, were so used to the confusion that they scarcely noticed.

For me, the Orleans means a wonderful summer memory from the early 1940s. Nearly every day, my girlfriend and I would go bicycling, and somehow we formed the habit of taking our bikes on the Orleans to Canada. There we rode around Fort Erie, shopping, looking at historical sites or simply loafing along the Niagara's shores. We used to joke that we and the spiders were the ship's steadiest customers.

By 1950, ferry boat patronage on the Niagara River was obviously sinking. Except when the Fort Erie race track was open, there were few pedestrians; to compete with the Peace Bridge, the Orleans charged only 25 cents per car, and this price could not cover the expense of operations. The time had come for the Orleans to sail into memory.

The Orleans, last of the local ferries, suspended service in 1951. After being moored on Grand Island for four years, it was cut up for scrap in 1955. The closest you can come to it now is a model on permanent display at the Buffalo and Erie County Historical Society.

But no model can duplicate those unforgettable snorts and clanks or the acres of lace spun by clever Niagara River spiders. ∞

OPENER CONJURES MEMORIES

FIRST PRINTED ∞ 04 – 20 – 85

*T*he return of Triple-A baseball to Buffalo stirs tender sentiments about past International League Bison teams and their triumphant home openers.

Opening Day for the Bisons used to be the equivalent of a civic holiday. Local courts and offices closed for a half-day, and schools were dismissed at noon so workers and students could see the Opening Day parades.

The parades were lavish. Bisons players in uniform, grinning self consciously, rode in open cars waving to cheering crowds. There were plenty of pretty girls in the cars, throwing out souvenir buttons, candy and even free tickets.

Bands marched in the parades and they always played "Take Me Out to the Ball Game." All the floats, bands and cars had the same final destination — Offermann Stadium.

Offermann Stadium…there's a memory to conjure.

Hot dogs, beer, the hearty aroma of cigar smoke, splendid cool summer evenings, friendly spectators — take these ingredients and wrap them in a package and it might look like the old stadium at Michigan Avenue and Ferry Street.

Part of the reason for the continuing success of the Bisons was that intimate, peppery stadium. To a boy of the 1930s, Offermann Stadium — named after Buffalo Bisons' president Francis J. Offermann — is unforgettable. The Ferry Street entrance had six arched doorways. Big, white signs mounted over each listed ticket prices: General Admission 50 cents, Bleachers 25 cents. In the stadium lobby were pictures of renowned Bisons, who helped carry the city's baseball fortunes to glory.

Through the turnstiles and into the grandstand…where the meticulously tended playing field appeared, a neat contrast of grass green with base-path tan. In England, groundskeeper Joe E. Brown would have been knighted for his civic service.

The high, black center field scoreboard listed the batting orders for the Bisons and their opponents. Billboard posters covered outfield fences, many advertising local products — Beck's Beer, Rich's Ice Cream, Manru Beer, Mel's $9.99 suits for men and MacDoel's Drum Bar Restaurant.

The porches of houses on Woodlawn Avenue were far higher than sta-

63

dium fences and became box seats for the lucky homeowners and their guests. As fans took their seats inside the stadium, these back porches (called the bootleg bleachers) also were filling with people, smugly propping their feet on the porch railing.

Many were the Depression children who watched those fortunate Woodlawn dwellers and wished their homes had such an exotic location. In the days before portable radios, they were probably the only spectators who could watch the game and hear Roger Baker's graphic radio descriptions.

Before the game, the Bisons, wearing spanking white flannel uniforms, practiced. The visiting team, dressed in grey, was equally formal. Compared to modern baseball garb, uniforms of that time were like white tie and tails. Suits were, of course, more restricting, more uncomfortable, but this was an age of ceremony.

The Bison manager would stalk the field. I recall vividly colorful Bison managers such as Ray Schalk, Gabby Hartnett or Paul Richards strutting about like field marshals.

Whether you were at the ball park or listening on the radio, one sound penetrated distance. There was a raspy-voiced vendor whose tenor notes scratched the atmosphere as he went through the stands — "Beer-ah-nice-ice cold bear-ah" — his voice cracking like Andy Devine's in the movies.

"Play Ball!" the chief umpire would command, and the evening's serious activity began.

A share of the popularity of the old Bisons belongs to Offermann Stadium. When it was torn down in 1955 and the team was transferred to War Memorial, somehow local baseball did not survive the change. The "Rockpile" always has been a cold, forbidding misfit, vainly searching for a mission in the world.

This year, let there be no sighs for the departed International League seasons. The umpire will shout "Play Ball!" to a new Bison affiliation with the Triple-A American Association. Furthermore, unless there is a major error — not by players, but by politicians — there ought to be a new baseball stadium clearly in sight.

Maybe Buffalo Bisons baseball still has its big inning ahead — bigger even than those in that spirited, feisty old Offermann Stadium. ∞

3RD GRADER LEARNS A LESSON ABOUT LOVE ON VALENTINE'S DAY

FIRST PRINTED ∞ 02 – 14 – 85

Long ago, when I was a third grader at Holy Family School in South Buffalo, all the boys and girls had seats on one side of the classroom; all the girls were arranged primly on the opposite side.

I suppose this sort of segregation was meant to keep students' thoughts on their school work. It did not accomplish the purpose for me. I had spied out a dark-haired, Irish beauty named Kathleen Doyle. She may have sat across the room from me, but she occupied a place near to my heart.

I used to cup my hands over my eyes and pretend to be intent on my book, but I really was studying Kathleen. My condition was akin to love, and Valentine's Day seemed an ideal time to tell her this.

Parochial school back then was dead serious. The nun teachers were strict and offered us few opportunities for levity. However, as Valentine's Day approached, our teacher, Sister Lucy, a dear and saintly woman, told us that she would save some class time on Feb. 14 for a Valentine exchange.

Perhaps valentines still come in the same varieties they did then. Some were printed on cheap paper with grotesquely insulting cartoons.

There were novel ones that pivoted and did unusual things. For example, a colorful cuckoo clock might have a movable pendulum: when the pendulum swung, a tiny bird would pop out a door. "I'm cuckoo over you," would read the caption. "Be my valentine."

A third variety was mawkishly sentimental: a big, red heart of satin would be mounted on a white background with ornate paper lace. The caption, dripping emotion, might read: "Because I love you deeply I want you to be my valentine." Such loving tributes cost a quarter.

Sometimes under stress of extreme emotion, we boys might shoot the remains of Christmas gift money to buy this king of tribute for our mothers. When I was in third grade, I decided to send such a valentine to Kathleen Doyle.

With trepidation, I gave my 25 cents to the storekeeper, hoping he wouldn't make a prying remark like "You must really be in love."

I wrote out routine valentines to my classmates, but the one to Kathleen

Doyle I studied and contemplated. There was the big, red, padded heart. "I want you to be my valentine," it sobbed. Somehow, at age 9, I didn't realize just how sickening the whole thing was.

I wrote "To Kathleen From George," put the throbbing message into an envelope and sealed it for delivery from Sister Lucy's mail bag.

On entering class on Feb. 14, all of us students dropped our valentines into a big sack. In the afternoon, Sister got some of the brightest girls to help her sort the valentines for delivery. One of them was Kathleen Doyle.

With hawk-like attention, I watched the proceedings. I saw my envelope for Kathleen, so much larger and heavier than the rest, causing a stir among the valentine-sorting committee. There were a few giggles as they pointed to Kathleen.

Sister Lucy's attention was caught and she picked up my weighty envelope, smiling amusedly. The curiosity of the whole class was arrested, and for the first time, I realized that I had made a mistake.

Several favored girls were chosen to walk around the room making valentine deliveries. Still watching closely, I saw my valentine to Kathleen laid on her desk. Gradually, all the cards and envelopes were distributed, and at a signal, we all started examining our valentine greetings.

Mild confusion surrounded Kathleen Doyle. I saw her pass my valentine to another girl, and they both broke into high-pitched laughter.

The big, red heart was making a sensation; it was passed from one girl to another, and then it found its way to the boys' side of the room. One laughing face after another turned toward me.

In the midst of this, Kathleen's eyes met mine. Far from the fond glance I had hoped for, her face was filled with scorn, the pretty features contorted in mockery. I burned in embarrassment that I had confessed my love.

One final humiliation lay in store. The ground that day was covered with wet snow. We students had dragged a lot of it into school, and the floors were streaked with dirty water.

As I was walking out in line with my class at dismissal, there lay my valentine in the grime of the vestibule floor. The red heart was torn and textured with the heel marks of students' boots.

"Hey, there's your valentine!" somebody taunted. I didn't need to be reminded.

Kathleen probably has had other men in her life since me. I hope that she has made them happier than she made me that soggy Valentine's Day many years ago. ∞

'THE CYCLONE' WAS THE TERROR OF THE MIDWAY

FIRST PRINTED ⌒ 05 – 19 – 85

*F*or years the most famous ride in the Crystal Beach Amusement Park was the spine-rattling coaster called "the Cyclone."

Like a huge and terrifying monster, the Cyclone lurked in the heart of the park's midway. Towering over everything, it dominated the acre of land adjoining the dance hall. Screams of its riders and the roar of its cars could be heard to the park's far reaches.

As mothers walked the midway with their families, toddlers would howl in fear when they approached the Cyclone. Teen-agers looked forward to the spring reopening of Crystal Beach because maybe this year, they might be old enough or big enough to ride the Cyclone. It was a rite of puberty for boys who desired to be men.

A long ramp led to its roofed entrance. There, glum-faced, suspicious operators eyed every rider, sifting out the small fry. "Get away, kid!" they'd bark. "You're too little!"

Accepted riders wore fated looks as they lined up for the next coaster car, like prisoners awaiting execution. When they boarded the padded seats, a bar, covered with some sponge-like fabric, locked into place over the rider's lap.

The Cyclone train was towed by a constant chain to the top of the first hill; on the way up, if you were in the outside seat, you could look down on the sleazy game stands that still flourish there. If you faced straight ahead, you might see that noble pleasure ship, the Canadiana.

At the pinnacle of the first hill, nonsense ended. There was a wooden plank arching the top on which the words "Hold Your Hats!" were painted. The words had a sense of destiny like Dante's "Abandon Hope, All Ye Who Enter Here!"

To describe the ride requires superlatives: breathtaking, startling, dynamic, incredible, fantastic. From the phenomenal first hill through turns where the car was absolutely vertical (held to the track only by centrifugal force), over the last, small ridge (on which the train sometimes stalled in windy weather and had to be cranked over), the Cyclone ride deserved its exalted place in Crystal Beach history.

Some showoffs — to dramatize their disregard for safety — would ride no hands, holding a handkerchief flamboyantly overhead.

Stories about the Cyclone abounded. A suicide was said to have jumped spectacularly to his destruction from atop Hill No. 1. A woman's hair reportedly turned from black to gray during the ride. One hapless rider trying to grasp a giant butterfly (affixed whimsically to the top of the third hill) broke his arm in the mad effort. Naturally, sensible riders, if there were any, did not place much faith in such tales.

Once, on a first date, I took a girlfriend to Crystal Beach. Roaring down the first hill, the poor girl slumped helplessly. I put my arm around her, trying to stir some sign of life, but she remained limp until the ride's end.

When we returned to the boarding platform, the sour-faced Cyclone crew realized the problem: another customer had passed out. With routine efficiency, they brought smelling salts and quickly revived her. Strangely, that girl never wanted to go out with me again.

The Cyclone was dismantled in 1949, and some of its steel was used to build its replacement, the Comet. Perhaps the Cyclone was just too frightening for ordinary people; passengers needed unusual prowess, bravery, sense of adventure, courage of heart. So at least I like to tell myself, because I was a frequent Cyclone rider. ☁

WILL REAGAN PULL A COOLIDGE STUNT?

FIRST PRINTED ∞ 1985

*W*ill Ronald Regan really seek nomination for a second term as president, or will he in the end walk down the steps of history as one who chose not to run?

Even the words "choose to run" are reminiscent of the last Republican president who stood in Reagan's place and astonished the world by declining to run for re-election. The year was 1927; the United States was enjoying the riotous prosperity of the roaring '20s. In the White House lived a steady, stable Republican president who was almost a sure winner should he run again — Calvin Coolidge.

Ronald Reagan does not conceal his admiration for Calvin Coolidge, but it is difficult to think of two men who are more different.

Reagan is friendly, witty (who else could say to his wife, "Honey, I forgot to duck," when he was still suffering from the shock of a near-fatal bullet wound?). Coolidge frequently ignored visitors, almost begrudging the few words he spoke. With a look of sour distaste, he weathered glumly the years of his presidency.

A famous anecdote tells of a Washington hostess who bubbled over Coolidge: "Oh Mr. President, everybody's been betting me that I can't get you to say more than three words at my party!"

The president's response was delivered with his usual, inscrutable deadpan: "You lose," he said.

In summer, 1927, President Coolidge was vacationing in the Black Hills of South Dakota and living at the State Lodge, not far from Mount Rushmore. It had been assumed that he would be a candidate for a second full term. On Friday, July 29, he summoned his secretary and said tersely, "I am not going to run for President again." He showed a 12-word announcement that he had written in longhand and intended to issue at 8:30 a.m., the following Tuesday.

Coolidge's secretary protested that it was not necessary to make the decision yet, that the country would be greatly disappointed, but the only concession the president would make was to defer his announcement from

69

8:30 until noon. By then, considering the time differential, the New York Stock Exchange would be closed — providing an interval for investors to digest the news.

Coolidge's announcement became a classic of his laconic style. As reporters assembled at noon on August 2, they were given slips of paper by the president. Typewritten was the famous message: "I do not choose to run for president in nineteen twenty-eight."

A gasp of surprise swept over the newsmen and hours later when their stories appeared, over the nation. Here was a president presiding over a prosperous economy, almost a certain winner for re-election, in his physical prime at only 56, letting down his party, the whole country.

Weeks of incredulous speculation followed. Did Coolidge really mean it? Doubt centered on semantics. Did "I do not choose to run" mean "I would prefer not to run" with the mental reservation that "I will run if you insist"? In short, was the president being coy and inviting a draft to establish his popularity?

Those who knew Silent Cal best said that "I do not choose to run" meant a definite no. And so it did. Despite all pressures and for whatever his reasons, Calvin Coolidge refused to seek re-election.

In the case of Reagan, some columnists suggest that his wife, Nancy, may influence her husband's decision.

Not so with Calvin Coolidge. Although he was married to an elegant, beautiful woman, Grace Coolidge could scarcely have been a motive in her husband's big announcement in 1927.

In fact, the afternoon of Coolidge's "I do not choose" statement, he had lunch with Sen. Arthur Capper of Kansas. After lunch, when the president had retired for his customary afternoon nap, the senator remarked to Grace Coolidge: "That was quite a surprise the president gave us today."

Grace Coolidge looked up, puzzled. "What was that?" she asked, and Sen. Capper explained that her husband was not to be a candidate for re-election.

"Isn't that just like the man?" said the first lady. "He never gave me the slightest indication of his intentions. I had no idea." ∞

'36 ST. PATRICK'S DAY STORM
DIDN'T FAZE IRISH REVELERS

FIRST PRINTED ⌘ 03 – 15 – 85

*B*uffalonians are experts on winter storms. They smile tolerantly at an early strike in November: "It'll all be gone in a few days."

This response differs from the guarded caution about a raw wind with snow in January. The Buffalo storm expert looks glum and thinks of blizzards like '77 and '85. He grumbles about the onset of a tough winter, the kind of snow that lingers for weeks, even months.

Or, there are the end-of-the-season storms that come in mid March, the kind that do not hit the city; rather, they sit down on it. Such a storm smothered Buffalo on March 17, 1936. It may have been St. Patrick's Day, but even the Leprechauns were white that day.

On Sunday, March 15, 1936, Buffalonians were imagining the first hints of spring. The day was cloudy but only 40 degrees; the annual St. Pat's Day parade was being held with Grand Marshal Michael Quinn.

The weather forecast predicted slightly colder weather with occasional rain. Nobody expected what happened.

Just after midnight on St. Patrick's Day, snow began to fall. The temperature hung just below freezing, and the snow fell not in inches but in tons. Indeed, it was the start of the heaviest snowfall — not in depth but in weight — ever to blanket Buffalo.

71

By 8 a.m. on Tuesday, March 17, for the first time in memory, the trolleys were unable to move. The snow was simply too heavy to be pushed around — and still it continued falling. City plows and trucks could not even budge out of their garages.

Oddly, there were no school closings — probably because schools then were strictly neighborhood groupings, and most students were expected to walk in any weather. In fact, teachers and administrators at many schools worked with shovels to clear school walkways.

As the morning wore on, several downtown stores closed; however, Hengerer's and J.N. Adam's tried to stay open. They promised to get their employees home in store delivery trucks.

The snow kept on, and soon a new anxiety struck. Roofs, first of houses and garages, began to collapse from the weight of accumulated snow. Later on in the day, larger buildings were threatened.

Elmwood Music Hall was closed because of the danger of roof collapse. Across the border, the Fort Erie Hockey Arena groaned complainingly, and toward evening, the roof of the big building thundered down under tons of snow.

The storm finally stopped near midnight on March 17, 24 hours after it had begun. About 20 weighty inches had padded down and left Buffalo quietly smothered.

Recovery from such a phenomenon was slow. By 3 p.m. Wednesday, the first trolleys were moving. Some 25,000 men were hired by the Depression WPA agency to help clean up. With shovels, they struggled away at the snow.

On Thursday the inevitable thaw followed, and finally on Friday, all city schools were closed for a big recovery effort. By week's end, nearly 1,000 buildings had buckled under the heavy snow.

Such was the great St. Patrick's Day storm legend of 1936. That year, the Irish proved that they were the world's most heroic partygoers (if anyone seriously doubted it) because few scheduled affairs were cancelled.

In fact, the roofs of two church halls caved in during Tuesday's parties — happily with no injuries.

Honey-tongued orator Monsignor Fulton Sheen was in Buffalo that Tuesday to discuss Irish humor before the Friendly Sons of St. Patrick. His lecture was delivered at the Hotel Statler before 500 loyal sons. There is no record of how they got there.

Perhaps Martin Flemming, the mayor's secretary, summed the situation up best. Asked to comment on the storm, Flemming was philosophical: "Thank God the St. Patrick's Day parade was held on Sunday." ∞

THE DL&W RAIL TERMINAL WAS A SCENE OF CLASSICAL SPLENDOR

FIRST PRINTED ∞ 07 – 28 – 85

*I*f there had been railroads in ancient Rome, the terminals would have resembled the Delaware, Lackawanna and Western Terminal at the foot of Main Street.

Opened in 1917, at a time when railroads were expected to outlast mountains, the DL&W Terminal was strategically located on Buffalo's harbor. There, freight and passengers could transfer conveniently from water to rail.

To enter the DL&W was to face a scene of classical splendor. Twin stairways of beige marble ascended gracefully to an upstairs waiting room, the sun projecting interesting patterns of light and shadow.

Throughout the terminal, heavy oak benches were mounted on white, marble bases with brass-shaded lamps rising over seated travelers' shoulders. At each doorway, imitation Roman flares, really electric lamps, extended the classical motif.

Anyone who has ever played with a model trains knows the difficulty of moving even a toy engine up a steep incline. Anyone who has ever felt the earth shake under a steam engine can imagine the problems of having such a weight on a building's second story.

Such obstacles were overcome at the DL&W. Huge iron horses of railroad legend puffed in to the terminal's upper floor. For baggage workers downstairs, the noise was thunderous as a train arrived. Only a glance at the massive circular supports convinced them that the ceiling could bear such weight.

73

I know because I was a baggage worker at the DL&W in the time of its greatness. My job in the basement was to unload Railway Express trucks onto wagons, to drag the wagons to an express elevator and from there to the second floor loading platforms. In ancient Rome, my work would have been done only by slaves.

During those years, three important railroads operated out of the DL&W Terminal: the Nickel Plate, the Baltimore and Ohio, and, of course, the Lackawanna. I loaded freight on all three, and on occasion, I rode the trains as a baggage-car guard or messenger.

Back then, I was studying Latin, and mornings in my classes, I read Virgil and Horace. Afternoons, toiling in the railroad's classical surroundings, I suffered a peculiar time warp, almost losing sight of the modern world.

Like all American railroad terminals, the DL&W fell on bad times. With the rise of air travel, patronage sagged; trains were discontinued; finally the depot shut down in 1962.

For nearly 20 years, that wonderful building lingered in abandonment and increasing desolation. During this period, I took my little children up to show them the place where their father had once worked.

The devastation was incredible. Nearly all windows were broken, and glass lay everywhere. Brass lamps were smashed and twisted. A mosaic drinking fountain set delicately into a wall recess had been systematically removed. The scene could have been used as a Hollywood set for a movie about the fall of Old Rome.

Although the terminal no longer stands, the adjoining freight buildings and repair shops survive. Shiny, new rails have been laid on their floors, and they are once more busy work places. The steam engines are gone, but the old DL&W is the garage site of the swank Metro subway rail cars.

One set of tracks has replaced another. Ancient Romans would have loved the irony: Sic semper transit gloria mundi! ☜

LEGENDARY DAYS AT LEWISTON HILL

FIRST PRINTED ⌒ 08 - 18 - 85

arning signs started two miles away. Approaching Steep Hill," they shouted. "Use Low Gear." Another mile, and another sign agonized, "Use Extreme Caution. Stop. Apply Low Gear."

One last admonition. Beside a big water barrel was the advice: "Check your radiator." All such cautions were appropriate; we were drawing near the Lewiston escarpment, a frontier legend since the end of the ice age.

Dad pulled our old 1927 Buick to a halt. The ladies in the back seat suddenly stopped talking, sensing the immanence of danger. The road didn't have much of a shoulder, but Dad got out and grasped the disc-shaped ornament that sat on top of the front radiator.

"You'd better put in some water," said a driver from the back seat.

There was a hiss as the radiator cap let go, and Dad gazed into the cauldron that was the Buick's cooling system. There were, of course, no water pumps on cars back then. "It looks okay," my father said. "I think we can make it."

The door clanked shut, and Dad settled behind the big, wooden steering wheel. He grasped the gear shift knob tightly and pulled it into low gear.

The car began to roll, slow at first; then, with a convulsive movement, Dad threw the shift up into second gear. The knuckles of his right hand were turning white with the tenseness of his grip. There was a steady moan as the gears of the Buick matched wills with the sheer ascent, left by the retreating glaciers of pre-history.

We crept up, up. Except for the gear groan and an occasional cough from the engine, hush gripped the car. Gradually, we sniffed a hot, metallic smell, and everybody knew that things were not quite right with the radiator. The motor was obviously overheating.

First a hiss, next a jet of steam shot from the radiator ornament; then all at once, rusty, boiling water was shooting all over.

"Holy Cow!" breathed Dad, who was entitled to use stronger language.

By this time, Dad had flicked the windshield wiper to clear off the brackish water and was looking frantically for a place to stop. Meanwhile, littered over the road's narrow shoulders were stalled cars of all sorts but one thing in common; they had challenged the Lewiston Hill and lost. Their radiators were cooking away in despair.

Part of a motorist's equipment was a water can. After Dad had found a place to stop, he gave me the can. "Walk up the road and get some water," he said.

As I started up the hill in search of a water barrel — these were placed at regular intervals along The Hill — I saw Dad burning his fingers loosening the radiator top. Steam was exploding convulsively.

When I returned with water, the sheet steel sides of the engine hood had been folded upward. Like a great bird with wings outstretched, the engine was cooling. Dad spilled water into the snarling radiator, and half an hour later, we resumed the uphill assault. When we reached the top, my father always unloaded the same line: "Well, she made the Lewiston Hill!"

Driving south from Artpark near Lewiston on a sunny afternoon in 1985, a motorist takes the gently turning hill without a twinge of anxiety. The climb is so gradual now that the car's automatic shift does not even change settings.

Gone are the warning signs, the steep, shoulderless roads, the water barrels for overheated cars. Engineers have used modern, road-building techniques to conquer the drop in the terrain, to take the danger — and the adventure — out of driving.

Climbing the Lewiston Hill was an achievement for any car half a century ago — like scaling the Matterhorn for a mountain climber. It is difficult to believe that today's four-lane highway is the famed escarpment, the legendary Lewiston Hill, once a terror to drivers, a thrill to children, an ultimate test to the spirit of an automobile. ∞

LIFE BEFORE THE BALL-POINT PEN WAS OFTEN A MESSY BUSINESS

FIRST PRINTED ⌒ 09 – 15 – 85

Turn back the calendar a quarter century to a time before the ball-point pen, before Bic, Scripto, Papermate were invented. What did people use to fill out applications, to sign official documents, to take notes, to write compositions in school?

The solution is that they relied on ink. There were inkwells and ink bottles everywhere.

When tots entered first grade, they learned to form their numbers and letters with pencil. It was a great day when teacher announced, "Boys and girls, tomorrow I want all of you to bring pens. We will begin to write in ink."

Buying a straight pen involved no great capital outlay. For a nickel, you could secure an acceptable one, but 10 cents bought a luxury model. In addition to this expenditure, the writer had to invest in a steel point of standard size, which could be wedged into the pen's stub end. Points sold for a penny each.

All pens were shaped the same. About as long as an unsharpened pencil, the pen's lower end was blunt; its shaft tapered gracefully to a rounded peak. Economy models were simply brown, varnished wood, but the luxury model might be a colorful enamel with a cork collar surrounding the point area.

Cork served a dual function: the writer could grasp his tool more firmly, and the cork absorbed ink. Especially for early graders, using a pen was a sticky operation, and often the student wound up with his writing fingers soggy with ink.

Thus in the pre-Bic age, the ink system began in school. Each desk had its individual inkwell, filled from a liter bottle kept by the teacher. The final item of penmanship equipment was a blotter. Because they generally bore printed advertising, blotters were plentiful and free of charge.

Back then, a common gift at grade-school graduation was a fountain pen. A fountain pen! The very idea was exciting — like smoking a cigarette or having a girlfriend. With a fountain pen neatly clasped in your pocket, you had arrived at adulthood.

Fountain pens carried their own ink supply and came in gradations of snob appeal. Parker was a name of quality, and the staid, cigar-like Parker pen decorated the vest of successful executives. Waterman's also marketed prestigious pens; Esterbrook was the aristocratic name of a neat, serviceable pen.

So on down to economy models which frequently had gimmicks like a plunger-type filler or a see-through tank for the ink. You had to be careful with cheap fountain pens because invariably they leaked.

In fact, sooner or later, all fountain pens leaked. The ink tanks were rubber, and in time, they grew dry and brittle. Then, one day, you felt a dampness at your breast pocket, looked…and everything was a blue blotch.

High-school students often carried private ink supplies in their purses or book cases. Plugged with tight stoppers, the portable bottles came in varying sizes and designs. Waterman's ink had a narrow-necked bottle; Parker's Quirk affected a pyramid design; Schaefer's resembled a square perfume container.

School ink, used exclusively in classrooms came only in large vessels, shaped like a whiskey bottle, with a pouring spout, depressed by the forefinger.

During the golden age of ink, some pens were unforgettable like the gems they hoarded at the post office for writing money-order applications. Post office inkwells were thick with sooty ink, but their pens had jagged, angry points.

Many is the customer who hacked away at his postal forms, cursing as the pen sputtered and spit ink over the paper. Climax of such an ordeal would be the moment that the pen suddenly belched up a big ink blob from its rusty point.

A messy substance is ink, and it is sobering to reflect how tense people became keeping pen points moist, inkwells liquid and fingers clean. It is the philosopher who is patient now when his ball-point pen snags, realizing that things were worse in the old, inky days. ∞

THE CARD THAT LEFT ITS MARK

PUBLISHED IN THE WALL STREET JOURNAL ☜ 01 – 30 – 86

A frugal document was the traditional elementary or high-school student report card. Its series of crossed lines left blocks for teachers to fill in by hand the names of subjects and grades. Such a system seems primitive in an age when nearly all schools have converted to computer-kept records.

Frigid in tone, spare of words, the pre-computer report card was the child's first brush with official accountability. Aside from squares for academic grades, accommodations were also provided to rate student behavior, generally under categories called "deportment and effort."

Often space was reserved for teachers to jot comments about their charges. This was an opportunity to personalize the report card with a word of praise or a studied ambiguity that might translate into something like "Your son is a bum."

A kind of morality play took form on the day designated for report-card circulation. It was the occasion of reward for virtue, disdain for indolence and neglect.

Usually students carried their report cards with them from one class to another. The teacher would look searchingly over the class: "Pass your report cards to the front," came the terse command.

With the somberness of a funeral director, the teacher would place cards on his desk. After setting students to work at their seats, he took pen in hand, consulted his record book and assumed the responsibility of administering just desserts.

Ominous silence gripped the schoolroom when such serious matters were conducted. Students worked industriously, wary that some last-minute quirk of behavior might exert an unhappy influence on their grade.

Dies irae, dies illa! This judgment day was a step in crossing to another world: from the world of children to that of adults.

As on all formal occasions, speeches were made on report-card days. They could all be distilled into one sequence by the teacher. Marks had been deserved by virtuous application or the lack; with more earnest effort, future improvement was possible and expected.

At the day's close, students took their report cards home for a parent's signature in acknowledgment of receipt; cards were mailed home from boarding schools. All were returned, signatures were scrutinized for validity, and the same cards were used for the entire year, guarded like negotiable security certificates.

Whatever criticism may be directed at the old-time report card, it was a living document, touched by human hands; to wit, the hands of teacher, student and finally of parent. Of course, reports had to be on cards to survive all this attention.

The traditional report card and much of the attendant mystique have ended with the new technology. Records are now put into a computer and eventually churned out for home consumption.

At some private time and place, the teacher makes arrangements with a computer. The chance to say anything on his own has vanished; any comments have been phrased in advance to suit large groups, common situations. Each student must fit into some group.

Over the years, the report card survived many assaults, especially at the hands of a generation of progressive educators. But now the computer has dealt a stunning blow.

While the school report has not been killed, the computer has depersonalized it. Student performance has been demoted to a data sheet. Likewise, along with the teacher, the student has been demoted from a name to a number. ∞

THE DAY THAT BUFFALONIANS HAD A DARKNESS AT NOON

FIRST PRINTED 10 – 20 – 85

When Buffalonians set back their clocks an hour to Standard Time in 1950 it was a strange experience — almost as if there had been a time warp.

On Sept. 25 that year (the switch was made in September in those days), dawn should have come an hour earlier. Instead, it didn't come at all. It was 8 o'clock, then 9. But where was the daylight? Resetting clocks could not affect the atmosphere, or could it?

People rubbed their eyes and wondered whether, Rip Van Winkle style, they had slept through the daylight and were beholding the next night. It was all a little spooky.

That Sunday, as worshipers went to church, they drove with headlights on, or they walked under street lights still shining from the previous night. Once inside their churches, they gazed at black windows with no morning light shining through the colored glass. On Main Street in downtown Buffalo, street lamps, store lights and advertising signs flickered just as on any night.

In 1950, only five years away from the horror of World War II, America was tense. Although peace had come, the nation found itself in an unpredictable nuclear age. Just recently, the Russians had tested their first atomic bomb.

Influenced by such tensions, people had all kinds of fears and speculations. Switchboards at newspapers and police stations began to jump with activity.

Many callers were convinced that an atomic bomb had been exploded somewhere nearby; some interpreted the darkness as an indication that the world's end was at hand. Meanwhile, weird reddish patches glowed occasionally in the inky sky. At 4 p.m., a man from the Boston Hills area said that he glimpsed the sun but that it looked like the moon in a nighttime sky.

As the afternoon wore on, radio reports explained that this daytime darkness was affecting not only Buffalo: the Cleveland Indians were playing their afternoon game under night lights. Some rowing races had been canceled in Toronto because of the extended night.

Then an airplane pilot flying over Erie, Pa., stated that he had flown at 25,000 feet, through what was apparently thick smoke. Other pilots agreed, saying that they had smelled smoke.

Huge forest fires were raging in Northern Alberta and British Columbia, and smoke from these Canadian conflagrations had covered parts of the northeastern United States. So thick was this smoke that it had almost completely shut out the sun. The New York Weather Bureau could not recall a smoke blanket as extensive: they compared it only to the famous eruption of Krakatoa in the Dutch East Indies in 1883, a grim event that shut out the sun.

The bleak condition was not without humor. Chickens and birds roosted in the afternoon thinking it was night. A disk jockey commented that his listeners had the daylights scared out of them. Arthur Koestler's popular novel "Darkness at Noon" was featured in special book-seller exhibits. A lady in Hamilton, Ont., claimed that the midday darkness reflected supernatural wrath at man for tampering with Daylight Savings Time.

Again on Monday, Sept. 26, there was no sun, but Buffalonians went to work in the dark. However, by late afternoon natural sunshine had begun to peep through, and two eerie days of darkness yielded to a friendly autumn sunshine. ∞

WHEN THE CITY RAN
ON HORSE POWER

FIRST PRINTED ∞ 05 – 25 – 86

*L*ike the blue whale and the Asian panda bear, perhaps the horse is a vanishing species.

In the normal course of present urban life, you rarely see one; yet, when I was a boy, horses on city streets were commonplace.

I do not refer to sleek, well-brushed animals that you find at riding academies or race tracks. When life was less mechanized half a century ago, horses did the city's work.

Back then, milk came in glass bottles, and nearly all of it was distributed door-to-door. In the dark of very early morning, the milkman hitched a horse to his delivery wagon. Sometimes the animal knew the route better than the man, stopping unerringly at each customer's house, while its master counted out quarts of milk and pints of cream.

Bakeries had routemen who followed neat, frisky horses. Such bakers carried broad, leather baskets strapped over their shoulders, and when they alighted from their wagons, they blew a double-piped whistle.

Hall's and Lang's (when Lang's had to suspend its brewery operation during Prohibition) had stables for their bakery-route horses. Bakery wagons were immaculate with varnished interiors, enclosed from the horse power by sliding doors and glass windshields.

Horse-drawn baker-trucks dispensed everything from the workaday loaf of rye to luscious cream confections that would delight the heart.

Neighborhoods were crossed daily by a plethora of other horse-powered vehicles. During the pleasant months, hucksters peddled fresh fruit and vegetables; the ubiquitous ragmen croaked out, "Rags-a rags, bottles-rags," as they sat atop ancient carts pulled by decrepit nags.

Then, there were the work horses who spent their lives in municipal service. Anything but pampered, these heavy-flanked beasts trudged through the streets in all sorts of weather pulling refuse wagons.

The wooden garbage wagons of bygone years were huge with side pieces splaying out to contain their cargoes. Big wheels with no tires, with only a strip of metal fitted to their wheels, turned ponderously.

Winters, the work horses had to assume added responsibilities. In an age when all homes were heated with coal, a second weekly collection was required to pick up coal ashes.

After snowstorms, horses also assisted in snow removal. Crews of men, equipped with shovels, used to fan out snow trouble spots and throw the snow up onto the horse-driven wagons for disposal.

Docile, obedient, uncomplaining, the poor city horses had no civil-service benefits. The only comforts they enjoyed were a burlap cloth thrown over their backs in bitterly cold weather — or in the heat of summer, rope tassels, hung from their backs, to stir off the flies.

I suppose the phrase "put on the feed bag" dates from these days when a canvas bag of oats was strapped around the horse's neck. After lunch, horses were led to cement watering troughs, common sights at city corners.

When the horse was replaced by the tractor and truck, some gentle aspects of life vanished. No more did the neighborhood resound with the pleasant, clip-clop cadence of horses' hoofs. Replacing the earthy smell which accompanied any horsey operation was the diesel exhaust odor of combustion engines.

Gone, too, was the ready source of fertilizer which could be scooped up in abundance for summer use on lawn or garden.

When early trucks would sputter and break down, kids shouted mockingly, "Get a horse!" Everybody felt a sneaking regret when the faithful dobbin ambled off into the sunset. ∞

TRANSPORTATION GOES BACKWARD

FIRST PRINTED ∽ 02 – 23 – 86

*I*n 1974, there were odd-days and even-days at the gasoline pump — that system whereby cars could be refueled only on alternate days, according to the final digit of their license plate number.

The Arab oil boycott was on then, and with frustrating frequency, signs began to appear outside filling stations. "Out of Gas," "No Gas Today," they read.

As a nation, America struck back against the boycott. Among many measures, Congress created Amtrak, a hopeful compromise by which the federal government in effect socialized passenger rail services. Although Amtrak involved federal subsidies, it was one way to keep trains running, to avoid promiscuous use of gas-consuming cars.

Back then, government planners had a dream. They thought that urban and suburban mass transit could become cheap and convenient, workers would leave their cars home or drive to some central pickup spot. From there, they would ride on public transportation to their places of employment; no more reliance on sheiks, emirs or oddballs.

To further the dream, Buffalo, like many big cities, was the recipient of federal transit aid. Millions of federal dollars were invested in a subway line designed to attract city commuters. With patronage, the trains might be extended to northern suburbs, and later on, who could tell where else?

Promises, promises.

Ten years after these ambitious plans, federal subsidies have been severely cut along the transportation line. As a result, Amtrak has reduced service and canceled some crack trains. Locally, the sleek, new, subway has not even reached its first goal by operating on Main Street to the city line, and already there are hints of curtailing service; already, fares have been raised, discouraging ridership.

Worse still, suffering from budget losses, the local transportation authority has begun to chip away at bus service lines. It plans to discontinue two city lines and to cancel runs to Alden, Angola, Boston, Holland. Riders from these towns are being pushed back into their cars.

Does this mean that America has attained oil independence? Far. from it: despite temporary market gluts and consequent price reductions, the

CONTINUED ON PAGE 88

85

MEMORIES OF A NEW YEAR'S EVE IN BUFFALO AT TURN OF CENTURY

FIRST PRINTED ∽ 02 – 23 – 86

$\mathcal{M}$y Aunt Barbara lived to be 93, but she never forgot the New Year's Eve she spent when she was a girl of 18. She loved to recall that night because it was the eve not only of a new year, but also of a new century: December 31, 1899.

Conrad Diehl was Buffalo's mayor back then, and he had promised the city a big display that New Year's Eve. After all, not everybody has the privilege of welcoming in a new century. There was to be an evening parade down Main Street properly glittering with gas illumination and even with a new lighting system called electricity.

"The mayor told us to expect some surprises," Aunt Barb remembered. "We couldn't wait to get downtown."

The weather that last night of the old century was cold and brisk, but clear — ideal for a parade. Marchers were to assemble in front of Buffalo's City Hall on Franklin Street (now the Erie County Hall).

All municipal workers had received orders to report to their offices by 9 p.m. because City Hall was to be shining with lights from basement to tower. Employees were needed to light the gas jets in their offices so that some 1,500 such lamps would be glowing by 10 o'clock.

As Aunt Barbara with some of her friends walked in Genesee to Main Street, she was amazed at the numbers of people she met along the way. Buffalo had a smaller population at the turn of the century than it has now, but a crowd of over 100,000 people converged that night in the downtown area.

The New Year's Eve parade was an ambitious affair: all units of the Buffalo Fire Department were represented, the firefighters garbed in formal uniforms with starched wing collars. It was too cold for the Parkside Wheeling Club's members to ride their bicycles, but they marched, each member jauntily swinging a cane.

There was a Rag Time Pleasure Club, whose members dressed as hoboes for the occasion. Delegations from nearby Indian reservations were conspicuous for their full head-dress and war paint.

Snow was starting to fall as the parade got under way. Athletes from Buffalo's German Turn Verein wore uniforms; another German group, the Sprudels, carried scythes to blend with Father Time costumes. Some marchers held torches, banners; others wore straw hats, rode on horses, mules, in carriages decorated with bunting.

Buffalo's Main Street that last evening of the old year was a great white way, picturesque with gas lights puffing up their flickering glows into the darkness. Electric lights, still a novelty, gleamed brilliantly from the tops of the Prudential and the Iroquois Buildings.

The snow was dropping steadily, and by 11:30, the last of the marchers tramped off, their footsteps muffled on the carpet of snow. Then, for the mayor's surprise.

The street lights dimmed; some were extinguished. A silence of expectation settled over everything. Just before midnight, as the old century gasped its final breath, the hush was broken by a piercing outburst of noise.

Bombs exploded, horns and trumpets blew, bells rang out from building towers and church steeples. Amid the clamor, the winter sky was set ablaze with fireworks, some shot from building roofs. For 15 minutes, there was pandemonium. This was the birth of the 20th century in Buffalo!

Gradually after the excitement, the huge crowd quietly dispersed on trolleys, wagons, carriages, special trains. A soft layer of snow lay everywhere as Aunt Barb walked home with her friends. They could hear their footsteps.

"I wonder what the new century will bring," one of them said, probably echoing the thoughts of all.

"Auld Lang Syne," the ballad so long associated with New Year's, is the saddest of all songs because it is a loving sigh for the past. As another year ends, I remember Aunt Barb and her generation and the wonderful New Year's Eve that she never forgot. For auld lang syne. ∞

— ∞ —

TRANSPORTATION GOES BACKWARD

CONTINUED FROM PAGE 85

Western World remains dependent for its present level of oil usage on the most unstable areas of the globe.

A crisis, a flare of emotion, a new sense of resolution among unpredictable OPEC nations, and America could be back with odd and even days at the gas pump, at the mercy of inadequate public transportation.

Cutting support to mass transit is especially regrettable since significant progress has been made. Passengers are riding regularly, for example, on commuter buses to towns, in a metro area. To cancel such service is a step backward from all common sense urban planning. ∞

EVEN CASTRO HAS
STOPPED SMOKING

FIRST PRINTED ⌢ 01 – 19 – 86

*F*idel Castro, leader of a small island nation whose shaky economy rests largely on cigar export, recently gave up smoking. I sympathize with anyone who has to discard too pleasurable a habit because years ago, I bit the same bullet-like cigar.

When I was in college, the large tobacco companies used to send representatives around to schools. Well-dressed young men and girls would set up brightly decorated stands and exhibits, usually in college cafeterias. The handsome salespeople always had free gifts for students — colorful lighters and starter packets of cigarettes. These latter were distributed generously: neat, little boxes of four cigarettes, attractively wrapped in cellophane.

Like many of my classmates, I willingly joined the community of cigarette smokers because smoking seemed mature, sophisticated, an adjunct to the beautiful life.

Quickly, my smoking vistas widened: I discovered pipes and collected a pipe for every occasion. I had racks filled with all kinds of them, small and large. There were shiny pipes, dull ones; some with straight, others with comfortably curved stems. Like friends, each had a personality, and I grew to love them.

Selecting blends of tobacco to feed my pipes was fun. I became a frequenter of little shops where I would experiment judiciously with different, delightful mixtures. At home of an evening, aromatic tobacco simmering in a favorite pipe, I would puff contentedly.

Finally, I graduated to the cigar. Grasping a panatela affectionately, I learned to discriminate among fine cigars and I luxuriated in sniffing tenderly at the clouds of smoke with which I surrounded myself.

For years, I conducted a romance with these companions. No day, certainly no evening, was complete without smoking. I carried my smoker's gear with me everywhere, always checking my pockets as I left home to be assured that I was equipped.

In 1956, I dismissed the first statistical evidence of smoking's tie with various diseases as an unfounded assault; a year later, when the evidence became not only statistical but clinical, a decision was thrust upon me. One thing I valued more than tobacco was my vigorous health. Feeling almost a victim to science, I quit smoking.

Dismantling my arsenal of pipes was a trauma. At first, I thought of retaining some as keepsakes; then I decided that it was better to shed them completely. Like the owner of a litter of favored pups, I bestowed my pipes on friends who would give them good homes.

Substituting a peppermint for an after-dinner smoke was hardly a fair exchange. Evenings alone were desolate without the company of my pipes and cigars. For a time, life seemed empty, but eventually I survived.

When I look back on my life as a smoker, I remember the habit wistfully. I still feel vaguely cheated that I had to give up as source of oral satisfaction which was not fattening. Sometimes on lonely nights, I reflect on the joy of picking a friendly pipe, pressing a moist blend of cuttings into its bowl, seeing the flash of a match, and then, the comfort of a leisurely smoke.

Strange that after 27 years of abstinence, I recall those days fondly. But I will never return to my smoking ways: the consequences are too gruesome.

Even Fidel Castro had to admit that. ☙

THE GREAT FIRE AT OLD ST. MICHAEL'S

FIRST PRINTED ⏪ 03 – 16 – 86

*T*here were severe rain storms in the late afternoon, then a temporary lull. In the early evening, with sudden fury, the rain resumed. Shattering thunder and jagged bolts of lightning pierced the sky that spring evening, May 24, 1962.

Programs on TV wobbled to the electrical interference; for those listening to the radio, in between scratches of static came news of local fires. In Tonawanda, for example, within 18 minutes, 10 houses had been hit by lightning. Neighborhoods echoed with emergency sirens.

More serious still, Buffalo fire equipment had been summoned to the Sterling Bag Company on Carolina Street, where six aerial ladders and an 85-foot snorkel were struggling at a wind-swept industrial fire.

So fierce was the blaze that Mayor Chester Kowal was on hand with his fire and police commissioners. As they watched, at 9:32, came another alarm, stunning and urgent: "St. Michael's Church downtown is on fire."

Old St. Michael's filled an intimate place in Buffalo's heart. Thousands had found sanctuary in the church: businessmen, office girls, the homeless, bundle-laden shoppers. People of all religions respected St. Michael's and the noble Jesuit priests who staffed it.

On May 24, after a deafening thunderclap, Father Thomas Reilly had looked toward St. Michael's steeple and discovered flames spouting from it. He put in the fire alarm and with the pastor, Father James Redmond, charged into the church.

The interior was already thick with blinding smoke. There was noise of falling timbers and shattering glass. The two priests groped their way to the altar to save chalices and Sacred Hosts. Very soon, they were aided by policemen, firemen, even passersby.

The city's heavy fire equipment had to be divided between the burning factory and St. Michael's. Calls went out to nearby towns for their volunteer units. Eventually about 1,000 firefighters were assembled.

A huge crowd had soon gathered in the troubled May night as flames spread quickly through the old, heavily timbered church. Despite the excitement, people were quiet, reserved, shocked by the calamity. No supervision was needed by police: as though beholding a solemn ceremony, spectators stood back.

Smoke poured into the heavy, black sky; firemen climbing their ladders seemed to disappear in the darkness. Mayor Kowal spent two hours aloft in a high pressure snorkel directing a stream at the church dome.

Then with a sudden, immense thud, the church roof gave way, setting off a burst of sparks into the murky clouds. Without being warned, onlookers retreated, fearing that the steeple would fall next.

The old church tower with its two mighty bells withstood the fire for a time. Finally with a terrible groan, it sank into the wreckage at 3:30 a.m.

Happily no one had been in the church: the last service had been held in the afternoon at 5:45. In fact, miraculously no one was injured in that night of conflagration.

But old St. Michael's! At noon next day, firemen were still shooting water into the embers. Only the church's shell remained — those thick walls of Buffalo limestone and Albion sandstone. Even in disaster, the edifice, dating from the Civil War, was uniquely local.

The story of the great fire at St. Michael's would be incomplete without a postscript. Affectionate outpourings from Buffalonians of all faiths followed the fire; dozens of Protestant pastors and Jewish rabbis offered use of their facilities to the priests and parishioners of St. Michael's.

The Sunday after the blaze, Father Redmond celebrated mass on a flower-decked altar at, of all places, the Town Casino. The nightclub's owner, Harry Altman, had volunteered his property to St. Michael's for as long as it was needed.

Father Redmond spoke that morning with a full heart. He thanked the brave police and firemen who had risked their lives. He asked the congregation for prayers that a new St. Michael's would arise to last for another 100 years.

Evidently these prayers were heard. This year, at Lenten masses, the new St. Michael's built on the ruins of its predecessor, is filled with worshippers. The church is nearly a quarter of the way into its second century. ∞

END OF ERA OF THE GREAT DIRIGIBLES

FIRST PRINTED ⌾ 06 – 01 – 86

*H*alf a century ago, in the spring of 1936, with hope and fanfare, the world's first transatlantic, air-passenger service was inaugurated. As a symbol of Germany's final rise from the humiliation of World War I defeat, the huge dirigible Hindenburg began scheduled crossings from Germany to America.

The Hindenburg was the climax of German infatuation with balloons. Before 1914, the Zeppelin Company had sponsored regular air service with five dirigibles operating among principal German cites. During the war, these dirigibles, or zeppelins, had spread destruction and terror over France and England.

Following German surrender, the airships were confiscated by allied nations. However, German zeppelins refused to perform at the direction of their new owners; and nearly all met frightening ends in wind and storm. One by one, European countries dropped their airship programs.

In America, the U.S. Navy saw possibilities in dirigible use. Two big ships, called the Akron and the Macon, were built at a cost of millions, but by 1935, in the face of disaster to these ships and others, dirigible flight was abandoned in this country.

Only the Germans persisted. Under guidance of the stubborn genius Dr. Hugo Eckener, the Graf Zeppelin was developed. This mighty airship made several Atlantic crossings and crowned its career with a 1929, 12-day flight round the world.

Based on such success, the Hindenburg was built at Friederickshaven for North Atlantic service. The length of a city block, the 804-foot ship was powered by four 1,000 horsepower diesel motors. It could attain a speed of 90 mph and complete Atlantic crossings in 2-3 days,

In luxury, the Hindenburg rivaled any ocean liner. It had two decks with 35 modern, two-bed cabins, a spacious, carefully insulated smoking room, sumptuous dining facilities with a stunning view through the windows on one side.

The Hindenburg's passengers were lyrical describing the flight of the new ship: a sense of floating on a cloud, every want catered to, the matchless view from the promenade whose windows actually looked downward. No wonder all passenger accommodations were sold out long in advance of each flight.

Old newsreels have caught the Hindenburg in passage over the skyscrapers of Manhattan. Infinitely graceful, like a bullet photographed in slow motion, the ship pondered through the skies, leisurely contemplating the city below.

Nearly everyone knows the tragedy that befell the Hindenburg only a year after it began regular service. A spectacular newsreel shows the great ship nuzzling into its tower at Lakehurst, New Jersey. Suddenly an explosion lights the nighttime sky, and in 30 seconds, the Hindenburg crumbles to the ground in twisted wreckage. Of the 97 people on board, 37 perished, some hurling themselves through doors and windows to the earth.

The cause of disaster remains a mystery. Since Hindenburg was inflated with highly flammable hydrogen, it could have been the target of an incendiary bullet. Barring such sabotage, lightning on an evening of electrical storm was another conjecture.

Despite Dr. Eckener's plans for a new zeppelin inflated with non-combustible helium, destruction of the Hindenburg ended the era of frame dirigible flight probably forever. ∞

INTERURBAN RAPID RAIL SYSTEM ONCE A REALITY ON FRONTIER

FIRST PRINTED ∽ 06 – 22 – 86

*T*hey used to come up the tracks along Main Street — those long, heavy, yellow cars. They bore signs on their front windows identifying the destinations toward which they shot: North Tonawanda, LaSalle, Niagara Falls.

These were the electric, interurban trolleys of a couple of generations back — the mass transit that made Western New York a little smaller for travelers. Shooting like rockets along smooth, well-maintained tracks, interurbans reached top commuting speeds of 70 miles an hour.

Like city trolleys, the Niagara Falls interurbans began their trip out Buffalo's Main Street, but resemblance stopped there.

Interurbans were all business: no dallying, with passengers at every corner. Boarding privilege was extended only at a few points along Main Street.

Just east of Hertel — you can still see the right-of-way — the trolley left Main Street and veered north. Then the fun began: liberated from city restrictions, those marvelous cars burst out in their plunge across open land.

Those who have ridden Buffalo's new electric subway know the ease with which the jaunty cars accelerate — no shifting gears, no odor, only a sense that all is well in the engine room.

It was like that on the Niagara Falls interurbans. With fixed determination, they headed for the Tonawandas. Inside the cars, passengers enjoyed comfortable seats and

95

the panorama of swiftly changing scenery. With absolute dependability, the yellow cars arrived in the Falls just an hour after leaving Buffalo.

Once there, riders could connect with the fabled Niagara Gorge Route and with trolleys to Youngstown and Old Fort Niagara. The web of rail service also included a strand at Queenston, Ont., to a steamboat across Lake Ontario to Toronto.

At the huge cost of $4 million, the Niagara Falls interurban began in 1919; only 18 years later, on Aug. 20, 1937, the line was discontinued because most of its passengers had deserted to private motor cars.

Recently, the possibilities of a mega-mall in Niagara Falls and of legalized gambling in Ontario have stirred recollections of the old Buffalo-Niagara Falls high-speed line. In the event of increased commuting, an extension of the present light-rail line has been suggested.

Perhaps it is an impossible dream, but such speculation quickens the heartbeat of all trolley fanciers. Much of the former interurban right-of-way is still available, awaiting a time when electric mass transit again makes practical sense. ∞

AT GAS STATIONS OF YESTERYEAR,
PUMPS HAD PERSONALITY

FIRST PRINTED ∞ 07 – 06 – 86

*I*n the 1930s, when the automobile was younger, gasoline filling stations were far different from today's complicated installations. There were no bays with leaded and unleaded fuel, there was no self-service, no office with monitor panels for individual pumps.

City gas stations back then resembled any other neighborhood store with two display windows, one on each side of a walk-in entrance. Gasoline pumps

97
∞

were located at curbside, and cars would simply pull into the parking lane to fill up.

A honk on the horn would fetch an attendant who was usually the station's owner. He had only one question to cover all transactions: "Regular or ethyl?"

Since but one car could be serviced at a time, curbside filling stations needed just two pumps, one to dispense regular gas; the other held the higher-octane blend, called ethyl. Before pumps were electrified, the attendant had to crank out the gas, turning a metal handle slowly.

Gasoline pumps looked like robots whose tall bodies were topped by a glass balloon. At night, a bulb lit inside the globe, and the manufacturer's logo shone out into the darkness.

If you used your imagination, you could endow those primitive gas pumps with human individuality. The bubble top was, of course, a head. It tapered into an elongated body, and jutting from the sides of the pump's body was a long hose.

The hose, depending on its random position, resembled the body's arms in various attitudes. At times impatience was reflected with arm akimbo; other stances looked casual, impertinent, lounging, even inebriated.

Today, such curbside accommodations would cause hazardous traffic problems; they would violate fire safety laws. Years ago, however, there were fewer cars on the road, and we didn't borrow as much trouble as we do now.

Driving through the country, we have all seen small abandoned tourist cabins, dating back to an early phase of motor car history.

Country-road gas stations looked something like those tourist cabins. In front of a shack, a half dozen pumps — sometimes more — would line up like soldiers on parade. Some were tall, skinny; others, fat and squat; all had the bubble head.

Few oil companies maintained their own franchised stations, and at the same country location, pumps bearing rival national brand labels would operate side-by-side.

Many of the old brands of gasoline have changed names or disappeared. Gone with them is the price gas used to command: about 15 cents a gallon.

No wonder old-time motorists could afford to smile expansively when they pulled up to the pump and said, "Fill 'er up!" ∞

LIFE CYCLE OF THE INNER-TUBE TIRE

FIRST PRINTED ∽ 04 – 13 – 86

*f*or 25 years now, automobiles have been hitting the road on tubeless tires. People are growing up almost ignorant, except for bicycles, of the inner tube — that soft, bulging balloon-ring that used to serve as an undergarment for the car tire.

Before tires went tubeless, when you had a flat, you knew that the first thing to do was to strip down to the inner tube. Along the way, you probably found the offending nail or glass shard, but it was elemental to get to the inner tube, find the lesion, patch it, reassemble.

Some tubes with wear and bad luck grew to look like old soldiers returning from the wars. Eventually they became battered, scarred and were withdrawn from service, or — wanting a better word — retired.

For an inner tube, retirement from road service was the start of a whole new phase of life. No more running around in circles, no more lurking in a stuffy, dark casing. Life became fun in the sun.

Retired inner tubes were carried to the beach and inflated there. Children loved to climb, cavort, romp in the water with them. Perfect beach companions, inner tubes were shiny, black, but with just the necessary degree of abrasiveness to help a swimmer catch on.

For beach use, the more patches on the tube, the better; the more colors for those patches, the more festive: blue, green, red, white. Wherever a patch had been applied, the inner tube's surface became distended — like the scar left after an appendectomy.

Much envied were the children who somehow secured the service of old truck inner tubes. Once lords of the road, such bulbous tubes were royalty at any beach, offering comfortable haven for a cadre of bathers. (Happily, inner tubes are still available for certain truck sizes.)

Old inner tubes stayed in the beach phase as long as they were inflatable, but they had an Achilles' heel — the valve.

Hard use gradually loosened the valve's mooring, and one day, the tube would let out a painful puff. With a gurgle into the water, it gasped out its final breath, and beach life was done.

It was time for another metamorphosis.

Children of the Depression often had to rely on imagination, rather than money, for their playthings. Ingeniously they contrived a rubber-band gun using sliced inner tube rings to join a split clothespin and a 10-inch length of wood.

The resulting product was a very rough suggestion of a cowboy's six-shooter, and it served in many shoot-outs with knotted, stretched inner tube pieces providing ammunition.

The ultimate phase of the inner tube's life cycle arrived when Dad cut out a 9-inch square of rubber. He tacked this over the garage door lock as a curtain to keep out freezing rain and snow. Only then was the inner tube through. The world is a poorer place without it. ☜

BACK-TO-SCHOOL AND
THE RADIO SERIALS CURE

FIRST PRINTED ∽ 09 – 20 – 92

*T*he same flip of the calendar that ended summer and sent us back to school also restored the late-afternoon radio serials. Suspended during vacation months, the daily lineup of cereal-sponsored serials was an engrossing world for kids of my era.

Many afternoon dramas drew their inspirations from popular comic strips: Dick Tracy, Skippy, Terry and the Pirates, Little Orphan Annie, Captain Midnight. Others relied on quasi-folklore: Tom Mix, Jack Armstrong.

Children's radio serials signed on at 5 p.m., each feature lasting a quarter-hour. Allowing for commercials at start and finish, actual drama time ran about 11 minutes.

Time passes more slowly for a child, and the daily segment seemed a fair allotment. It ended too soon — that was life — but there was always the next day. "Tune in tomorrow," as the announcer said.

It was amazing how quickly we kids could make the transition from one afternoon story to the next. Yet there was no problem keeping straight the characters, the situation. Of course, the announcer tried to help.

"You remember yesterday, boys and girls: Terry had lost his way in the jungle. Stumbling through the thick, wild brush, he suddenly heard a low moan... " Late-afternoon radio was in session.

Many serials wove music into their introductions. "Jack Armstrong, the All-American Boy!" started with Jack's school song: "Wave the flag for Hudson High, boys/Show them how we stand."

Subtly, this melody blended into a commercial: "Have you tried Wheaties? ...They're crispy, they're crunchy the whole day through/Jack Armstrong never tires of them/And neither will you."

At 5:30, Tom Mix would gallop on with a song to suit his cereal sponsor: "When it's Ralston time at breakfast/ Then it surely is a treat... " Tom's story generally involved cattle thieves or wolf packs that preyed on sheep.

The final afternoon slot opened with a musical question: "Who's that little chatterbox/The one with pretty auburn locks?" For any child, now well-aged, who can't identify the program, I'll drop a hint: She had a dog named Sandy whose cachet was "Arf."

The drama and revelry to which I allude was but a prelude to the unfurling glories of autumn. Within weeks, announcers were cooing about enticing free offers whereby kids could obtain lucky charms, secret decoders, lapel pins, breakfast mugs, club badges, engraved spoons.

I still have some of the prizes I received by return mail during that golden age of serial radio. Still better, I cherish a barrel of memories of programs that helped me forget the misery of being back at school. ∞

THE ICEMAN
CAME AND WENT

PUBLISHED IN THE WALL STREET JOURNAL 07 – 03 – 86

A lthough I corrected myself at once, my daughter laughed at me. I had meant to say refrigerator, but the word became icebox. "You've never gotten over that habit," she chuckled indulgently.

In many ways I feel that I grew up in the Ice Age; certainly I did with regard to refrigeration. To keep unused food, to cool beverages; we relied on the icebox, a wooden chest of stained oak. Like Cinderella, it used to sit in the unheated back hall or on a cluttered porch.

The icebox! This harsh name derived from an exactness of description. Effective in winter, the big box needed help from a big cube of ice when cold temperatures outside yielded to summer sunshine.

A dimension of life grew up in the service of the icebox. Community businesses sprang up: The local icehouse, a squat brick or stone edifice, stored tons of ice and supplied the iceman.

A word about this dexterous tradesman. In the North, the iceman of summer became the coal man of winter. Thus, a common neighborhood enterprise, "Coal and Ice," provided year-round employment. Tools of the iceman's trade were a gaping pair of tongs with which to wrestle the ice, and a leather pad for the shoulder.

Children followed the ice truck, pleading for a piece of ice to suck on a scorching July day. Sometimes, the burly tradesman would throw back the gray, canvas tarpaulin covering his dripping ice. With a pick, he chipped off a wedge and bestowed it with royal largess.

Carrying ice is a heavy soggy job, and no iceman wanted to lug a 50-pound block into a house only to discover that the housewife didn't want it. So a signal system emerged.

Every ice company provided a square card, and it was the customer's task to hang this card conspicuously in the front window. The card would be suspended diamond-fashion by its angle with one corner pointing upward. On each corner was a number — 10, 25, 50: these numbers referred to the size by weight of the ice cake to be delivered.

A problem for the icebox owner lay in its incontinency: What was to become of the water as the big ice cakes melted?

Several options were offered. Some iceboxes had a catcher-pan underneath, but this required regular emptying. Other models accommodated a hose connection and the hose might be strung down a step and out a lower window to drip freely.

However, if you lived in a house beautiful, there was the latest futuristic luxury. Designers had provided a pipe protruding through the floor. This pipe burrowed inside walls, under steps, finally spilling into a basement drain. Ah, technology!

Smile as you will, daughter, the name and character of the icebox are frozen into the crevices of my mind. These days, the young know only the blessings of easy refrigeration. Ice cubes are delivered, all right — only now they appear magically with a nudge to the door of the box. A free sample doesn't thrill like it used to. ∞

BUFFALO'S ROLE IN 100 YEARS OF HOLMES

FIRST PRINTED ∞ 04 – 13 – 86

*E*very follower of the adventures of Sherlock Holmes knows that the great detective had a brother, the brilliant but effete Mycroft Holmes. As to any other family members, Sherlock is very stingy with information.

However, fact and fiction often intersect — a real person becomes intimately related to a fictional one. There are several important real people closely associated with Sherlock Holmes who visited Buffalo, among them Holmes' creator, Sir Arthur Conan Doyle.

It is just a hundred years since Dr. Doyle conceived Sherlock, his most famous brainchild. Business was slack in the young physician's Plymouth, England, consulting room, so he diverted himself by sketching plots about a master detective. The author's notebooks, in his own handwriting, show that he wrote "A Study in Scarlet" in March and April of 1886.

Like many new fathers, Conan Doyle wondered what name to give his offspring. He considered "Sherringford Holmes," then "Sherrington Hope" before settling on Sherlock Holmes.

By 1891, his stories had made Dr. Doyle so renowned that he abandoned medical practice to rely fully on his writing for support. This decision freed him to travel, and twice his wanderings brought him to Buffalo.

105

The first visit was in October of 1894. Accompanied by his brother Innes, a British army subaltern, he registered at the posh Iroquois Hotel, which stood at Main and Eagle Streets, the present site of the M&T Plaza. He was 35 years old, six feet tall, and prematurely portly.

Like his countryman Charles Dickens a generation earlier, Doyle was scheduled for a Buffalo lecture and readings. Unlike the theatrical Dickens, he was shy by nature. Buffalo reviewers wrote that he read without the least attempt to bring out dramatic tones, but "there was a calmness, a solidity, an air of self-possession that his listeners found attractive."

By the time of this 1894 visit, Doyle had wearied of the detective-story genre despite how rewarding it had been. So definitely had he made up his mind to try something new that he had "killed" Sherlock Holmes by plunging him and his arch foe, Professor Moriarty, over the falls at Reichenbach in a Wagner-like disaster.

However, lovers of the Holmes stories were unwilling to accept the death of their hero. Questions from the Buffalo audience in 1894 prodded Conan Doyle about Holmes' fate. No body had been discovered at Reichenbach. Had Holmes really died, or might he somehow have survived to solve future mysteries?

The author dodged the question by saying that he awaited unfolding events, developments, reports, which might shed light on the Reichenbach disappearance.

Twenty-eight years passed before Doyle returned to Buffalo. It was a cloudy spring afternoon, May 12, 1922, when he arrived on the 20th Century Limited at the old Terrace Street Station. Again he stayed at the Iroquois Hotel, but many changes had occurred in his life.

By this time the Buffalo question about Holmes' fate at Reichenbach had been answered — Holmes did survive and return. But events more momentous had befallen his creator. Now Sir Arthur Conan Doyle, the writer, physician and medievalist, had been knighted by his king. And he had suffered through the terrible years of World War I.

During the awful carnage of that war, Doyle had shared the grief of a nation, most of whose families had lost sons, brothers or fathers in the fighting. His own son Kingsley and his brother Innes had died, along with some 12 to 15 other members of his and his wife's families.

The presence of death haunted Doyle, and he sought relief from its inevitability by embracing spiritualism. Immersed in study and practice in spirit migration (he claimed to have arranged reunions with their dead soldier sons for many families), he abandoned all other pursuits. Although he was the highest-paid writer in the world, he discontinued writing fiction to detail his experiments with what he called "the other world."

It was in this capacity, as a researcher and lecturer on the occult, that Sir Arthur Conan Doyle came to Buffalo for his second visit.

Approached by a Buffalo News reporter in 1922, Doyle claimed fatigue and agreed to only a five-minute interview outside the Iroquois Hotel. When a crowd gathered around the famous writer, he moved the newspaper interview into the hotel and extended it to a half-hour. The News reporter commented on Doyle's "child-like faith" as he spoke of his psychic beliefs.

That evening, over lamb chops in the Iroquois' dining room, he left the subject of spiritualism and talked with another reporter about sports. He was especially interested in boxing. Who would be Jack Dempsey's next opponent? Doyle had been offered the opportunity to referee the Jeffries-Johnson fight in Nevada, but declined, he said.

Doyle was reluctant to speak about Sherlock Holmes, and during his after-dinner coffee and cigar, he returned to the subject of the spirit world. He said he was planning to visit the Western New York psychic colony at Lily Dale, where some vivid, significant experiences had occurred.

On the evening of May 12, 1922, Doyle addressed a large cosmopolitan audience at the Teck Theater. He presented a "commanding figure, an earnest rather than oratorical manner."

A contemporary reporter referred to "warm applause from an audience, some of whom had come to scoff, and remained for the opposite reason." A breathless hush reportedly fell over the listeners when Doyle described his dead soldier son telling about seeing Christ in the afterlife.

At one time Doyle had considered writing a play about Sherlock Holmes, and had even sketched the four acts and written several scenes. Then, dissatisfied, he had dropped the subject until he was contacted by the popular British actor William Gillette, who was to become another Sherlock Holmes "relative."

Gillette was then the rage of London theater. He had written and starred in a suspense play called "The Professor." He had some definite ideas about writing a Sherlock Holmes play, and he presented Doyle with these plans.

Impressed, Doyle showed Gillette his own scenario for a play centering around Holmes. He suggested a collaboration, but the idea didn't appeal to Gillette, who wanted the production to be completely his own.

Doyle relented, and William Gillette wrote and later staged a play appropriately called "Sherlock Holmes." It had its world premiere at the Star Theater in Buffalo on Oct. 23, 1899. It became so popular that for the next 30 years, Gillette continued to play the role of Doyle's great detective all over the world.

He also chose Buffalo as the site for his farewell performance of Sherlock Holmes, on Feb. 18, 1930, at the Erlanger Theater.

Nearly every moviegoer knows another figure closely associated with Sherlock Holmes. In 13 moving pictures and a long-lasting radio series, the great detective was played by the fastidious British actor Basil Rathbone.

He often came to Buffalo. One triumphant stay in November of 1933 featured him in two plays with Katharine Cornell as his co-star: "The Barretts of Wimpole Street" and "Romeo and Juliet."

In the Shakespeare play, Rathbone and Cornell were, of course, the star-crossed lovers. That cast also included a highly mercurial Mercutio, a young Orson Welles.

Rathbone's last appearance in Western New York was on Feb. 17, 1962, as part of an ambitious theater series at Lackawanna High School. A one-man show, he read many selections, including one from a Sherlock Holmes story. He skipped the familiar deer-stalker hat, but the audience chuckled at the familiar voice and manner so long associated with Holmes.

During the past two seasons, the PBS Mystery Theater has had a new Sherlock Holmes, British actor Jeremy Brett, in a scrupulously faithful adaptation of several of the adventures.

To date, this latest Holmes associate has not paid a visit here. But if he follows the path of his predecessors, he will. It's elementary. ∽

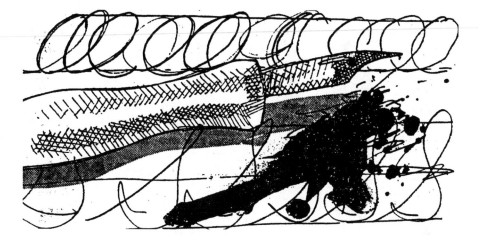

'PALMER METHOD' DOMINATED AGE OF BEAUTIFUL HANDWRITING

FIRST PRINTED ◌ 08 – 31 – 86

Some of the world's neatest penmanship was molded at those old-fashioned, wrought-iron desks. With a shelf for books under the writing surface, students struggled from a folding bench-seat.

Years ago, schools were very big on teaching pupils not merely to write, but to write beautifully. Any dunce could be trained to form characters crudely; it was the hallmark of the lady or gentleman to impart an elegance to letters.

Students from these days will remember the Palmer Method. According to this system, developed by the founder of chiropractic, writers would hold the pen loosely and pivot from the wrist. This movement was said to keep penmanship uniform and relaxed.

Palmer Method involved countless exercises in making flowing, graceful circles. The teacher would croon rhythmically, "Over, over, over, round, up!"

As she spoke, she produced on the blackboard some neat, harmonious ovals. Students would try to imitate these designs, hacking away sedulously with pens and ink.

Part of the trick of good penmanship was a graceful dip of the pen into a recessed ink well. Every line or so, the writer had to refuel by reinserting pen in ink: It was as regular as the shift of a typewriter's carriage.

The indifferent student who overindulged his pen would wind up with messy blots on his paper as the pen's point disgorged excess ink. Technique exercises in Palmer Method to develop graceful handwriting style haunted school rooms. For hours, students practiced generous ovals or bold, upward thrusts and retreats called push-pull drills.

Some would make a stab at all this, before settling back with a characteristic conviction that what was worth doing was worth doing sloppily.

But others soared with a craftsman's satisfaction in turning out script of delicate excellence. With true flair, they took to penmanship as a duck-to-water.

Exotic shadings, balanced, artistic handwritings surfaced. Words bowed, glistened, sparkled as they found life on the lined page. Penmanship became a mark of individualism, a manifestation of character. It assumed the effortless style of a folk song, the symmetry of a medieval tapestry.

Blame the ball-point pen for writing an end to the age of elegant handwriting. With its constricting stress from the writer's hand, the ball-point pen choked the freedom integral to any art form. It is convenience at the price of grace.

Occasionally, one encounters still a sample of the beautiful Palmer penmanship that has survived a bygone time: It is as refreshing to see as the warm smile of a lovely face shining in sunlight. ∞

THE LEGENDARY TELEGRAPH BOYS
OFTEN BORE FATEFUL MESSAGES

FIRST PRINTED ∞ 10 – 05 – 86

*O*nce my mother received a telegram and stared at it all afternoon, afraid to open the envelope. When she finally did, it turned out to be a novel wedding anniversary greeting which my father, in a moment of expansiveness, had arranged.

Dad was later reprimanded because such a spendthrift gesture was not only costly; it was also scary. Most often in those days telegrams were harbingers of disaster, especially during the two World Wars, when they carried the government's official notification of a service tragedy.

In an age when only a fraction of American homes had a telephone, instant transmittal of news depended upon the wire service. Developed from the Morse Code, the sender tapped out his message; the receiver transliterated it into ticker tape. This tape then was pasted to a sheet of Western Union stationery.

The page wore a look of stark urgency, particularly because all letters were in upper case, and there was no punctuation. To simplify transmission, the word STOP signified period, comma, question mark, change of thought. Verbs were usually omitted.

Thus a well-planned telegram might read: BABY KATIE BORN 5:30 AM STOP MOTHER DAUGHTER FINE STOP ALL LOVE STOP JIM AND MARCY. The trick was to keep the number of words to 10 for the standard minimum rate.

After the telegram message was typed, pasted, sealed in an envelope, delivery was entrusted to Western Union's legendary telegraph boys.

People of my generation will recall these boys, dressed in neat khaki suits, with black tie, peaked hat, mounting their bicycles and driving, undaunted by weather or time of day, to deliver their message.

Brave boys to bear the tidings they did! After they rang the doorbell, the boys waited. When the door was flung open, frequently the message boy would be greeted with a gasp, a look of terror.

What a relief if the news was felicitous! Then the happy recipients dug deep and produced a tip.

Otherwise, like any bearer of bad news, the Western Union messenger felt vaguely responsible.

With near universal telephone service, printed Western Union messages became rare, and the telegram lost its macabre reputation. Gradually, the hand-delivered message assumed a ceremonious function: varied forms of congratulation — new parenthood, job promotion, graduation, but especially birthdays.

Out of birthday greetings came the famous singing telegram. When the door was opened, a plum-cheeked Western Union boy asked to see the jubilarian. Face-to-face, he began to sing: "Happy Birthday to You..."

Somehow, those musical telegram boys never faltered or lost a note. Often, their performance was so successful that an encore was demanded.

Today, you can arrange all sorts of singing or novelty messages, but not through Western Union. The singing greeting was discontinued in 1971. There is still personal delivery of telegrams in certain areas of the country, but messages are now typed directly on paper — no more glued tape. The magic word STOP has yielded to conventional punctuation.

And the renowned Western Union telegraph boy is no more. He has tipped his cap for the final time and pedaled off on his bike, carrying with him a bit of authentic Americana. ∽

FIRST PRINTED ⌒ 11 – 02 – 86

THE OLD LEHIGH VALLEY TERMINAL WAS A RAILROAD PALACE

Anyone who liked railroads loved Buffalo's Lehigh Valley Terminal. The building was picturesque, majestic and yet, in a way, cute. If it had been reduced to model railroad size, the Lehigh would have blended perfectly with any Lionel or American Flyer layout.

Situated on Main Street across from Memorial Auditorium, the Lehigh Terminal was built in 1910. Lower Main Street was then a bustling center for transportation with all major railroads, as well as the big passenger excursion ships, operating from there.

The Lehigh Valley Terminal was a gleaming, marble structure with eight classical columns soaring upward to an entablature on which huge letters spelled out the railroad's proud name.

It is a commentary on the age that a comparatively insignificant system like the Lehigh should have constructed such an impressive Buffalo base.

To walk through the terminal's entrance was to be a traveler in a great tradition.

The waiting room was gracious with a tall ceiling from which chandeliers were suspended. Heavy, oak benches, comfortably separated, stretched laterally.

Front windows were set into recessed arches. More arches were in the building's sides, providing doors to a marble-walled cafeteria and to the baggage room.

To reach trains, the traveler walked through a tunnel under Washington Street. There he stopped, surveying the platform and tracks, once firmly embedded on the present location of the Buffalo News building.

Lehigh and Erie railroad trains started from here on their journeys toward New York City. Legendary trains like the Lehigh's Black Diamond operated out of this center.

Many are the times I boarded the Black Diamond, but alas, never as a passenger. During college days, I was a Railway Express employee, shuffled between the Lehigh and Lackawanna terminals. My acquaintance with the famous trains was limited only to the baggage and freight cars, as I stacked up shipments bound for big, eastern destinations.

When my work was done just before train departure, I would stand aside to escape the first surge of steam power as the Lehigh's Black Diamond engine exhaled with an enormous whoosh and began its journey east.

The streamlined locomotive was followed by the coal tender; then, by baggage cars. I'd catch a glimpse of people already settled down in the diner, being catered to by white-coated waiters.

Daily, I watched this tableau of gracious traveling. With similar scenes being enacted simultaneously at Buffalo's three large railroad stations, no one guessed then that rail service would soon be attacked on two fronts.

After the war, buses proved cheaper; airplanes were faster. Faced with this double assault, the Lehigh, like most American railroads, suffered drastically. A terminal like the one in Buffalo became too costly to sustain.

In 1952, after a brief 42 years of use, the stately Lehigh Valley Terminal was demolished.

The property site was sold to New York State for construction of the Gen. Donovan State Office Building, a structure of bland design and small artistic flair. Architecturally, the exchange was not a fair one. ∞

DECO EATERIES HAD
A SPECIAL AURA

FIRST PRINTED ☞ 11 – 30 – 86

ong before Wendy and Ronald McDonald were born, before Burger King was even an infant prince, Buffalo had fast food eateries. They were called Deco Restaurants, and over 50 of them were scattered around the city.

Logo of the Deco chain was a steaming cup of coffee, nestling securely in a heavy saucer. With the slogan "Buffalo's Best Cup of Coffee," this picture was mounted at the front of each Deco restaurant. At first, the ad's prevailing colors were brown and tan; later, they were jazzed up with a red-blue combination.

Ranging in size from small to tiny, all Deco installations had a certain sameness. Walking inside, the customer found a counter with accompanying stools fastened tight to the floor.

Removed from the counter area, there were tables and chairs with chromium-pipe legs. Ashtrays were on each table, simmering glumly with the butts of a previous customer. Often it required keen appetite to enjoy a meal.

During the day, a waitress presided at the typical Deco lunch counter, but at night, especially for the 12-8 closing shift, a counterman took over. Every counterman wore an assistant manager tag and arranged at all times to have a rancid cigarette end dangling from his lips.

I can see him now behind his counter on a frigid winter night. After a late date, I would duck into a Deco to keep warm while waiting for a streetcar home. Clad in a yellowed white shirt, a soiled apron and an overseas cap with the embroidered Deco name, he would scowl at me. A quiet surliness was the counterman's abiding avatar.

Deco restaurants touted their coffee, whose quality depended on the assistant manager's generosity. Sometimes, it was average; at other times, when a budget needed stretching, the coffee's flavor weakened drastically.

Never headquarters for gourmet treats, Deco featured a menu of hot dogs and hamburgers. Familiar advertisements claimed that customers received "that extra bite."

Started by Gregory Deck in 1918, for a time the Deco restaurants multiplied like rabbits; at their height, there were six Decos on Main Street alone. Judiciously placed at busy transit stops, near schools, dance halls or popular taverns, the chain thrived during the Depression.

Deco business was cut into by a surge in the 1950s of small fast-lunch shops like the Toddle House, Your Host, Hull Dobbs, White Tower. But the telling blow was delivered by the current tidal wave of junk-food dispensaries, and the name Deco gradually faded from the local scene. The last surviving unit on Washington Street next to the Hotel Lafayette closed in 1981.

It's hard to forget the aura of a Deco Restaurant, particularly in the early morning hours: a large griddle with grease snapping away under a hamburger, the smell of stale smoke, clacks and pings from a pin-ball machine, the eternal drunk at a counter stool trying to sober up with Buffalo's Best Cup of Coffee. ∞

THE OLD POST OFFICE CAME ALIVE EVERY YEAR FOR CHRISTMAS SEASON

FIRST PRINTED ⬭ 12 – 14 – 86

*T*he building is now the handsome downtown site of Erie Community College, but for me, it will always be the Central Post Office.

Furthermore, Christmas spirit surrounds it because only at that happy season, did the Post Office come alive.

The old Post Office was not only the center for directing letters, packages. It was also the merging point for all those souls who, at holiday time, needed extra money. Every Christmas, the downtown post office hired hundreds of temporary employees.

Although the postal service still hires holiday help, the volume is not near what it used to be. When a 3-cent stamp paid the freight of a greeting card, Christmas mail fell on the Post Office like an avalanche.

To cope with the rush, an army of temporary help was enlisted. You might meet anyone: distant relatives, neighbors, fellow students, former girl friends. The whole city seemed to need money at Christmas.

In my youth, seasonal work was scarce so if you were provident, you put in a post office application in early September. If you were an eager-beaver (as we used to say), you would commit yourself to learning "the scheme."

The scheme, veteran postal employees will recall, was a plan for sorting Buffalo city mail. There were no zip codes then, no postal zones on letters. Mail was routed according to a system whose complexity rivaled the 1944 allied landing in Normandy.

Employees who had mastered the scheme were summoned earlier for Christmas work; they were given longer hours, better jobs. Other workers, not so enterprising, might be assigned to the "east-west" case. Here, the job of the mail worker was to sort letters roughly, according to their destination east or west of Buffalo.

Still other temporaries might "face" mail: arrange envelopes so that they were facing upwards with stamps all in the same position for canceling.

Such jobs were, of course, hopelessly dull, but while workers shared benches side by side, conversation relieved monotony. New friendships proliferated.

One Christmas season, I worked beside a temporary known by the sobriquet "Cuddles." Cuddles was a tall, cow-eyed girl who spoke little but looked devastating even in the harsh light of the post office basement.

With large, vacant eyes, Cuddles sorted mail beside me on the east-west case. "Is Chicago east or west of here?" she would ask. "I always get directions mixed up."

Friendship with Cuddles was stopped short that year by my transfer to the Parcel Post Division. Healthy-looking males were often shunted there, a sexist preference that ought never to have been challenged by women. Parcel Post was dreary, dirty, drafty.

In cold, joyless surroundings, I sorted packages and loaded canvas bags onto trucks.

Because of assignment to this Siberia of the Christmas operation, I never saw Cuddles again.

Whenever I pass the Old Post Office — now spruced up for its new mission in life — I recall those long, mid-winter nights inside, sorting letters or packages, dreaming of the pay check I would receive several weeks later.

Back then, those checks had to stretch a long way into the new year. ∞

TICKETS RECALL GLITTER
OF ERLANGER OPENING

FIRST PRINTED ∞ 01 – 04 – 87

*T*ickets to Buffalo's old Erlanger Theater always brought excitement and a joy of expectation. But tickets seldom last. An usher collects them and tears them.

Yet some tickets, like some memories, do not tear.

Consider four tickets that belong to Mary Murphy of Snyder for an opening-night performance at the Erlanger on Sept. 4, 1927. Mrs. Murphy still has her tickets, undamaged even though the box seats were occupied that night years ago.

But these are not your usual tickets.

Mary Murphy's father was Frank X. Schwab, Buffalo's mayor back in 1927 when the Erlanger opened. The tickets were presented to him, ceremoniously engraved in metal, enclosed in velvet pouches and meant to be retained as souvenirs.

The tickets bring cherished memories of a festive Buffalo evening for Mary Schwab Murphy.

The two marquees, the main one on Delaware Avenue and the side entrance on Mohawk Street, were swarming with elegantly dressed first-nighters. Through the heavy mahogany doors they passed, anxious for a look at the new 1,500-seat theater, which had been nearly two years in construction.

The bill that premier night was a musical called "Criss Cross," with songs by Jerome Kern, already famous for the melodies in "Showboat." Fred Stone was starring in the C. P. Dillingham production. And equally important was the spectacle of glamorous people in the audience.

119

These included David Belasco, Florenz Ziegfeld and George M. Cohan.

The Erlanger's lobby had a soft green ceiling; the walls were inlaid with Alabama cream marble. Steps to the mezzanine used more of the same marble, while stairway walls bore crests of America's 13 original states.

The mezzanine, paneled in fine walnut with cove lighting, was like a drawing room of an English estate. At its south end were theater offices; at the north were restrooms.

A sleek ladies' lounge, octagonal in shape, had a parquet floor, hanging lights, a half-dozen mirrors. The men's lounge imitated a private club with walls sheathed in pine.

Mary Murphy, clutching the durable brass tickets, remembers the orchestra performing when she arrived. Max Joseffer was directing a permanent house group of 18 musicians in the orchestra pit in hit tunes from "Showboat": "Why Do I Love You?" "Make Believe," "Old Man River."

A huge chandelier, gleaming with 486 lights and clusters of crystal, was suspended from the theater's dome. In front of the stage was a tapestry curtain of gold and old rose.

There were three boxes on either side of the stage. Mary Schwab Murphy recalls taking a seat between her parents in one of them. Smoothing her new party dress, bought for the splendid occasion, she luxuriated in the grandeur of it all and dangled the brass tickets in their purple pouches as she waited for the curtain to rise that glittering opening night.

Only the four outside walls of the theater survive today. The Georgian exterior is still handsome, but the old Erlanger has been converted to an office building, and its name has been changed to a less nostalgic one — The 120 Building. ∞

CLASSY COLUMNS ADORNING UB LAKE COME FROM BUFFALO BANK

FIRST PRINTED ∞ 01 – 18 – 87

*T*he State University at Buffalo frequently shows them on its publications. Picturesque, like relics left over from classical Athens, they soar into the blue Amherst sky.

Those majestic Corinthian columns that reflect so beautifully on the placid waters of Lake LaSalle could tell a story, but not of Ancient Greece.

Once upon a time, at the corner of Main and Seneca streets in downtown Buffalo, stood a massive stone edifice, called the Federal Reserve Bank.

Six mighty columns fronted the bank, and for years, they embodied the stability that a great government likes to associate with its finances. However, in the 1950s, operations had outgrown even this towering repository, and plans had been made for a larger Federal Reserve Bank on Delaware Avenue.

In America, it is the unfortunate custom to tear down buildings, even though they have not nearly exhausted their useful life span. So it was with the old Federal Reserve bank. In 1959, powerful demolition equipment converged at Main and Swan and the last days of the stately building were at hand.

Yet, so appealing, so impressive, were features of this structure that everyone, the wrecking company included, stopped wistfully and wondered.

Inside were eight graceful, green-marble columns that the demolition company tried to give away. Only after a fruitless search, were they regretfully knocked down.

The six exterior columns facing on Main Street were another matter. Contract agreements dictated that demolition move swiftly, but again it seemed a pity to have the outside columns follow their inside cousins to destruction.

Each exterior column was 35 feet high, 24 inches in diameter, and consisted of five sections. Weight of each section was estimated at 10-15 tons. Hardly a hot item for a liquidation sale.

Enter a Maj. Burt Hamilton, a training officer for the Buffalo Air Reserve Center, with a suggestion. He proposed relocation of the columns to the UB campus on Main Street for some unspecified future use.

The idea caught on. Gently, the columns were disassembled by the wreckers and put on caissons, bound 6 miles out Main Street to UB.

For 20 years, the orphan columns lay behind Baird Hall, like remnants of antiquity. Meanwhile, had come incorporation of UB into the State University system and construction of the huge Amherst facility.

When Lake LaSalle took shape in the landscaping of the new campus, somebody remembered the Federal Reserve columns. Wouldn't they be dynamic on the lake's shore, to be used as a backdrop for recitations, drama, music?

In 1977, the columns began a final odyssey to their present academic home. They were reassembled and formally dedicated in September 1978.

From a bank in central Buffalo to a university in suburban Amherst is a big change, but to see the columns gleaming evenings in flood-lit dignity proves that classical style can surmount any alteration. ☙

BUFFALO WAS RAVAGED BY DEADLY FLU EPIDEMIC OF 1918

FIRST PRINTED ∾ 03 – 01 – 87

uring the terrible, final winter of World War I, a new killer stalked European battlefields. Not manmade, this death exploded with no less fury. It was called Spanish Influenza.

Buffalo, like other large American cities, had been warned that the new strain of virus would not halt in the trenches of France. Wounded, returning soldiers would carry the disease back with them.

And so they did. A violent flu outbreak struck first at the port cities of New York and Boston. Then it systematically traveled west.

In September 1918, Buffalo's Health Department recorded only 33 cases, but the situation changed suddenly. During the first week of October, there were 1,281 instances of flu, with 119 fatalities.

On the single day of Oct. 19, 112 deaths were attributed to what was speedily becoming a pandemic.

Buffalo Mayor George Buck met with his health commissioner and severe control measures resulted: all indoor assemblages of more than 10 people were banned.

Thus, all schools, churches, entertainment places, had to close. When a few church congregations tried to hold services in the outdoors, the ban was extended to these likewise.

No visitors were allowed at any city hospitals. Bodies had to be sealed in coffins immediately after death and buried within 24 hours, only the direct family in attendance.

123

Police were ordered to enforce strictly a new state law making it a misdemeanor to cough or sneeze in public without proper cover from a handkerchief. Everyone was encouraged to wear a cloth mask at all times.

With schools closed indefinitely, the 2,000 idle, public school teachers were employed canvassing the city house-to-house, searching out any unreported sickness.

Luckily perhaps, the worst weeks of the epidemic coincided with a citywide transit strike. This temporarily removed an occasion when large numbers of people would have met under close, poorly ventilated conditions.

During the month of October, a frightening total of 23,544 cases of Influenza were reported; of these, 1,895 victims had died.

Old Central High School, occupying then the Genesee, Franklin, Court Streets triangle, was converted into an influenza hospital, beds and cots filling classrooms. Children from homes racked by flu were cared for at Children's Aid on Delaware Avenue or at other emergency shelters.

For several months, Buffalo remained a ghostly town of fearful, white-masked citizens, but gradually the desperate measures proved effective.

Except for an added flare-up after Christmas — probably due to a holiday relaxation of sanitary precautions — disease rates steadily fell. It was March, however, before local restrictions were ended.

Although epidemic regulations continued in force for other parts of the country, in spring Buffalonians took off their masks and breathed freely again. ∞

THE DAY THE 'SPIRIT OF ST. LOUIS' CAME TO BUFFALO

FIRST PRINTED ⌒ 05 – 17 – 87

Through the rain and fog, the famous airplane "The Spirit of St. Louis" skimmed over the building roofs in downtown Buffalo. The pilot, Charles A. Lindbergh, waved to people on city streets, and dipped as close as 50 feet above the Marine Trust Building.

When the silver plane touched down at Buffalo Airport, a huge crowd cheered, sirens shrilled, horns of thousands of cars honked. Appropriately, as Lindbergh climbed out of his cockpit, afternoon sun came out, and clouds began to disperse.

"You have brought youth and sunshine to Buffalo," said Mayor Frank X. Schwab in a graceful speech of welcome.

Sixty years have passed since the tall unassuming aviator made his storied flight from New York to Paris. At that time, a hysterical throng of 100,000 Frenchmen shrieked as the wheels of the "Spirit of St. Louis" hit ground at LeBourget Airfield. Lucky Lindy, the tousle-haired, shy American from the Midwest, became an international hero.

Only two months after his epic flight, the same hero, piloting the same plane, in which he crossed the Atlantic, arrived in Buffalo for a 3-day visit.

Immediately upon landing, just as he had in Paris, Lindbergh showed concern for his plane. Like a rider for a beloved horse, Lindy felt an ineffable attachment to "The Spirit of St. Louis." With the plural pronoun "we," he always referred immediately to himself and his plane.

When the craft had been stabled in a Buffalo Airport hangar, Lindbergh boarded Mayor Schwab's limousine for a trip to Niagara Square. There, a parade had formed with infantry and cavalry marching units, an American Legion band wearing snappy uniforms and tin hats—about 3,500 soldiers in all.

While Lindbergh changed cars, aerial bombs were exploded, but their detonations were drowned in the roars of excited people. Lindy took his place in an open car beside Mayor Schwab as the parade began.

That summer day, Buffalonians lined the streets in unprecedented numbers. Out Main Street the parade wound: to North to Delaware. On to Delaware Park meadow with cheering hordes of people along the whole route, straining for a glimpse of the self-effacing hero.

Reporters wrote that Lindbergh looked exactly like his pictures: hat off, hair disheveled, tan leather coat.

Some 50,000 people had assembled in Delaware Park meadow when Lindbergh arrived; the ceremony was brief and formal, speeches only by the Mayor and his distinguished guest.

Later the visitor returned to the Statler Hotel to rest before a 7 p.m. banquet in his honor.

Fifty police were assigned to the Statler, simply to keep back the endless crowds.

Lindbergh's airship was on display to the public at Buffalo Airport for the weekend and over 100,000 passed to examine it before its owner left the city on Monday afternoon.

The "Spirit of St. Louis" hangs today in Washington's Smithsonian Museum.

It is the same plucky plane that flew to Paris — and to Buffalo — 60 years ago. ∞

I'M GONNA SIT WRITE DOWN AND GRAMMERIZE

PUBLISHED IN THE WALL STREET JOURNAL ⚬ 02 – 24 – 87

*N*ow that I am halfway through my second year of retirement from public-school teaching, I can read statistics about low writing scores of American high-school students and remember, with a small shudder, the agony on a typical day of correcting composition papers.

There are the little wasps' stings, the casual misspellings: "gonna" for "going to," "are" for "our" and "Febuary" minus its often unspoken "r." The fact that such egregiousness reflects the sloppy pronunciation prevalent in society is small comfort. And, inevitably, there are apostrophes appearing consistently at odd places: yours' or childrens' or did'nt.

High-school students also overuse language fads: "the bottom line," "that's what it's all about." Such tiresome expressions accompany the discursions of many teen-age compositions. Meanwhile, thought development staggers through the written page with a drunkard's agility.

Faced with such ineptness, a conscientious teacher has difficulty mustering up a grade other than "D," accompanied by the marginal comment "careless."

But at this point, composition review becomes excruciating for the teacher.

In a suburban school such as the one at which I taught, students and parents have the notion that, with the aid of computers and television, today's high schoolers are the brightest things to hit the classroom since paint. Therefore, custom insists that each composition, no matter how slipshod, be dignified not only by a grade but by an explanatory note with a positive tone.

The teacher then is under the strain of diplomacy. His basic note might read: "As long as your bad spelling and basic sentence errors continue, I cannot give you a good grade. You do not understand apostrophe use; see me for a review sheet."

But such sternness must be tempered by adding something like this: "You have some original ideas. I liked the example in Paragraph 3, but you did not relate it clearly to your main thought. I sense some improvement. Grade: C-."

Time-consuming, nettlesome complaints always follow such notes, and a tired teacher often caves in. A high grade and a bland statement make friends and influence students, and after all, a teacher has to live with these kids for only a year. So if a "B" will buy happiness and avoid friction, why not?

I'm not certain a student learns much from the painful routine of practice writing. But as a teacher, I reached a few rueful conclusions: First, students do not take seriously the mechanics of writing. They think spelling, punctuation and grammar exist only in the crabbed world of the English teacher. Second, some students are naturally good writers, but for most who are not, improvement comes only with humility and application. The situation is aggravated because many modern students feel their opinion of good writing is at least as sound as their teacher's. Further, they are convinced that outline and revision hamper spontaneity and are to be disregarded.

Until there is a change of attitude, student writing will continue at a shallow level and English teachers will continue to suffer. Practice, without sincere effort, will never make perfect. ∞

IN DAYS GONE BY WHEN MOVIES
WERE INNOCENT

FIRST PRINTED ☞ 06 – 07 – 87

efore my mother gave me a Depression dime to buy a ticket for the Saturday movie matinee, she fumbled through papers on the dining room table. Finally she would emerge with a clipping from the Catholic diocesan newspaper, listing all films and their ratings by the Legion of Decency, a national Catholic board of censors. Unabashedly, this agency rated films, and unquestioningly, Catholics adhered to its judgment.

My life was suspended as Mother's finger ran down the column. If the Saturday matinee film was rated acceptable for children, Mother would fish up a coin from the depth of her purse. If not, I would hear arcane muttering about scenes objectionable for children, and Mother would seal my afternoon's fate with a succinct, "You'd better not go."

Most movies were innocent things back then, and the Legion of Decency aimed to keep them that way. Excessive violence might concern a shoot-out between cowboys and cattle rustlers. Kisses on the silver screen were rare — fully timed because an extended embrace contributed to a "sexually suggestive" sequence. On such grounds, many films were banned even for adults.

Sometimes, to the narrowed eye of the Legion of Decency, a film presented "a threat to faith and morals" and was totally "condemned." For an occasion like this, Catholic pastors would hoard their most reverberating tones.

"Under pain of serious sin," they would boom, "you are forbidden to attend this film." The thunderous hush gripping a congregation was proof that such an interdiction would be effective.

Human nature being what it is, curiosity of the prurient no doubt was whetted even then by mention of "sexually explicit scenes." Such allurements, however, could not be gratified because ours was a disciplined generation.

Thus the Legion of Decency held a power altogether different from that of the contemporary Motion Picture Association of America, whose bland "General" rating is an automatic kiss of death in the box office. Today's children regard a "G" movie as insipid, sterile, naive, moralistic, divorced from what they called the "real world": in a word, a drag. Parents have a hard time standing up against such scorn.

It is almost laughable to recall the Legion of Decency today. What shocked our elders would pass on prime-time TV casually. Bedroom sex scenes are commonplace, assuming an audience bankrupt of imagination. We have all become blunted to violence, adultery, homosexuality, incest or vulgar leer of talk-show hosts. The picture of the TV screen would have driven those long-gone decency legionnaires to apoplexy.

I'd like to think that somewhere there lies a compromise between the guilty compunctions of my generation and the weak permissiveness of today. However, if no such middle ground exists, even though Mother sometimes ruined my Saturday afternoons, I rejoice in the good fortune to have grown up when I did. ∞

THE DAY I SAVED A MAIDEN FROM DISTRESS

FIRST PRINTED 11 – 22 –87

*L*ike any man who grew up on Gary Cooper movies, I wanted to be a hero. Like most dreamers, I have never had the chance to stand tall and rescue a beautiful girl in distress.

Only once did I come close; perhaps that's a reason why I love the Buffalo Zoo, because it was there that I approached hero status.

On the day of my heroism, I had taken my children to the zoo. Katie, my tenderhearted middle daughter, was perched with me at a railing at one end of the circular duck pond. From a bag we had brought from home, we were casting bread upon the waters. Ducks would paddle quickly, comically, towards us, their voices all aquack.

That chilly autumn day, Katie was wearing a pair of knitted, rust-colored mittens, a gift that she prized highly. She would reach into the bag I was holding and take out bread pieces to throw to the ducks.

I recall the moment well. As she threw, her right-hand mitten came loose and fell gently onto the water below. When she realized the loss, her silver laughter stopped.

Just then, a goose, swimming among the ducks, saw the mitten, picked it up in its bill and darted away gleefully. Katie, forever sensitive, puckered out her lower lip and let go: "My mitten!"

While mittens do not grow on trees, I tried to explain that the lost article was not irreplaceable. Meantime up the stream, the goose, perhaps discovering that the knitted cloth was inedible, had dropped it and swum away. The poor, orphaned mitten lay 10 feet from shore bobbing on the water's surface.

More than she should have, Katie blubbered out her grief. This was my chance to be a hero. What would Gary Cooper do? Definite, unhesitating, he would seize the moment.

131

I tried to seize mine. Taking my daughter by the hand, I guided her along the mud at the water edge until we came as close as possible to the mitten.

I picked up a stick which, when I extended it, was about four feet from the mitten. Then I began to stir the still waters, causing a tide. Gently, the mitten floated over in my direction. Katie's whining diminished as she sensed method in madness.

More paddling of the water, and the mitten was near enough so that I could spear it with my stick. In a second, I had fished in one soggy mitten.

Katie beamed at me with joy. Although she did not kiss me at that moment, I knew she should have because I had attained hallowed status: I was a genuine hero. I had conquered evil forces and saved a maiden from distress.

Granted, my antagonist was only a dumb goose and the distress was only a 5-year-old's loss of grubby mitten. Yet, the girl thought I was a hero, and I knew she thought so. That's what really mattered.

At that moment, I stood as tall as Gary Cooper. ∞

IN THE DAYS OF THE 'FRUIT EXPRESS'

FIRST PRINTED ∞ 10 – 12 – 87

*G*od Shed His Grace on Niagara County and every year, all Western New York shares in that blessing. Sharing begins with a harvest of cherries in July and follows with peaches, pears, apples as the summer draws on. Those fruit farms toward Lake Ontario never let us down.

Bulging trucks roll into local markets from Niagara County. They are loaded with baskets, bushels, of the world's choicest fruits, ready for distribution to area super stores.

When I was a boy, the fruit was just as bountiful as it is now at harvest time, but the method of distribution was altogether different. Trucks and automobiles were few and undependable; roads were meager. Produce from Niagara County had to be carried by rail — electric rail.

Those were the days of the mighty interurban, electric rail lines. People of my generation will recall the heavy, stolid, yellow interurban cars lined up along Main Street, ready to rocket off to Niagara Falls or Lockport.

Rockets they were, even by the standards of 1987. Once they left the traffic of Main Street and started off on their own right-of-way, they shot up to speeds of 80 miles per hour.

The Interurban for Lockport left Main Street just east of Hertel and bulleted due north. With only a few stops around North Tonawanda, cars were in Lockport in under an hour. Continuing north, the line extended all the way to Lake Ontario at Olcott Beach.

Back to Niagara County's delicious fruits. Someone had the happy idea of using what had been designed primarily as a passenger line for fruit runs during the summer nights. If a fruit car left Olcott laden with produce, it could easily make its way over the web of deserted city street rail lines to Buffalo's Elk Street Market in time for morning distribution.

What an exciting idea for days before the efficient truck and roadways of

133

more modern times! The interurbans to Olcott stopped at Burt, Newfane, Corwins, Wrights Corners — all big fruit-growing centers. Farmers could get their produce to the rail line by nightfall and then ship it overnight to population centers like Buffalo.

The system caught on, and for years, farmers were using what was called the "Fruit Express."

The transit company, the International Railway Company, designed 10 special cars for this detail, and at the height of the fruit harvest season all of them were kept busy.

In fact, often when freight cars were unable to meet seasonal demands, passenger cars were converted to the harvest chores. Baskets of peaches and pears perched on seats and lined the aisles ready for the rush trip to Buffalo.

As shipping schedules were refined, with passing years freight cars were left on side tracks for loading during the afternoons; at night, they were picked up for delivery. Some choice cargoes were packed on refrigerator cars that had been iced at Hodgeville.

All this was going on efficiently while Buffalo slept.

Over the same city street tracks that would carry people to work next morning, rumbled the night cars hauling fruit to market. ∞

'WRONG-WAY' CORRIGAN WAS A HERO IN BUFFALO

FIRST PRINTED ⌘ 04 – 10 –88

No matter how old, lies have a way of working their way to the surface and exposing the prevaricator. Truth, it seems, will out.

But there is the stubborn case of Douglas "Wrong Way" Corrigan.

Once a mechanic on Lindbergh's "Spirit of St. Louis," Doug Corrigan had often boasted to friends that he intended to fly his own ramshackle plane across the Atlantic. Repeatedly denied official permission, Corrigan had to content himself with routine flights about the United States.

Then, one Sunday morning 50 years ago, Corrigan flew off from Floyd Bennett Field in New York City on his way to Los Angeles. The ground crew gasped because they watched the plane head straight out over the ocean: Instead of flying west, Corrigan was traveling toward Europe.

Utterly illegal, if deliberate, the flight without federal authorization was punishable by fine and imprisonment.

Two days later, when he had landed in Ireland, Doug Corrigan had a story ready. Enveloped in clouds after take-off, he read the wrong end of the compass needle. The same clouds prevented him from seeing the ocean beneath him.

In the course of the following day, Corrigan could not see lights from American cities supposedly beneath him — again, naturally, because of the clouds.

Didn't the absence of sunlight alert him that he was moving in the wrong direction? "Never thought of that," was the insouciant reply.

Finally, 26 hours after departure, Corrigan looked down through a clear-

135

ing and saw water. At first, said he, he imagined that he had flown across the American continent and was over the Pacific. Then, on further examination, he saw the compass, realized his elementary error and nearly fainted from shock.

The story continued: fuel was now short so Corrigan had no choice but to fly on.

Happily, when he looked over the side again, he just happened to see the green hills of Ireland in prospect. Corrigan dropped down for a perfect landing on the old sod.

The Irish welcomed Corrigan as an errant son come home. But when he tried to explain that his flight was all a mistake, they guffawed.

"Ah, Doug boy, you can tell us the truth."

The world did not know quite what to make of "Wrong Way" Corrigan. Despite its obvious contradictions, the genial flyer stuck to his story. When he came to Western New York a few months after his flight, he was cheered as he rode in an open car through the streets of Irish South Buffalo, surrounded by pretty girls.

Later, wafted on the winds of his brief fame, Doug Corrigan acted in two Class B Hollywood movies.

Then, the hapless aviator disappeared into the clouds of history.

Now at the respected age of 80, Corrigan still sticks to his wrong-way story.

His name will never be recorded on the honorable scroll of aviation pioneers, but in 1938, Doug Corrigan was awarded lifetime membership in the Liars' Club of America. ∞

SHOWBIZ GREATS TROD BOARDS OF THE OLD TECK

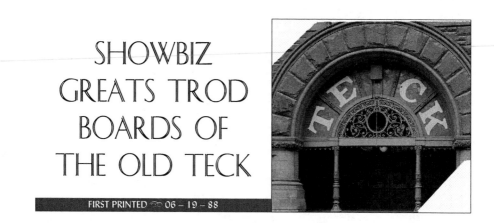

FIRST PRINTED ∞ 06 – 19 – 88

T he Teck Theater has all but disappeared from Buffalo. Yet, once the name shone brightly, a jewel in the city's sprawling theater crown.

The Teck was a vast, fortress-like edifice that vied in dimensions with its neighbor at Main and Edward Streets, St. Louis Church. Historians say the theater reached its peak at the turn of the century during the Pan American Exposition.

On its massive stage, in that halcyon age, the Teck played haughty host to performers whose names still are woven into theater legend: Lillian Russell, Ellen Terry, DeWolf Hopper, Madame Ernestine Schumann-Heink, Weber and Fields. The renowned Scotsman, Sir Harry Lauder, danced and sang his bawdy Highland ballads there, and James O'Neill was the perennial Count of Monte Cristo.

As American theaters go, the Teck enjoyed a long life of nearly a century. It began as the New Music Hall, but in 1885 a gas leak in one of the footlights jumped to canvas drops nearby. Soon firemen were struggling with a blaze that consumed a large part of the auditorium.

Enter Jacob F. Schoellkopf, Buffalo empire builder and music lover. Distressed that German singing societies no longer had a proper local home, he took control of the charred remains of the New Music Hall.

He redesigned the building to imitate several great opera houses of Germany. Its Munich-Romanesque towers gave the theater a Teutonic flavor. And mindful of fires that were a constant threat to showplaces, architects provided for stone walls three feet thick in places.

Over the main arch on Main Street were stone busts of Beethoven, Mozart and Schubert, and a massive German imperial eagle with the royal Hohenzollern crown further decorated the stonework. With old-world pride,

Jacob Schoellkopf names the structure Teck, after his native province in Germany.

Two prominent Buffalonians were early managers of the Teck: John Oishei, president of Trico Products, and Dr. Peter Cornell, father of the great actress who brought fame to her native Buffalo, Katharine Cornell.

In 1908, New York City's Shubert family leased the Teck, and in the decades that followed booked a stunning string of performers: Al Jolson, Eddie Cantor, Otis Skinner, Jeanette MacDonald, Amelita Galli-Curci, the mighty prince of ballet Nijinsky.

In 1914, when George Arliss was playing the title role in a drama appropriately called "The Devil," a fire broke out in the front part of the building. Luckily this time it was extinguished with only minor damage.

The Teck had other tenants outside professional show business. On its second floor it housed offices, the German YMCA and Jane Keeler's original "Studio School of the Theater."

Losing out in downtown audience competition to the Erlanger, the Teck faded and closed in 1937, but its career was not ended. Although the front section was demolished in 1942, the auditorium was left standing for eventual conversion to movies.

This change in role had to wait until after the war, but the doors swung open for films at Shea's Teck in 1947. The theater was all new inside: Louis XIV style with bright shades of red, green, and ivory. It was a costly, ambitious effort, with several fine shops and stores in the building, adjoining the marquee. One of them had an outstanding book selection and took its name from the theater: the Teck Pharmacy. (A suburban branch bore the name until 1985.)

Perhaps because it was situated too far out Main Street, the movie operation floundered, and once more the Teck shut down. One more revision remained to be made in the script. Front rows of seats were torn out to accommodate a wide, curving screen. Thunderous sound equipment was installed, and a battery of projectors to operate simultaneously. This was Cinerama, the gimmick approach to movies that was intended to battle the rising television craze.

In August of 1955, the Teck flashed open in a final burst, but Cinerama failed. The structure was battered down in 1985, except for the lobby and movie marquee.

They survive today, and figure in a proposal by the Alleyway Theater Inc. for renovation and restoration into a small theater. If it comes to pass, it's hoped the new theater could be given a proud old name: The Teck. ∞

A YANKEE GETS AN EARFUL IN OTTAWA

FIRST PRINTED ⌁ 11 – 01 – 87

An unusually large crowd had already assembled when I joined the wait in the hallways of Canada's House of Commons. The subject for debate was to be a hot one: the proposed Canadian American Trade Treaty.

It was the first visit of my wife and me to Canada's capitol at Ottawa, and we had split up for the afternoon because I have no interest in shopping and parliamentary discussion has small fascination for my spouse.

Being a foreigner, I was lucky to get a place in the crowded visitors' gallery. I was even more fortunate because a genial constable saved me an excellent place in the front row.

Canada's Parliament is, of course, bilingual, some members speaking in French, some in English. Conveniently, each seat in the gallery is equipped with an earpiece enabling an observer to dial an instant translation to his own language.

The chamber itself is carpeted in gleaming green. It is easy to see a kinship to Mother England in the quaint touches of British tradition: presiding officers wear robes and wigs; messenger boys in black britches scurry through the aisles delivering notes.

"Are you sure you want to sit in on this one?" the constable had asked me when he discovered that I was an American. I quickly learned what he meant in the ensuing debate.

As soon as I got settled, I heard a speaker refer to the U.S. as a "hungry glutton south of our border." Was this the same friendly Canada of Crystal Beach and Fort Erie, I wondered. "Mr. Minister," the representative called out with heavy irony. "Until I read this treaty, I was not aware that Canada is up for sale, that our country with its history and customs is about to be handed over to the Americans."

Evidently this sentiment struck sympathetic chords because widespread applause and cheering exploded along with shouts of "Hear! hear!" The speaker continued: "My question, sir, is: are we to apply for admission as America's fifty-first state?"

139

The august British tradition of restraint prevails. "Such a question is unworthy of an answer; it is even unworthy of the speaker," came the withering reply from a cabinet minister.

A French-speaking member inquired whether, once Canada had increased its American imports, it would also import American crime and criminals. His tone was antagonistic, bellicose.

Other speakers read statistics to prove that Canadian unemployment would increase with implementation of the proposed treaty. "We are dealing with a menace," one said, referring to the United States. "America wants to solve its unemployment problem at our expense."

One after another, representatives rose to interrogate Prime Minister Brian Mulroney and his cabinet. Some were moderate in their criticism; others were vitriolic. All had one thing in common: sharp suspicion for what I grew accustomed to hear called the American "giant," "bully," or "colossus."

After two hours, the question-answer session concluded. I was left with the uncomfortable feeling of having overheard people talking about me — people who didn't like me very much.

When I walked past my friend, the constable, in leaving, he said, "Sorry about the heat of the argument, sir. Nothing personal, you know."

I was glad, at any rate, to know that. ∞

PARADISE FOR 10¢: SHEA'S MATINEES

FIRST PRINTED ∞ 01 – 10 – 88

*I*t began with a shout heard round our world. As the house lights went down, 700 young voices bellowed out of the darkness and another Saturday movie matinee was under way in one of Western New York's Shea community theaters.

The Seneca in South Buffalo was my local emporium, but every Saturday afternoon the same excitement swept through Shea theaters throughout the Buffalo area. At various times those theaters included the Bailey, Kensington and Roosevelt on the city's East Side and the Elmwood and Niagara on the west. North Buffalo had the North Park; beyond city borders were Shea's Kenmore and Lackawanna and the Riviera in North Tonawanda.

Saturday matinees at those community theaters were festivals for kids. Although the films didn't start until 2, a long line had already formed by 1:30. In all sorts of weather, a ribbon of children wound out onto the sidewalks.

Shea movie houses had impressive entranceways. At the Seneca, for example, once you had bought your ticket for a Depression dime, you walked through a long, mirrored promenade. Sparkling chandeliers were suspended from a high rococo ceiling.

Such grandeur was not lost on the tots. They would gawk from side to side along the mirrored walls, seeing themselves reflected to infinity. This experience was part of the afternoon's entertainment. It was like walking through the Hall of Mirrors at Louis XIV's Versailles Palace: anyone would be impressed.

Sometimes to drum up business, the Shea theaters would advertise free gifts. On entering, each kid was given a foreign postage stamp album; on succeeding weeks, packets of common stamps were distributed. We thought it was marvelous.

At precisely 2, wild, simultaneous action erupted: house lights dimmed, kids shrieked, the projector churned. Generally for openers at the Saturday matinee, the management threw a car-

toon at us — Porky Pig or Donald Duck. Then came an interminable string of blurbs for "Coming Attractions" — movies to play the following week.

Every Saturday matinee carried two full-length feature films, one unvaryingly a Western. Bumbling, confused, dumb, the cowboy muddled into all kinds of villainy: cattle rustling, Indian warfare, stolen mining claims, stage coach robbery.

Between features, there was the serial, a 20-minute segment of a continuing story. Each installment ended in a climax of imminent danger for the hero. The closing words "To Be Continued" were a snare to lure the audience back next Saturday.

Serials led into the piece de resistance, that big feature wisely reserved for last. Among my most cherished recollections are Harold Lloyd, the Marx Brothers and my life-long favorites, those gentle fools, Laurel and Hardy.

My brother Joe was my usual matinee companion: at 5:30, we would emerge after a long afternoon, blinking at the real world outside. In the darkening, autumn twilight, we would walk home together.

There were still two things left from the Saturday matinee. We would retell the story of the afternoon's movies to Mother, who always convinced us that she was interested. Then, after dinner, we settled down to paste those world-weary postage stamps onto the flimsy pages of the stamp album.

Ten cents admission had provided a day of wonderful entertainment; Saturday matinees at the Shea theaters were the best bargain in town. ∽

HE JUST MISSED
SEEING BRIDGE
FIRST PRINTED ⊂⊃ 01 – 20 – 88 FALL

*F*or days, the threat to the legendary Honeymoon Bridge over the Niagara River was a subject of excited conversations. "Is it down yet?" such discussions would begin.

There is always a desire to be present at history-in-the-making, and despite the bitter cold, thousands of people had assembled to watch the actual collapse. I was almost one of them.

During school hours that day at old Canisius High School on Washington Street, our teachers had kept us informed about the radio reports. From them, we students learned that the bridge was swaying and that its end was imminent.

Right after dismissal, hoping to be present when the bridge fell, two friends and I boarded a Niagara Falls high-speed trolley. As soon as we climbed onto the car, I realized that our idea was not an original one. The long trolley was filled with passengers, most with the same intention.

During the hour's ride to the Falls, the streetcar hummed with amateur engineers giving their predictions and assessments of chances to arrive for the crucial moment.

It was after 5 p.m. when we reached Niagara Falls. I knew immediately that we had arrived too late because the phrase "it's down!" was on everyone's lips.

Despite this, with my classmates I hurried to the gorge. There lay the bridge twisted and gnarled like a strange beast, with its limbs broken, lying half-in, half-out of the water. Peering down, into the abyss, I imagined that I could still hear the dying shrieks of the bridge, suffering like an animal in pain.

Most people remember what they were doing when they heard about great events like the bombing of Pearl Harbor or the assassination of President Kennedy. I always remember where I was when the Honeymoon Bridge crashed into the Niagara River: on a streetcar that would arrive just a little too late to make me an eyewitness to history. ⊂⊃

WHEN THE FRONT PORCH WAS A HIVE OF SUMMER ACTIVITIES

FIRST PRINTED ∽ 07 – 10 – 89

*H*alf a century ago, every self-respecting house had a front porch. To walk down a street in summer was to be dazzled with an array of color: khaki, red, green awnings, most with jolly yellow stripes. The world was different then, and summer living centered on the front, rather than, as now, in private rear terraces and patios.

Part of early summer ritual was to reinstate the front porch to its status as the warm-weather living room. People couldn't wait to take hose to porch and to flush out months of soot and dried leaves. Awnings came out of storage, and eyes were fit into place on a row of hooks.

Pipes slipped through peripheral loops, and with an intricate network of ropes, rings and pulleys, the householder could raise or lower the awning at will. For growing families, a latticed gate at the entrance could combine with porch railings to form a commodious playpen.

Since the porch would serve as family center, floor covering was a delight because familiar but cast-off pieces were resurrected: odd lamps, wind-up Victrola, a card table and of course, rockers: cane-seated, ladder-backed, cushioned, wicker. A porch without a rocker? Unimaginable!

With furniture cozily arranged, the area was ready for a variety of warm weather activities: pinochle games that made a hot night even hotter; family dining; listening to the radio; visits across driveways with neighbors; sampling the latest batch of near-beer that dad brewed in his continued fight against Prohibition.

Each porch had individuality and reflected patterns of family use. In two-family houses, a lower porch was more accessible so guests could come and go easily, but an upstairs porch offered seclusion. Additionally it provided a panoramic view of the street below.

Referring to this aspect, anyone who has ever occupied an upper front porch knows how it feels to be on a spy satellite. Few moves in the world below are able to escape close scrutiny.

"I see that Doris has a new boyfriend."

CONTINUED ON PAGE 146

144

ON SUNDAY EVENINGS WHEN
RADIO RULED THE LIVING ROOM

FIRST PRINTED ☞ 03 – 20 – 88

*I*n years when radio ruled the living room, everyone looked forward to Sunday evening. Barely had the Shadow crackled out his ironic sneer of the late afternoon, meditating on "what evil lurks in the hearts of men," then one by one, family members started assembling in the living room.

Those were long winter nights when the wind howled outside drafty windows, when the coal furnace was not quite up to its heating job. We bundled up to keep warm with full attention fixed on the wooden, table-model radio, shaped like a Gothic cathedral window.

Right after dinner, broadcast entertainment began in earnest with the Jack Benny Jello program. Anybody over 40 recalls those vintage voices: Mary Livingston, announcer Don Wilson, Kenny Baker singing with Phil Harris' orchestra; raspy, revered Rochester.

Indisputably, the jewel in Sunday's radio crown was the Chase and Sanborn Coffee Hour, which perked on at 8. For years, Eddie Cantor was master of ceremonies: "I'd like to spend an hour with you, as friend-to-friend..." he always sang with a display of gentle sentiment.

Those Chase and Sanborn Hours were a potpourri of all kinds of pleasant hits: Eddie would quip with an invincibly stupid sidekick called, of all things, Parkyerkarkas; a long-forgotten musician named Rubinoff played his "magic violin"; Edgar Bergen and Charlie McCarthy matched wits with W.C. Fields; Don Ameche acted in short dramatic skits.

Although the Chase and Sanborn show had been the climax, Sunday's lineup on radio continued: the Manhattan Merry-Go-Round ("Step on the Manhattan Merry-Go-Round/We're touring alluring old New York Town") pretended to be a visit to a nightclub of the big town; the American Album

145

of Familiar Music (sponsored by Bayer aspirin) vibrated with homey light classics.

Finally at 10 p.m., listeners thundered into "Grand Central Station," which any radio veteran knows was "the gigantic stage on which are acted a thousand dramas daily." Each week, America sampled one of the thousand.

We were an odd set of people, sitting together in utter silence, as though hypnotized, occasionally catching each other's pensive glance. While eyes were vacant, our ears were wide-alert. We had been conditioned to use fantasy, to respond to sound effects so the pictures on the screen of our imagination were far larger and more vivid than anything that television can show.

Sometimes now, when I watch Sunday TV programs even as justly prestigious as Masterpiece Theater, I can't stifle a sigh for those rollicking, fast-moving radio evenings, filled with an innocent mix of music, laughter and drama. ∞

— ∞ —

WHEN THE FRONT PORCH...

CONTINUED FROM PAGE 144

"It must be serious because they were parked together in his car in the driveway for half an hour last night."

"And her father was at the saloon again. He was walking home about eleven o'clock. I'm sure because 'Ellery Queen' had just gone off on the radio."

"Was he steady on his feet?"

Not many houses are built with front porches any more. Certainly this decline has closed off a fertile source of conversation, an entertainment more absorbing than television. Summer in America has not been the same. ∞

LORDS OF THE SIDEWALKS IN THOSE DAYS GONE BY

FIRST PRINTED ⌘ 05 – 29 – 88

*T*he present generation of tots possesses history's most varied selection of riding-wheel toys. Molded plastic has spawned a family of colorful, miniature pedal and battery-powered cars.

Conventional bikes have yielded to a breed of big-wheelies with laid-back seats. Often outfitted with their own noisemakers, such vehicles imitate teen-age hot rods.

How I wish that I had had the fun of these toys when I was a boy in an age whose most popular wheel-toy was a contraption, home-made of wood. Referred to variously as a soap-box car, a box scooter, it was known in my neighborhood as a gig.

Wherever it plied the roads, the basic gig was the same: a wooden box nailed to a plank of wood.

Wheels were fastened at both ends of the plank. Naturally, power was supplied with the pump of a strong left foot.

Back then, wood crates were plentiful because many things were shipped in such containers: oranges, eggs, milk, and of course, soap. It was no trick to select a wood carton of desired size from the refuse outside any grocery store.

Similarly, scrap wood was always in abundance, left over from assorted neighborhood projects; with a wood box and a 4-foot length of reject timber, you had the ingredients of a gig's chassis.

Wheels were scarcer. It was necessary to scavenge for odd discards; broken, outgrown, mismatched roller skates; worn wheels from baby pushers. Almost anything round could be adapted by the gig engineer.

While the basic soap-box scooter consisted of only three pieces, yet in his heart, every driver yearned for the accessories that would convert mere transportation to glamorous cruising. He longed for a deluxe model.

Luxuries included: extended wooden handles attached to the box's top, black electrical tape wound about the final six inches. Such tape was tacky to the touch, but high living exacted a price.

Jar covers, treated with luminescent paint, were fixed to the front to resemble auto headlights. Pieces of tire tread might be nailed around ends of the platform plank as bumpers. Candles, burning in inverted glass jars, supplied illumination in the dark.

No self-respecting gig-builder would be seen on an unpainted vehicle. Paint remnants reclaimed from the basement were frequently blended, producing vividly nauseous shades of green, blue or red.

Atop this color, each gig bore an escutcheon, usually a number, sketched proudly on its face. My best model, for example, sported a big " 2".

Kids with mechanical flair embellished the basic gig design still further, devising seats and a brake system. Refinements led eventually to contests called Soap Box Derbies.

Once equipped, gigs could be employed in errands. You might go to the grocery for your mother and bring back a loaf of bread, a pound of baloney and a bottle of milk and bring all conveniently stashed in the box cavity.

Primarily however, the gig was a vehicle of pleasure, intended to gratify its owner's fantasies of luxury and grandeur.

No possessor today of a roaring, sleek Trans-Am could be more haughty than these lords of yesterday's sidewalks. ∞

THE AGING OF PETER PAN

FIRST PRINTED ∽ 12 – 04 – 88

hen I was very young, aunts who seemed ancient in years used to caution me. "Cheorchie," they would pronounce my first name in their great German accents. "Some day you'll be our age, and you'll be surprised how quick the time went by."

I listened to them because I was trained to be patient with the elderly. But for me to grow old was such a remote thought that I banished it instantly. I was Peter Pan, the boy who would not grow up.

However, years did slip along, and I can recall a few milestones along the way when I paused and wondered about my eternal youth. When I registered for the draft, I realized, for example, that I wasn't a kid anymore, and at 21 having attained a technical maturity, I was able to vote.

One evening sometime during my 30s I took a long inventory around the living room. I was holding a baby and administering a bottle of its formula. — The baby was mine (and my wife's), and moreover, there were four other children — all ours — toddling about the same room.

With responsibilities like these, I knew that Peter Pan and I had parted ways. To compensate, I began putting faith in comfortable sayings like "Life begins at 40 (later 50)" or "You're as young as you feel."

A new decade of life is always startling: turning 40 was a surprise; age 50 pounced on me, but 60 descended with a thud. It takes imagination to feel young at 60. Yet, so long as I stayed active and kept fairly slim, I insisted intuitively that I didn't look my age.

But now I must make a confession. Two things have happened recently that have shaken confidence once and for all in my lingering youth — er, middle age.

Several days ago, I was pushing an empty supermarket cart to its corral when I met the lad whose job it is to collect wagons. "I'll take it, Pop!" he said.

That "Pop" staggered me. The only "Pops" I had known were codgers who took care of lockers and towels at the YMCA. Benign, bespeckled, bald. "Pops" of my memory were vaguely comic fellows, tolerated, patronized. It couldn't be that I...

The other shock was delivered by the mailman. In a rough, brown envelope, he brought me a red, white and blue Medicare card. I was being invited officially to join the national medical program for the elderly.

So I have to face it at last. Peter Pan has grown old, and what the boring aunts used to tell me was true: I am surprised at how speedily I have become an identifiable, card-carrying senior citizen.

The attainment is not without comfort. I don't think any aging generation in history has been better treated than mine is, and so long as my wife can stand me, we'll continue in the autumn sunshine to hike state park trails (free admission with a Golden Park Pass).

Furthermore, if the kid at the supermarket calls me "Pop," I guess I have that coming to me. ∞

IN THE DAYS OF THE ITINERANT
POPCORN MAN

FIRST PRINTED ⬡ 07 – 31 – 88

*O*n hot summer nights, I can hear him yet, the shrill whistles penetrating the silvery, moonlit darkness. As eerie light glows from a flickering, benzine flame.

Through the streets he trudged those long, torrid evenings, part lifting, part pushing his wagon. I am remembering the itinerant popcorn man of my boyhood. Maybe he was a Depression phenomenon, but every neighborhood seemed to have at least one.

Popcorn men were lookalikes: Each wore a battered straw hat, striped shirt with a little kerchief tied at the throat. Their hair was grey; a bushy mustache, also gray, hung luxuriously with a faint suggestion of departed rakishness.

All popcorn men of that time spoke with a foreign accent and rather wearily, as though they had lost part of their energy along with their native tongue.

The wagon they tended was a shallow, rectangular box on wheels, with a 3-foot cube of glass mounted at the back. Two front wheels enabled the vendor to lift one end and push his portable store. Popcorn wagons were painted in gay colors — reds and yellows.

These were years when the country was about one-quarter younger, when a larger proportion of the population was an immigrant one. It was also an age when the dollar, or the dime, was preciously hard to come by.

So the immigrant popcorn man plied his route, the whistle sending out a piercing signal to boys and girls to run to their parents, to say urgently, "Mom, the popcorn man is here! Can I have a nickel?"

A heavy, Indian-head or bison nickel would buy a caramel fritter, round, carefully wrapped and rolled in a slip of wax paper. The brown-sugar syrup would stick to your teeth, as you crunched into the confection.

If Mom didn't have a nickel, two cents would buy a bag of warm popped corn. The man would set down the back legs of his wagon, and now it became a portable restaurant, the far end a counter.

In our excitement, my friends and I would all be screaming out our requests together.

"Wait-a-min-oota," the popcorn man would plead for some order. "How many you want?"

He would open the glass door and scoop out with a bent ladle a measure of popcorn that he slid into a flimsy paper bag. Then he juggled bottles: in would go a shake of this, a dash of that. The ceremony completed, the calloused, brown hand was held out for payment. Two cents!

Memories for me of those far-gone dealings with the popcorn man are illuminated with the gentle glow from the benzene burner. There we children stood making our big deals, the faces of youth contrasting with the leathered features of the older man.

After finishing a sale, out would come a bandanna handkerchief: wearily, the popcorn man would wipe his forehead, sometimes removing his hat. Then again, he stood between the staves of the wagon, lifted and pushed.

We children sat on the curb munching, as the light and the whistle receded, blending with the other sounds of the muggy summer night. ∞

WHEN MILK CAME IN BOTTLES AND WAS DELIVERED TO THE HOME

FIRST PRINTED ∞ 10 – 02 – 88

watched the little tot at a flea market as she gazed at a counter display of vintage milk bottles. "Milk used to come in those bottles?" she asked her grandfather incredulously.

Had I been that grandfather, I could have given the kid an earful — and not of milk. Imagine not knowing that, while cows did have something to do with it, milk was dispensed from bottles.

In my era, the clank and jingle of milk bottles formed an early-morning cacophony as milkmen worked their routes. Daily home delivery was a carry-over from a time that predated the electric refrigerator, when, especially in summer, milk might sour if kept for longer than a day.

Before dawn's early light, milk routemen reported to their dairies. There, they loaded wagons with heavy glass bottles — quarts for milk, pints and half-pints for cream. The mouth of each bottle had been sealed with a tab-disk that snapped into place, the entire top neatly encased by a paper wrap.

Having loaded the cargo, the milkman began his day: picking up yesterday's empties and replacing them with a fresh supply.

The focus of this activity was a milk chute whose small door opened next to the side entrance of every house.

For big families, the milk box might not be large enough and then extra bottles had to be left beside the doorway. You could almost gauge the size of the family from the number of units delivered.

"Milkman, Keep Those Bottles Quiet!" So ran the lyrics of a popular World War II song, reflecting the night-shift, war-factory worker's need for a morning's rest in the face of milk delivery noise.

Milk bottles came in an infinite variety which probably accounts for the current interest in collecting them.

There were the old timers with squeezed neck and bulge top; tall round ones, sleekly tapered near the mouth, or later models squared off for improved refrigerator storage.

Every bottle bore the name of its home dairy either stamped or embossed on the side. Since each suburban or city neighborhood had its own dairy, those names were many: Weckerle, Beale, Rich, Jones, Beres, Sparks, Sterling.

That was an age before milk became homogenized, and cream would rise to the bottle's top. Thus before using, consumers had to shake a bottle vigorously to blend the contents. Some folks achieved their own low-fat "2 percent solution" by draining off the cream for use in coffee or on desserts.

Gradually after the war, dairies converted to paper cartons. First came models whose wax coating flaked into the milk; then efficient plastic crept into the operation and milk distribution was revolutionized. Home delivery faded into memory.

I can't stifle a sigh for the milkmen and their bottles. Like town criers, their gentle jangle assured sleepers that all was well and that another day was soon to commence. ∞

IN THE DAYS WHEN WOMEN SLAVED OVER A FLATIRON

FIRST PRINTED 02 – 28 – 93

*M*onday's family laundry was only a respectable start for the housewife's workweek. In my boyhood, the next day was reserved for ironing the freshly cleaned clothes.

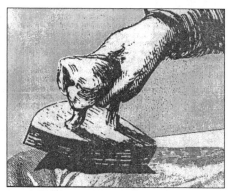

My mother, a neat, methodical woman, prepared for Tuesday's toil with what was almost a vigil ceremony. Monday evenings, she sprinkled and starched those pieces that were to be pressed wrinkle-free in the morning. Each item was rolled into a compact cocoon.

In the background, Jessica Dragonette warbled on the "City Service Radio Music Hour" while Mother worked silently. She burrowed through a pyramid of soft linen, heaped on the kitchen table: sprinkling, starching, rolling.

In those days housewives had no electric irons, so their basic tool was the flatiron, warmed over a flaming burner on the gas stove. Like thieves, flatirons usually operated in pairs: While one was busy, the other was at watch — heating on the fire.

Tremendous weight was concentrated in the iron's bricklike base. Pointed in front, armored on the sides, the instrument was treated with respect. A falling iron was a threat to foot or floor.

Some models accommodated a detachable wooden handle, so that in seconds a deft housewife could shift a cool iron back to the stove and switch its handle to a sizzler.

In my reverie, Mother stands before me in our South Buffalo kitchen. She stretches a shirt over the padded ironing board, lifts the flatiron from its trivet and tests it for temperature with a moist fingertip.

Like a plated metal gunboat, the hot iron sails over the wavy linen surface. The iron hisses, steams and occasionally spits as it meets droplets of moisture. Mother captains her ship over these shoals.

Because my father was a storekeeper, he needed a starched white shirt every day. Collars and cuffs had to be stiff and shiny. The sticky starch would often gather on the hot iron and need scraping.

After shirts, Mother attacked bed linens, table cloths, napkins, handkerchiefs. She even pressed things like pajamas and underwear, garments that did not warrant such pains.

Clothes were easily scorched by a weary or careless worker; fingers were frequently singed by contact with the hot edge. Flatirons exacted a toll from the woman's hands, wrists and psyches.

When her first electric iron entered Mother's life, she was lyrical with appreciation. True, there was no temperature control, but emancipation from the ponderous flatiron rotation wrought profound domestic bliss.

From a changed world, I contemplate that generation of embattled housewives turned laundresses. Current lightweight steam irons would have filled them with ecstasy.

Wash-and-wear fabrics would have perched those noble women in an earthly paradise. ∞

NEW YEAR'S 1939 –
IN A DIFFERENT BUFFALO

FIRST PRINTED ᨏ 01 – 01 – 89

*O*n a Sunday morning, half a century ago, 1939 was born. During its life span, that new year would bring a terrible war to Europe, but in Buffalo, 1939 received a customary welcome.

Although a winter blizzard had blasted the city on Dec. 28, Mayor Tom Holling had promised to have streets open for "New Year's Eve Midnight Shows."

SALE! *Thrift Shop Bursts Into Lively Bloom*

8 O'CLOCK DRESSETTES

Cottons so fresh and sparkling that they will take you all through the day looking your charming best! Cottons that are new in styling . . . vibrant in color. Cottons that you simply can't resist!

$1.59

● Thrift Shop—A. M. & A's, Second Floor

Shea's Buffalo was the most alluring. For a 99-cent ticket. D'Artega and the Shea Orchestra performed live with the Fraser Sisters and the Kidoodlers. On screen, Jeannette MacDonald and Nelson Eddy warbled ecstatically in "Sweethearts."

Other Shea Theaters, the Great Lakes, Hippodrome and Century, had special New Year's Eve shows, but without stage entertainment. Off Main Street, the Lafayette Theater had a midnight showing of the movie "Swing, Sister, Swing." The newspaper ad urged: "C'mon You Jitterbugs, Alligators, Rug Cutters — Celebrate 1939!"

The stodgy Erlanger Theater on Delaware Avenue boasted the "Rolicking Musical Revue — Pins and Needles" with tickets at inflated prices: $1.10 to $2.75. Across the street, the Statler Hotel had a New Year's Party with dancer-impressionist Paul Hartman.

Out Delaware, pretentious Chez Ami offered stage revues, dancing from 7 p.m., and supper for $5. Lorenzo's prestigious restaurant on Pearl Street would provide an orchestra, favors, entertainment and surprises, with dinner — all for $3.

Never to be outdone, Main Street's Palace Burlesk staged a $3\frac{1}{2}$ hour "New Year's Eve Midnite Show" with Evelyn Nesbitt Thaw and a cast of 40.

Those naughty Buffalo nightclubs were busy: McVan's at Niagara and Hertel billed the sexy Jingle Belles and "Pickert and His Seal performing tricks never before seen in nite clubs." The Havana Casino had "Shapely Dancers" while Andy's on Lower Terrace billed a torch singer.

Buffalonians who listened to a different drummer were invited to the Delaware Roller Rink. For 40 cents, including skates, you could attend a New Year's Eve party and "skate out the Old Year and in the New."

If anybody wanted to drive out to the country — all the way out to Williamsville — the Glen Park Winter Garden offered "Music, Dancing, Stage Revue and a turkey dinner for $2.25."

After the excitement of the holidays, on Jan. 1, stores advertised their first sales of 1939. At Hengerer's there were silver fox collars on sale at $48, dinner dresses for $10; thread chiffon hosiery for 79 cents.

Oppenheim's had "better dresses" marked down to $15.50. Elegant Flint & Kent featured a special purchase of Beaver Coats for $49.95.

Of course, irrepressible Sattler's exploded with "1939 Spectaculars" including Evening Gowns at $3.94, Men's Suits: $9 (made to sell for $15); Tuxedos: $11.50. You could go downstairs at the "one-stop wonder store" and buy oranges or lemons for 10 cents a dozen or wieners for 19 cents a pound.

A New Year is, of course, an occasion for looking ahead. It is also a time for nostalgic remembrance of a bygone era like 1939 — for Auld Lang Syne. ∞

THE DAY A B-25
HIT THE EMPIRE
STATE BUILDING

FIRST PRINTED ∞ 01 – 29 – 89

All airline disasters, like the recent tragedy in Lockerbie, Scotland, are spectacular. But the accident that happened on July 28, 1945, was bizarre.

Think of the soaring Empire State Building, the greatest building of its time, surpassing in height any edifice that man has constructed. Next, think of that superb flying machine, the B-25 "Billy Mitchell" bomber, which dominated the skies, which reaped chaos and destruction on America's World War II foes.

Bring these two man-made achievements together: Imagine them at the same place, at the same time, and what happens? Explosion, fire, confusion, death, 79 stories over midtown Manhattan.

Through heavy morning fog, the 15-ton B-25 was groping its way from Bedford, Mass., to LaGuardia Field in New York City. Airport authorities had warned the ship by radio that it was flying too low and the three-man crew was struggling to lift the plane's altitude. Then one of the engines quit functioning.

Since it was Saturday, a comparatively few people were at work in the Empire State Building. An accountant was sitting at his desk on the 75th floor when, incredibly, he saw the nose of a huge plane heading for him. The man dashed in panic for the corridor.

At street level, a barber whose shop was on 33rd Street heard a terrible explosion; and immediately his glass window shattered. Since the country was still in war, he thought the city was under a bomb attack and fell to the floor.

What the barber had heard was a collision of huge dimensions. Moving through the haze at 250 mph, the B-25 had struck the 102-story building with such force that the plane's nose penetrated through the corridor to an elevator shaft. This concussion caused three elevator cars to plummet from the 80th floor to the basement.

On the 78th and 79th floors, where the bomber hit, there was instant disaster. Upon impact, high octane gasoline ignited, spreading flaming fuel through offices and corridors. One survivor later said that her whole office burst into flame.

The aircraft's left wing was cut off and fluttered down into Madison Avenue. One engine crashed to the same street; a propeller struck the roof of the Waldorf on 33rd Street. Debris and shattered glass were strewn over a five-block area.

While fire trucks and ambulances converged on the wounded Empire State Building, a cadre of mounted police helped within 40 minutes.

The wonder of this terrible accident remains that more lives were not lost. The accountant who rushed from his desk escaped injury; only one passenger was on the three plunging elevators.

On the 86th floor observation tower, 60 sightseers had been gazing at the city below. Although terrified, everyone was brought safely to ground. In all, 13 persons were killed; 26 were injured.

The great building under stress had behaved exactly as it was designed to. It swayed like a boxer rolling with a punch, but despite the gaping wound, remained absolutely stable. Except for the two gutted floors, Empire State offices reopened on Tuesday.

New Yorkers like to say that they have seen everything. Occurring within a month of the close of World War II, this accident confirmed that belief. ∞

NORTHERNERS FIND HAVEN IN WINTER HAVEN

THE WINTER HAVEN NEWS CHIEF ⌒ 04 – 02 – 89

*W*had shoveled snow the February morning I boarded a train from Buffalo for Winter Haven. The weather was dipping toward zero and the notion that somewhere in this country the temperature might be moderate was enticingly incredible.

So when my wife and I spotted our cousins at the Amtrak depot in sunny Winter Haven, the situation had all the flavor of wonderland. To step into the sunshine was miraculously to sample not spring but summer.

Oddly in lives that have included a fair share of travel, we had never reached Florida, and the change from frozen North was all the more spectacular for having waited into retirement years. Furthermore, we could afford the additional luxury of taking the train.

Let me describe the Winter Haven that was spread out before two Northerners. The Amtrak station itself is a pleasant relic that has slipped into gentle neglect. The station is clean inside, and sunshine makes up for a need of exterior paint outside.

My cousins drove us through a city that holds charming traces of small-town America, like its central post office. Everyone is friendly in Winter Haven. Up north, we are unaccustomed to greeting strangers. In Florida, any casual passerby exchanges a pleasantry.

In my daily walks, I was constantly invited to agree with complaints about increasing heat. Of course, I felt like saying that it was my fervent wish to bottle it to take home with me.

What did we do while in Winter Haven? Of course, there were Cypress Gardens, Epcot, Bok Tower. However, more intimately, the cousins introduced us to friends who nourish several citrus trees in their back yard. There we picked delicious oranges and grapefruit, my first such experience.

We went to a Theater Winter Haven production of "The Music Man," that tender, tried-and-true hit of the 1950s. An imaginative performance in an acoustically perfect hall before an enthusiastic audience provided a delightful evening.

I hadn't seen baseball in months — until opening day at Chain O'Lakes Stadium. The Sox beat the Detroit Tigers, and there were some spectacular hits. Somehow, the atmosphere was more relaxed than I could recall at previous ball games.

Dinner on Saturday at Christy's gave us a chance modestly to return hospitality for the lovely dinners at my cousins' overlooking Lake Howard.

My single adverse remembrance is the angry noise during evenings of an overpopulation of motorcycles. Otherwise, Winter Haven is spectacular with its lakes and lush vegetation, its modern plazas and its citrus groves.

Having found haven from Northern winter, my wife and I will come calling again. ∞

BLUE EAGLE WAS SYMBOL OF HOPE IN HARD TIMES

FIRST PRINTED 03 – 27 – 94

"NRA — We Do Our Part." Between the three initials and the four words stretched the picture of a haughty blue eagle. This sign, symbol of a resurgent America, was displayed in millions of locations.

Although I was only nine, I'll never forget the hope and dedication that NRA — 1933's National Recovery Act — inspired. If President Clinton thinks he has an ailing economy, he should have been around 60 years ago.

For example, there was my father. Owner of a small men's clothing store in Lackawanna, he was disheartened. The steel mills had shut down and his business faced failure. Despite frugal living, our family situation was grim.

The new President Franklin Roosevelt had to act fast. Like candidate Clinton, he had made the economy central to his election campaign. Creating "alphabet agencies" (AAA, CCC, PWA, etc.) to stir phases of the economy, Roosevelt eventually established NRA to coordinate the whole show.

The president's program aimed to reduce work hours, thereby spreading employment, to raise wages, to provide money for public projects, to eliminate child labor. NRA called on Americans "to do our part."

The Blue Eagle was a symbol of compliance, and it became as popular as a flag. With enthusiasm, my dad displayed an NRA banner in each of his store's front windows. At our home, the Blue Eagle perched on our front door.

We were not alone. Rare was the business that failed to show an NRA sign; few were newspaper ads that omitted the eagle from a corner. We kids liked walking about the neighborhood, spotting versions on nearly every house.

Big cities staged massive rallies to demonstrate support of NRA codes. In New York City, 250,000 people paraded up Fifth Avenue, marching to the rhythm of 200 bands.

Meanwhile, at Holy Family Parochial School in South Buffalo, our teachers distributed book covers bearing the Blue Eagle symbol and little tin NRA buttons to wear on our shirts.

163

Touring groups put on puppet shows in the school auditorium, a huge NRA banner suspended above the stage. To this day, I recollect a wonderful program about the life of Stephen Foster and the spirited renditions of his songs that followed — all sponsored by WPA/NRA.

How much good did all this hoopla do? Judging from my family, I'm sure it at least lifted our spirits: Something was being done, and the whole nation was cooperating.

At Lackawanna's steel mills, while work hours were reduced, more men were employed. Gradually, slowly, Dad's prospects improved. Maybe, I prayed, our family would survive; thanks partially to NRA, we did. ∞

THEY DON'T MAKE
PHONE BOOTHS THE
WAY THEY USED TO

FIRST PRINTED ∞ 08 – 20 –89

An ultimate in privacy was the old-fashioned, wood-frame telephone booth. When a caller slid the folding, glass-paneled door shut, it was like pulling up the drawbridge on a medieval castle: entry was closed off.

The buffalo nickel bought many things in those days — candy bars, ice-cream cones, bottles of Coke but the biggest bargain was the pay-station telephone call. As a five-cent piece dinged into its slot, it paid for not only use of communication wires, but also seclusion and even a measure of comfort.

A standard, bare bones phone booth of old provided a light that flicked on with the closing door and a varnished stool, polished to high gloss by the seats of many pants. Walls of textured metal imparted a hollow echo so a call could generally be identified if it was being made from a booth.

However, there were levels of booth refinement. Pretentious stores, night-clubs or hotels contained luxury call booths.

Inside such an installation, the talkers enjoyed padded walls and seats. Sometimes, small fans were mounted in an upper corner, and the blades would whirl, cooling hot air generated by the speaker.

The Buffalo Statler Hotel, for example, had a small room beside the stairway to the mezzanine, lined with about 30 posh telephone accommodations. In the center of this room were neatly arranged phone books from cities around the country.

By the hour, if so motivated, one might talk on for a nickel. Calls of massive proportions were negotiated: sticky business dealings, renewed friendships among old acquaintances, heated arguments with girl friends. Regardless of how protracted the conversation, no snotty operator ever cut in to demand more money: a nickel covered the total cost.

Yet, while a phone occupant might savor isolation, consider the outsider's plight — the frustration of a would-be telephoner. Impatiently needing to place a call, he might rush into a store, only to discover himself hopelessly shut out of an available booth.

Such a customer might pace, he might fret over his wristwatch, finally in extreme dudgeon he might rap on the phone booth window to draw attention to his urgency. Blood pressure could skyrocket under this stress as the booth occupant basked in his squatter's right, haughtily turning his back on any intruder.

Veteran pay-phone users can recall booths with the black funnel to speak into and a separate sound piece to hold to the ear. Those incidentally were days before the dial system, when "Central" would sign on with her immortal greeting, "Number plee-az?" She often followed up with the information: "The li-on is busy."

What became of all the telephone booths of yore? You can still find one occasionally in a country hotel, but a combination of vandalism and practical plastics spelled their doom.

People nowadays who have to crouch and mumble hurriedly at a wall pay phone don't know what amenities old Ma Bell used to provide for her customers. ∞

THE YEAR THAT THE
TALKIE CAME TO BUFFALO

FIRST PRINTED ∞ 09 – 17 – 89

Since early years in this century, silent pictures delighted Buffalo audiences, but like most of the nation, sound movies did not catch on here until much later.

Warner Brothers, a near-bankrupt Hollywood studio, in a last fling at financial solvency, had explored a movie sound system called Vitaphone. They sought a performer whose talents cried out for sound and came up with popular vaudeville singer Al Jolson.

The resulting partially sound film was the famous "The Jazz Singer," which opened in New York City in 1927. Buffalonians read eagerly about "the motion picture triumph of the age" in which viewers could actually hear Al Jolson sing "April Showers."

Just after Christmas, technicians at the old Great Lakes Theater (whose battered facade still frowns on Main Street near Chippewa) installed Vitaphone Sound. On Jan. 28, 1928, "The Jazz Singer" came to town to open the era of talking pictures in Buffalo.

Although the film was accompanied on stage by four vaudeville acts, the spectacle did not knock Buffalo on its ears. In fact, a skeptical 1928 critic for The Buffalo Evening News wrote, "The movies are safe from the inroads of Vitaphone and similar mechanical contrivances purporting to synchronize speech with pictures."

After a two-week run, "The Jazz Singer" packed his bags and left town. The Great Lakes returned to the silents while live vaudeville acts, a theater organ and a succession of captions made up for lack of speech on the silver screen.

But out in Hollywood, Warner Brothers was still making sounds and the rumblings re-echoed in Buffalo. By May 1928, the Lafayette Theater (across Broadway from the downtown library) was adapted for Vitaphone and advertised a new sound movie "bigger than `The Jazz Singer'": "Tenderloin" with Dolores Costello and Conrad Nagel.

In September, the Hippodrome (at the current Main Street location of Norstar Bank) heard the call and wired for phonics. Proudly, the Hipp featured "Wings," formerly a silent, but now remade with sound. Clara Bow, Buddy Rogers, Gary Cooper: with a cast like that, now accompanied by sound, "Wings" had to be a high-flyer.

Reflecting the national trend, one of the hit songs that year was a jaunty number that began "If I had a talking picture of you-oo..." Gradually, downtown Buffalo movie places converted to the new dimension.

In early 1929, Shea's Century was advertising that "Buffalo's Thousands Are Getting the Thrill of Their Lives in this ALL-TALKING Triumph." The movie that caused such excitement was a now forgotten opus: "The Green Murder Case" with William Powell.

The final downtown house to install sound equipment was the largest (and the only survivor), Shea's Buffalo. Just 60 years ago, the theater became "All Talking"and ran a complete talking picture with Norma Shearer: "The Last of Mrs. Cheney." The following week, to prove that the marvel was real, Shea's Buffalo billed urbane Ronald Colman in "Bulldog Drummond," accompanied by Laurel and Hardy in "The Great Comedy Team's Newest All-Talking Picture — Men o' War."

There was no doubt about it: 60 years ago, like thunder following lightning, sound had caught up with the flicks. It had taken a year for Buffalo to convert, but the movies had finally become the talkies. ∞

A SHORT BUT COLORFUL HISTORY OF THE TRADING STAMP WAR

FIRST PRINTED ∞ 11 – 05 – 89

"**D**o you want Green Stamps?" the cashier in a small specialty shop asked me recently.

Green Stamps? For a moment, I was confused because I hadn't heard of them in years. Then it came back to me: the day of the trading stamp and all the purchasing hype that once went with it.

One stamp for each 10-cent purchase. You pasted them in books and redeemed the books for exciting merchandise — anything from toasters to diamond rings.

Sperry and Hutchinson (S & H) Green Stamps were championed by Buffalo's Hens and Kelly department stores: in fact, H & K had a big S & H redemption center on the second floor of the store at Main and Mohawk streets.

This center was a bustling store-within-a-store to which shoppers came clutching their Green Stamp books in quest of the premium dear to their hearts.

Green Stamps suddenly spread in Buffalo in the late 1950s, as the Loblaw grocery chain got stuck on stamps. So serious was Loblaw's sponsorship that special dispensers were installed at every cash register to help — somewhat — the harried cashiers.

Not to be outdone by Loblaw's Green Stamps, the rival Acme Food stores brought out another certificate — the Red Stamp. Immediately many shoppers became savers of two species of premium stamp.

Back then, A & P grocery stores were the grand-daddy of Buffalo food markets. Ancient in years compared to Loblaw's and Acme, the stuffy Great Atlantic and Pacific Tea Co. held aloof from the trading stamp frenzy.

But finally pressures mounted and the A & P announced that it was about to issue trading stamps to shoppers. By this time, nearly all the common colors had been used by competing stamp operations, so what shade would A & P choose? Magenta, mauve, beige? Suspense grew.

At last, the announcement. A & P would sponsor Plaid Stamps, a brilliant ploy to break the color barrier. I remember the date in 1962 well because my first daughter had just been born.

When I paid the cashier at the hospital, I asked, "Do you give Plaid Stamps?" The question caused giggles and remarks about what kind of stamps they would think of next.

Trading stamp hysteria raged: Stores offered double, even triple stamps for purchase of certain items. Stamps were issued in multiple denominations: 10, 20, 50. Redemption centers popped up everywhere.

Meantime, gas stations caught the fever, and up went big signs: "Green Stamps at the Red Texaco Star"; "Double Plaid Stamps With Every Fill-Up."

Dispensing trading stamps could be a nightmare. Imagine a service station operator with greasy hands counting out 39 tiny, sticky stamps on a wet, windy day.

Yet the fury spread. Even small stores got in on the act with arcane, spurious issues: First Dividend Stamps, Easy Fun, Big Gift, Perrywinkle. Then as if by mutual consent, the stamps lost their appeal, and one by one, they were canceled.

Today, Buffalo has a completely new set of supermarkets, and stamps have been licked by coupons as the principal sales lure. However, occasionally the stamp idea is revived — with Turkey Stamps at Thanksgiving, for example.

Then, like misers, we itch to go home and count certificates the way we did in the golden age of the trading stamp. ∞

ICE SKATING ON CAZENOVIA POND IN THE OLD DAYS HAD A MATCHLESS CHARM

FIRST PRINTED 7 – 3 – 83

In my boyhood, before modern indoor rinks, only ponds and freezing cold could provide ice skating opportunity. Back then, outdoor rinks were set up in various Buffalo neighborhoods: Humboldt and Schiller parks on the East Side, Riverside on the West.

Delaware Park welcomed skaters on its frozen waters, and in my neighborhood in South Buffalo, there was Cazenovia Park with its stunning lake.

All these outdoor sites waited on an extended cold snap for safe freezing. Only then would the water form an ice thick enough to sustain the weight of snow-clearing equipment.

Snow-clearing equipment! I turn the calendar back to a time before the tractor-scraper, when burly horses used to pull a plow across Cazenovia Pond.

I recall watching one winter day when the ice was insufficiently frozen. A sharp crack of splitting ice was followed by a frightened neigh from a horse and the sound of heavy weight plunking into deep water.

Onlookers gasped as a horse sank into the lake. Eventually the frenzied animal struggled back to a solid ice surface and survival, but I never forgot the chaotic sight.

Whenever Cazenovia Pond had been frozen solid, word spread quickly that there was skating. As kids, we couldn't wait to get home from school and to dig out the ancient skates that had been gathering mildew in the basement.

Cazenovia Park erupted with a feeling of winter carnival. The shelter house, which still stands, was opened, and as if from nowhere, vendors appeared selling hot dogs, popcorn and a diluted beverage they dared to call hot chocolate.

A smell of wet wood permeated all as we sat in the shelter on green park benches and changed from shoes to skates. As we edged down the cleats of a wooden runway leading to the frozen pond, ankles were turning like the jelly legs of a newborn calf. Yet, as soon as we hit the ice, the talent of skating returned, and impervious to the cold, hours spun by.

Evenings, our parents came along to watch us. Spotlights flashed on, and huge trees that surrounded the pond took on an eerie appearance, their empty boughs reaching like arms into the night sky.

I can recall vividly how pretty the girls were, their faces red and shiny with the stinging cold. On daring occasions, some of us boys would skate side-by-side with girls, holding their hands. No ride at Crystal Beach could equal this thrill.

In the darkness, the scene assumed the charm of a Currier and Ives print. Skaters glided smoothly, rhythmically, around the pond in a gentle counter-clockwise progression.

Although today's indoor rinks are more convenient, I would not trade the frozen lake of my memory. There is a matchless beauty about the outdoors, and no modern music, piped over a sound system, is so sweet as the clean swish of steel blades on ice. ∽

THEY STILL TELL OF THE GREAT CHASE TO SAVE A NIAGARA GORGE TROLLEY FROM DISASTER

FIRST PRINTED ☞ 03 – 04 – 90

$\mathcal{OS}$ ome grandparents still tell stories about the Great Gorge Trolley Line, that incredible route that burrowed at the very base of the Niagara River Gorge from Niagara Falls to Lewiston.

Everyone who ever traveled those spectacular eight miles within feet of the tumbling, rushing currents has his own remembrances, but perhaps the most dramatic Gorge Route story involved a trolley-car chase in a frantic fight to head off catastrophe.

Over its 40-year operation, dangers from falling rocks and swelling rain tormented the Gorge Trolley Line. So imminent were these threats that each morning before daily trolley runs began, a pilot car was sent over the gorge line.

In case of hazards that occurred during the night, the skipper of the pilot car was to report immediately from a telephone station about the track condition.

Like 1989, the early summer of 1917 had been unusually rainy. Constant downpours had undermined the roadbed under a section of track near the **173** gorge whirlpool. The conductor of the scout car did not observe this, but as his trolley passed the waterlogged stretch, a soldier did.

Stationed at the border, the soldier-guard observed an area of roadbed crumble and sink into the river. At once the soldier telephoned railway officials of danger; however, the day's first regular trolley, loaded with sightseers, had already set out from its depot in Lewiston. A special pursuit car was dispatched from Niagara Falls to avert disaster.

Unsuspicious of danger, the passenger car proceeded on its route, a guide lecturing through a megaphone about gorge history and geography. Busy with cameras and binoculars, tourists enjoyed the breathtaking panorama.

Trolleys never traveled over 15 mph in the gorge, but the rescue car accelerated as fast as its own safety permitted. Signaling wildly when they spotted the tourist car, pursuers were in time only to witness a frightful accident.

As the passenger trolley arrived at the washed-out area, it derailed and toppled toward the river. Helpless company officials watched the doomed vehicle somersault into the turgid waters. The motorman and several passengers leaped to safety; a few more managed to keep afloat and clutch ropes thrown to them by rescuers, but most sightseers perished.

At an investigation following the tragedy, transit authorities were reprimanded for not having cut off electric power as soon as the warning was received. The soldier bore his share of criticism for not stopping the oncoming car himself by either flagging it or firing warning shots. There was enough blame to go around.

No accurate accounting of deaths from this accident was ever made, because the fare register was lost in the deepest section of the turbulent Niagara.

Considering the potential for danger, the Great Gorge Line was remarkably free of accident. The catastrophe of July 1, 1917, involving a bizarre trolley chase, was by far the worst. ∞

BUFFALO BUBBLED WITH REVELRY ON THE EVE OF PROHIBITION

FIRST PRINTED ∞ 03 – 27 – 94

*U*nheralded, unlamented, unobserved, an anniversary crept by early this year. Seventy years have passed since Prohibition laws changed the mores of America.

Enacted by Congress the year before, the new program took effect on Jan. 20, 1920. Thereafter, it was illegal to buy or sell a beverage with any alcoholic content. In plain terms, this translated: no more beer, no wine, no whiskey, no saloons, no champagne at weddings. Many Americans wondered how such a drastic law had befallen them.

Prohibition was the result of various abrasions. For one, recent immigrants with a beer-wine tradition, who had settled in large cities, were resented by abstemious rural families.

Also, World War I rancor against Germany was transferred to brewing and distilling industries where many German-Americans flourished.

During January, newspapers publicized Prohibition. John J. Barleycorn, the personification of an intoxicant, was to be officially declared defunct.

But not without some last-minute kicking. On a rainy, cold Prohibition Eve, New York City's Times Square was as lively as on New Year's Eve.

Buffalo also bubbled with pre-Prohibition revelry. The staid Ellicott Club held a formal funeral for John Barleycorn at its dining room. Special skits featured members dressed in prison, convict garb, anticipating violation of the anti-drinking laws.

Although police had been alerted, arrests were comparatively few.

One drunk at Main and Seneca streets, clinging to a fire box, had tripped a false alarm: another at Eagle and Michigan mistook a snowbank for his bedsheet and was thus reposing before a patrolman found him better quarters at the city jail.

The case of one Fritz Dieter reached the pages of the old Buffalo Express as Prohibition's first fatality. Depressed at the prospect of a dry world, he committed suicide by inhaling gas.

Once Prohibition Eve had slipped by, there was the morning after.

In New York City, Daniel Foster, supervisor of Prohibition enforcement, destroyed 500 cases of whiskey that had missed export. Foster promised that the Empire State would be "dry as the Sahara."

The Yarmouth was the last ship to leave New York harbor with a liquor cargo. Because of hasty loading, the Havana-bound ship foundered off Virginia and had to be emptied. More liquor was confiscated and destroyed.

William Anderson, commissioner of the Anti-Saloon League, was almost plaintive in his newspaper message on Jan. 20: "Be a good sport! Shake hands with Uncle Sam and board his water wagon!"

Feelings were strong on the opposite side.

Sen. David Walsh of Massachusetts said that if Christ had performed the Cana water-wine miracle in modern America, he'd he arrested and probably crucified again.

Such conflicting behavior greeted the 18th constitutional amendment.

No wonder that after 12 years of unenforceable failure. Prohibition would be repealed. ∞

GROCERY SHOPPING IN THE DAYS BEFORE SUPERMARKETS

FIRST PRINTED 05 – 06 – 90

*T*he convenient, accessible grocery supermarkets are so much a part of modern America that it is difficult to imagine life without them. Yet, many people my age can remember another era.

Every afternoon, my mother used to dispatch me to the store. Back then, before refrigeration, shopping was a daily thing, and as a customer, I ordered food from a clerk who wore a visor and stood behind a counter.

"A box of cornflakes," I read from Mother's list. Mr. Schlee, who owned the Red and White Store on South Park Avenue, would take along pole with a clasp at its end. A neat thrust to the top shelf would send the cornflakes (which came in only one size) tumbling down to his hands.

"What else, young man?" jolly, round Mr. Schlee asked.

"Half a dozen eggs." For this, I held out my own small bucket, lined with newspaper, into which the grocer delicately counted six eggs.

Similarly, for items like sugar, butter, pickles and jelly, Mr. Schlee measured out a portion from a bin and emptied the goods into a bag or container.

When I had exhausted my list, Mr. Schlee pulled a pencil from behind his ear and tallied up my purchases on a slip of paper. I knew from practice that Mother would insist on examining this sheet when I got home.

Our grocer pushed some tabs on his cash register and cranked the handle. With an explosive ringing, the bottom drawer burst open. Money changed hands.

"Have a jelly bean, son," Mr. Schlee said, proffering a small dish from under the counter as if to close our transaction.

An inside door connected the grocery to Herold's Meat Market. As I entered, burly, red-faced Jim Herold looked over his chopping block.

"Got your list?" he asked me. Jim preferred to read Mother's notes himself. Her writing was always neat, precise.

"A 10-cent soup bone," the butcher muttered to himself, shuffling about on the sawdust floor. Our family thrived on Mother's soups.

The heavy meat ax swung down with a thump. Jim changed tools next, grasping a shiny knife to cut a pound of liver. We kids were never crazy about liver, but we ate plenty of it. It was a law of Depression economics.

On a lucky day, while Jim Herold was shearing off five slices of baloney for tomorrow's lunches, he would hand a chunk to me — one of the reasons why I liked to go shopping.

Finally, he wrapped up my purchases in a length of meat paper, torn from a thick roll. He tied the package firmly with string. "Put this in your grocery bag," Jim said, watching as I obeyed.

Walking home, I hugged my cargo tenderly: in one arm, the big, brown bag; in the other, the bucket of eggs.

Although the ease of today's supermarkets offers sharp contrast, I miss the honest faces of tradesmen like Mr. Schlee and Jim Herold. Afternoon shopping used to be fun, and when I got home, it would be just time to listen to Dick Tracy, Orphan Annie and Jack Armstrong on the radio. ∞

BAND CONCERTS IN THE PARKS
HELPED RELIEVE DEPRESSION

FIRST PRINTED ⌒ 07 – 01 – 90

At least once a week during Depression years, there were band concerts in Buffalo's principal city parks. Those were times when many musicians were out of work and welcomed an evening's pay as well as a chance to perform.

"Can we go to the band concert tonight?" As kids, we started nagging our parents early in the day.

"Well... if the weather clears up," Mother responded dubiously. The skies had been changeable and rain always turned concert into catastrophe.

As kids, we liked the music, especially the Sousa marches, but even more we wanted to meet our friends, to chase each other around the park. Also, Mother used to pack refreshments: popcorn and a few bottles of home-brewed root beer. Made from yeast and Hires Extract, this stuff, once aged, packed a hefty punch — good for shaking up and shooting in jets at other kids.

Most parks had bandstands, those square parcels of Americana, with elevated platforms. My neighborhood park, Cazenovia, had such a bandstand near the park casino.

On special occasions, like the Fourth of July or Labor Day, band members organized a parade and marched triumphantly through nearby streets to the bandstand. On such holidays, they dug out uniforms with festive hats and gold braid. Ordinarily, dark pants and tie with white shirt were de rigueur.

This night, despite distant rumblings of thunder, my parents were persuaded to take us to Caz Park for the band concert. Members of the Buffalo Civic Orchestra, a WPA sponsored project, were playing.

Recitals frequently began with a stab at culture. "We're going to start our program." the leader shouted, "with Rossini's 'William Tell Overture.'"

Since we kids recognized this rousing selection from its use on the "Lone Ranger" radio program, we applauded loudly. Wind, meanwhile, was whipping through the trees.

After bows, the second feature was announced: "A medley of songs from 'The Desert Song' with Cynthia Klarp as soloist."

A clap of thunder augmented audience applause. The poor singer, dressed ornately in a gown, poured her heart into the syrupy words of "Night Divine." When we could escape our parents' angry glances, we howled and mimicked the struggling soloist.

All at once, with sudden gust of wind and a scary bellow of thunder, a torrent of rain burst in.

Although the bandstand had a hip roof to protect performers, the wind swept under it. Even in our family confusion, scrambling for shelter, I remember watching the girl singer huddling pathetically in a corner in her fancy gown. I felt sorry for her.

Troopers that they were, musicians resumed the concert after the cloudburst, even though most of the audience was too drenched to stay.

My last recollections as we piled into the Chevrolet were of seeing a soggy Cynthia Klarp warbling again as the band heroically played on. ∞

MAYBE THE STANLEY STEAMER SHOULD HAVE WON AUTO CONTEST

FIRST PRINTED ∞ 09 – 09 – 90

*H*istory is filled with ironies: consider, for example, the gasoline automobile engine and resultant world dependence upon Middle East oil.

At the turn of this century, transportation was running away from the horse. Man's sophistication led him to neater sources of energy: electricity, steam, oil.

In fact, a century ago, automobiles of various sizes and designs were hitting the mud highways — all of them driven by one of the above three energy sources.

No fuel was perfect. Electric cars had to submit their batteries for regular recharging. Steam-powered cars had to be heated 20 minutes before use, to get the boiler operating.

Gasoline-powered cars were the worst. Their engines had many moving parts; they were dirty and emitted smelly, noxious, polluting vapors.

Since electric cars lacked investment backers, their general use dimmed. But steam and gasoline-powered engines had aggressive champions.

Steam power was boosted by the Stanleys, identical twins who were erratic geniuses. They had dabbled in dry photographic plates, an invention they later sold to George Eastman's Kodak Company. They bought and managed resort hotels in Colorado. But their longest, continuing interest was in a steam-driven auto, the Stanley Steamer.

Most people think of a steam boiler as ponderous and huge. But the Stanley steam cars of 1917 looked very much like other contemporary autos. Their boiler could easily be mounted today in, say, a Ford Escort.

Acceleration in a steam vehicle was totally smooth: no spark plugs, no transmission, no gearshift. Stanleys consistently won speed contests; in 1907, a racer hit an estimated 197mph before it went out of control.

So free from mechanical defects were the Stanley Steamers, with only 15 moving parts, that they carried a lifetime warranty for free repair; but few things went wrong.

The weakness was that, while the eccentric Stanley twins were indifferent about merchandising, their rival competitors of the gas engine, notably Henry Ford, were brilliant salesmen and advertisers.

About 1914, the gas engine guys shot into the lead because they invented the self-starter. Soon Ford was mass-producing more cars in a day than the Stanleys did in a year.

Ironically, about this time, new devices solved most of the steam car's inconveniences. An electric starting discovery could get boilers ready for use in under 2 minutes; condensers trapped escaping steam for reuse, eliminating the need to fill the boiler.

The Stanley twins were not fighters. They quickly recognized the gas-car victory; their only comment was a wistful, "Steamers were a lot more fun."

With more steam power, today's world might be a cleaner place; without need of Middle East oil, it might be safer. Sometimes in history's rivalries, one feels that the wrong side won. ∞

THE MARCH OF TIME USED TO BE MEASURED WITH GRACE AND DIGNITY

FIRST PRINTED ∞ 10 – 21 – 90

*f*or Uncle Bill to look at his heavy, gold watch was a ceremony. First, his face assumed the furrows of deep solemnity, then he leaned judiciously to one side, Reaching reverently with his right hand, he slipped the engraved watch out of a vest pocket.

"What time is it now, Uncle Bill?" I would ask, knowing that, however small, I played some part in the unfolding ceremony.

My uncle cradled the hallowed piece in his leathery, calloused palm, while he snapped open the disc cover with his left. "It's two-thirty-eight," he said, and his voice reverberated with the authority of Big Ben.

Uncle Bill gave the stem a few pensive turns, caressed the watch for a moment and replaced it into his vest pocket. A gold chain trailed the movement across his stomach, disappearing through a bottom hole.

On favored occasions, when I was allowed to behold Uncle Bill's watch face-to-face, I saw a dial of masterful precision. Roman numerals lined the periphery; two black hands pointed sharply to the numbers. A thinner hand ticked out the seconds, dancing around the dial with light-hearted, unfailing, joyous rhythm.

Perhaps because he was an engineer on the New York Central Railroad and because time was part of his business, Uncle Bill regarded his watch as a symbol of trust. His life and those of others demanded accuracy and credibility.

I cannot help comparing that redoubtable instrument to the digital watches and clocks that flood the markets today. Like miniature hockey-game scoreboards, they light up with a hysterical outburst of information.

Hour, minute, second flash on; day of week, date of month, year. Such pieces can be set to buzz with nagging reminders. No winding, no ticking, no indication of how one minute relates to the total day's framework of hours, they shout out only the statistics of the instant.

I wish that I could scorn the digitals on grounds other than aesthetic. I wish they were undependable, inefficient, inaccurate, but they are not. Their offense for me is that they lack face and character. The passage of time, like growing old, should assume a dignity of measure as well as a measure of dignity.

I cannot get over the outrage that such digital timepieces would deal to the grace of Uncle Bill's softly ticking railroad watch, whose honest face wore an expression of quiet beauty. ∞

AN INSTITUTION WORTH REMEMBERING

FIRST PRINTED ⌘ 10 – 08 – 90

*N*ow that the Erie County Savings Bank has gone, let me breathe a sigh of regret for a bank that was once my friend.

In 1950, I bought my first new car at South Park Chevrolet. A basic two-door, the car cost $1,624. I paid $624 in cash and financed the rest at the Erie County Savings Bank.

I worked downtown that year, and I used to make biweekly payments on my loan at the bank's central office, on Shelton Square.

I remember the experience vividly, because to climb the heavy stone steps resembled crossing a medieval moat: The mighty, brownstone main office was a castle.

Rich with turrets, arches and deeply indented windows, the edifice balanced with its Romanesque splendor St. Paul's Cathedral, its neighbor across the street.

An old-world charm pervaded the structure; guards, elevator operators and tellers perpetuated the bank's general dignity. A customary greeting — even to me — was, "How do you do, sir?"

The main office had been decorated in the age of bronze. I would fill out my payment coupon at a desk lighted by bronze lamps. I dropped my empty pay envelope into a bronze wastepaper basket. Even the water fountain was encased in bronze grillwork.

Corinthian columns, gold leaf and classical friezes soared overhead on the first floor. My footsteps reverberated as I handed my papers to a teller.

"Thank you, sir," she always said crisply.

When my loan payments were completed and the Chevy was mine, I felt a satisfaction that was shared by my bank. Within a week, I received a letter praising me for promptness and inviting me to use the bank's services again.

This I did. In 1964, when my wife and I bought our house, we climbed the brownstone steps once more to arrange our mortgage — at $5\frac{1}{2}$ percent interest.

Again I admired that graceful building. Upper stories were fitted with bronzed balustrades embossed with royal fleurs-de-lis. Pigeons found apartments among the countless dormers and crannies of the tile roof.

This fine edifice was demolished in 1967 to make way for a new head-quarters building. The local flavor vanished — especially when the bank adopted that tacky name, Empire of America.

My car and my home are long since paid for. But I'll always remember the Erie County Savings Bank, which helped me to get my life in order. ∞

'SCARLET FEVER' USED TO GET YOUR HOUSE QUARANTINED

FIRST PRINTED ⟶ 11 – 11 – 90

While I was waiting at the doctor's office for this year's flu shot, my mind drifted back to a time before preventive medicine, before routine hospitalization. I was remembering an era when winter diseases were fought by quarantine.

Names like typhoid, diphtheria, smallpox, even measles mean very little today. But half a century ago, if someone fell victim to one of these contagious diseases, he and his family were sealed up in their home for the duration.

It was in the 1930s that my older brother Bob had been sick. Dr. Nash would stop by our house each afternoon and shake his head gravely after examining the patient.

One day, I overheard him talking to Mother, and I caught words like "contagious," "health department" and "quarantine." To a boy of 9, such syllables carried the sound of doom.

As was his duty, Dr. Nash reported my brother's illness to the county Health Department, and it was only hours before a grim-faced man made his dour appearance.

After studying our house number, he produced a glaring sign, took out a hammer and tacks, and started to fasten the card to our house front.

"Scarlet Fever," the yellow sign proclaimed. Because of contagious disease, our family was quarantined.

Those first days, we all felt under siege. It was like being a leper in biblical times. I would see people who walked by our house shudder as they saw the mark of pestilence. Groceries were left at the side door.

I fretted that our family would perish. However, after a week of our

187

30-day quarantine my brother was much improved, and we other three children showed no symptoms of his sickness.

Gradually our problem became boredom. How do four healthy children pass weeks closed up in a small lower flat? Scarlet fever changed to cabin fever.

We quickly got hooked on the radio soap operas: "Just Plain Bill," "David Harum," "Young Widow Brown." Afternoons, we played endless card games of rummy and old maid. On pleasant days, Mother let us into the backyard, but we felt shunned like convicts being put out for exercise. My best friend would wave to me from a 20-foot distance.

At the end of our quarantine, a public health nurse came out to inspect us all. A massive woman in a blue uniform, she examined our throats, chests and hands. Only then did she write out certificates permitting us to return to school, and the hated sign was removed from our house front.

"Are there still cases of scarlet fever?" I asked my doctor after the flu shot.

"No, that's been gone since the antibiotics," he replied with a smile.

Gone, I thought, but not quite forgotten. ∞

DEATH OF VICTROLA
WAS LIKE LOSING
FAMILY MEMBER

FIRST PRINTED ☜ 12 – 23 – 90

When I was a boy, my father made some impulse purchases from a music store that was closing its business. Among the acquisitions was a Victrola.

The top of this heavy, mahogany console lifted, revealing a felt-covered turntable ready to accommodate phonograph records. Two doors in front swung open to emit sound.

Our Victrola came equipped with dozens of those thick, platter records, some classical, others dramatic. In the center logo of each record a dog was pictured, head cocked, listening obviously to noise emanating from a cone-shaped horn. Under the picture was the caption "His Master's Voice."

When played on the Victrola, such records produced sounds that would drive any modern hi-fi listener to run for cover. Steel needles hit grooves with a deafening combination of clacks, thuds and non-stop scratch. But hidden behind the crackle was a performance.

I grew up on the stew that these records brewed: Sousa's "Washington Post March," the quartet from "Lucia di Lammermoor," John Barrymore agonizing over Hamlet's question, "To be or not to be."

I was close to tears when Al Jolson sang "Sonny Boy"; I knew the first movement of Beethoven's Fifth before I could tie my shoelaces. For the Christmas season, a very gritty Madam Schumann-Heinck rendered "Stille Nacht, Heilige Nacht."

At a time when the phonograph was a novelty, I felt in possession of a wondrous invention. I was allowed to have school friends in to observe the marvel, and we marched around the living room to the compulsive beat of the "Notre Dame Victory March."

Sometimes the tempo slowed, and the sounds became distorted because the Victrola was "running out of winding."

Back then, many devices ran on springs, and from the Victrola's side protruded a 10-inch handle. To keep the turntable spinning, we had to pump this handle for every five minutes of music, a motion reminiscent of Dad cranking the engine of his Model T.

Sadly, this spring mechanism caused the end of our Victrola. One day while I was cranking there was a terrifying snap, and the handle flew wildly round in the reverse direction. I gazed at it until the convulsion ceased and a strange silence fell.

It was like losing a family member when our Victrola died, when dust and silence settled on those scratchy, beloved 78 rpm records. ∞

RUDENESS WAS JUST PART OF THE SATTLER'S SHOPPING EXPERIENCE

FIRST PRINTED ⟨⟩ 06 – 02 – 91

*E*very store has its own flavor: Some are elegant, sophisticated; others are ordinary, drab. One Buffalo department store was none of these because it was unique: Sattler's, at 998 Broadway.

Ask anybody who remembers the old Sattler's, and words will bubble to the lips: words like bedlam, pandemonium, chaos.

Sattler's made a retail policy of cramming the maximum number of people into its store. This strategy entailed, of course, a push-and-shove approach to shopping.

Because there were no parking lots, all cars had to be left on crowded side streets, often a mile away. Like ants, customers crawled along narrow sidewalks, Whether they arrived by auto or streetcar, they carried shopping bags with handles.

Sattler's liked to call itself the home of bargains, parceling these out to shoppers in cycles. Early each week, newspapers ran huge blocks of Sattler advertising characterized always by screaming banner headlines.

"Miami Department Store Closes All Merchandise Sold to Sattler's," a typical lead might shout. Following would be a brief explanation of some retail exigency: a lost lease, a fire, death of an owner, a tragic business miscalculation.

Whatever the accident, the moral was ever the same: "Their Loss Is Buffalo Shoppers' Gain. Hurry! Hurry!" Next, an advertisement would detail prestige-brand labels: London Fog, Land's End, MacGregor, Brooks Brothers, Zenith, General Electric, Simmons, Serta.

All these desirables could be purchased at fractions of their usual prices. The best part of Sattler's ads was that they were on the level. The store's agents penetrated far corners of the retail world and brought back bargains to Buffalo.

Only one impediment pertained: crowds! Massive, aggressive, undulating swarms of bargain hunters descended on 998 Broadway. The mood of a Sattler's sale was always near frenzy.

Rudeness was part of the mystique. "Hey, you grabbed the Size 16. I laid

191

it down on the corner of the counter" brought an immediate invitation to go to hell.

Above the fury of the bargain tables, announcements thundered over a primitive PA system. "Attention, shoppers," a piercing voice would yell. "We have a Sattler's super special on children's underwear on the second floor."

With a deafening thunk, the sound system would turn off for a breather, but then the voice barked on again. "We have a little lost boy who was found in the ladies' restroom. He says his name is Harry."

The building on Broadway near Fillmore bore the city's best-known address, because singing commercials on radio droned on: "Shop and Save at Sattler's, Nine-nine-eight Broadway in Buff-alowww…"

The Sattler's edifice was demolished two years ago, but today there's fresh activity on the site as a new department store prepares to take shape. The location, close to the Broadway Market, is an attractive one, but Sattler's is a hard act to follow. ∞

NIAGARA RIVER STOPPED FLOWING FOR 30 HOURS IN 1848

FIRST PRINTED ∞ 01 – 27 – 91

*I*t is part of folklore that surrounds the Niagara River that once upon a time, the great stream ran dry. Only stones and puddles remained, and the mighty falls themselves were reduced to a dead gulch. Unlike many folk stories, this one is true.

Early on a March morning in 1848, people in Niagara Falls were awakened by a strange stillness because the familiar roar of water was absent. One by one, they stepped out of their homes in the light of early dawn to investigate.

What folks saw was astonishing: The reason there was no noise was that the Niagara River had ceased to flow. The riverbed and the falls were dry; rocks were exposed; turtles and fish were struggling in crevices.

On the river's Canadian side, a miller named Samuel Street discovered that his water wheel had stopped. With his daughter, Street walked midway across the top of the Horseshoe Falls and fixed a small flag near the brink.

In amazement, other Canadians were walking across the riverbed to Goat Island, picking up sticks and lumber fragments. At Chippawa, Ont., villagers found bayonets, rifles, swords — weapons discarded by the American troops after the Battle of Chippawa in 1814.

A reporter for the Buffalo Express wrote: "All the people of the neighborhood were abroad, exploring recesses and cavities that had never before been exposed to mortal eyes. This writer went some distance up the shore of the river where huge fields of muddy bottom were laid bare."

For the whole day, this mysterious freak of nature continued. Experts shook their heads in disbelief, the superstitious canted about planetary imbalance tipping the water awry. Then, after 30 hours of silence, came a rumble like distant thunder, from upstream. Residents heard a far-off echo that grew louder and nearer.

As though by magic, the Niagara River was reborn, rushing again into its channel, soon surging over the cataract, filling the gorge with water and sound.

Such odd events demanded an explanation, which proved to be simple. After a severe winter, huge deposits of ice lay on Lake Erie. Driven by easterly gale winds, these ice packs had jammed into the Niagara River's mouth at Buffalo.

On March 29, when the winds switched direction again, the water resumed its natural course.

No one now alive remembers these phenomena, so we must accept evidence of our forebears who peopled the Niagara Frontier during that cold winter of 1848. ∞

DYING ART OF TYING A PARCEL WITH A PIECE OF STRING

FIRST PRINTED ⟳ 04 – 21 – 91

*T*he other day I found myself hunting for, of all things, a piece of string. We used to wind up miscellaneous lengths and deposit them in a kitchen drawer.

That drawer was empty, and I slowly awoke to another small realization of changing times. The span of a piece of string is running out: String is becoming another casualty of progress.

It seems that yesterday all stores were equipped with string. Fat coils of it were mounted at each cash register. Like beehives, a hank of string sat on an elevated perch, dangling down a tail to be pulled at consummation of a sale.

In department stores, a clerk would lay the new blouse she had just sold onto a sheet of wrapping paper. Knowing that she was being observed, the clerk carefully folded the paper, tucked the edges and reached for the string end. Pretentious stores used jazzy shades of yellow, green, red.

Bags came only in very small sizes. A purchase of any consequences demanded pieces of wrapping paper — and string.

Sales people became very skilled in packaging, With speedy efficiency they scrutinized an object, calculated the necessary length of paper and applied the string.

Knots were signatures of resourceful employees. Any novice could pull together a shoelace-type knot. But to apply a formula that was neat, compact, form and tidy — that took experience, and flair.

String was everywhere. Children wound it around their tops for spinning. Butchers used it to encase that waxy paper they wrapped meat in: 5-and10-cent stores, dry good stores, groceries, bookstores, post offices. The world was held together by string.

One Christmas season, I was employed at the counter of the U.S. Parcel Post Office. That year, I learned some varied knots to fit special situations;

I even cultivated a trick of cutting twine without a knife — by snapping one strand against another.

Blame plastic for the end of the ball of string. The crinkly, unecological plastic bag suits every size and situation. Plastic tape grips every shipping box in a crushing embrace that defies weakening.

Plastic may be practical, but it lacks the individuality of a neat package, tied skillfully with a sturdy, reassuring piece of string. ⌒

'IT TAKES MORE THAN A BULLET TO KILL A BULL MOOSE'

FIRST PRINTED ⌒ 04 – 07 – 91

*I*n Buffalo, 90 years ago, Theodore Roosevelt was inaugurated as the 26th president of the United States. He succeeded to this office because of the death of William McKinley, victim of a mad assassin.

Some years later, Roosevelt was himself the target of a crazed crank. His close escape from death offers a glimpse into Teddy's robust personality.

The year was 1912, four years after Theodore Roosevelt concluded his second term in the White House. Roosevelt was again running for president, this time as an independent candidate of the Bull Moose Party.

On Oct. 14, he was outside the Hotel Gilpatrick in Milwaukee. He stood on the sidewalk, shaking hands, meeting friends before leaving the hotel for a campaign speech.

In the darkness of the lovely autumn evening, a stranger pushed his way to a position about six feet from Roosevelt. Suddenly, the man pulled out a Colt revolver from his coat, took quick aim and fired the powerful weapon.

Jovial conversation ceased at the loud report, and Theodore Roosevelt, hit by the bullet, fell flat on his back as if kicked by a mule.

He lay there for only a moment; then he bounded to his feet. At first, he touched his breast; next, showing great presence of mind, Roosevelt put three fingers to his lips and coughed.

With full composure, he examined his hand. When he saw no blood, he realized that the bullet had not reached his lungs.

Reassured, Roosevelt demonstrated characteristic bravery. He ordered the crowd to stop punching the gunman. "Bring him to me!" he commanded.

Face to face with John Schrank, the fanatic who had tried to murder him, Roosevelt eyed the man with scorn. "You poor creature!" he said. No words could have been more expressive.

Instead of seeking medical treatment, Roosevelt insisted on making his scheduled speech at a Milwaukee auditorium. "I will make this speech or die," he exclaimed dramatically. "It is one thing or the other."

In the cab, the ex-president had a chance to examine his wound. The bullet had struck a very crowded breast pocket containing a steel case for his spectacles and a 50-page speech. Encountering such heavy resistance, the bullet stopped four inches from Roosevelt's chest, fracturing a rib.

The rival candidates, President Howard Taft and Gov. Woodrow Wilson, suspended their campaigns during Roosevelt's hospital stay of a few days.

As always, Theodore Roosevelt had a perfect comment after the incident was closed: "It takes more than a bullet to kill a Bull Moose. I do not care about being shot — not a rap." ∞

THAT OLD GANG THAT USED TO HANG OUT AT THE NEIGHBORHOOD ICE CREAM PARLOR

FIRST PRINTED ⟳ 08 – 04 – 91

An old aunt used to grumble that I was turning into one of "the gang that hangs around the ice cream parlor." Poor Aunt! Could she but have known how innocent were those ice cream emporia of my youth!

Every neighborhood had at least one, and on hot summer nights, teen-agers would naturally drift there. During my era, South Buffalo cherished Sullivan's, a super ice cream parlor at Abbott Road and Columbus Street.

Owned by a glum, hatchet-faced man named John "Turkey" Sullivan, the establishment played host nightly to droves of teen-agers.

"Where you going tonight?" was a common question.

"Probably over to Sully's," was the familiar reply

During summer months, more teen-agers than sandflies, moths and mosquitoes put together clustered around Sullivan's corner. There we boys stood and talked by the hour, observing the passing scene. Occasionally a policeman in a squad car would tell us to move on, but his heart was not in the request, and we knew it.

The most intriguing thing to observe, of course, was the girls. They would start arriving primly in twos and threes, dressed neatly in delightful summer frocks.

The girls would check into Sullivan's Ice Cream Parlor looking for a place. There were plenty of booths, tables with bentwood chairs, even a bar with revolving stools. But so popular was the Sullivan ambience that frequently lines formed to wait for a vacant spot.

Ice cream parlors used to have specialties, and Sully's put together a hot-fudge sundae that was, in the parlance of the time, "out of this world." Dark, warm chocolate sauce oozed over a rich vanilla ice cream; whipped cream covered all.

We boys swarming on Abbott Road would peer in the store window, and when the girls had ordered their confection, we pounced. "Mind if we move in, girls?" was the conventional opener.

On lucky occasions, they did not, and a friend and I would slide onto the bench, each of us beside a girl. Bring on the Sullivan specials: Aside from the aforementioned hot fudge entry, there were extravagant banana splits, indecent maple walnut floats, shameless butterscotch dips. The list was endless.

Meanwhile, across the table, words were flying. We tried to be charming, witty, because if fate was smiling, we would leave Sullivan's with the girls amid looks of envy from the assemblage outside.

It was a short walk to Cazenovia Park, resplendent with flowers, silent but for the creek and the cicadas. By now, my friend and I were strolling hand in hand with our girlfriends, filled with ice cream, youth and the beauty of a summer night.

If Mr. Sullivan had given diplomas for steady attendance at his institution, many familiar names would appear: Diggins, Curtin, O'Connor, slews of Murphys, generations of Griffins, Malley, many Meegans, McNamaras and Moriartys, Dolan, O'Brien, Monahan...Such alumni often did graduate work at Joe Cooley's famous saloon across Abbott Road in later years. ∞

THE DAY THE SECOND MAID
OF THE MIST GOT CAUGHT
IN THE WHIRLPOOL

FIRST PRINTED ∞ 09 – 09 – 90

*F*or generations, ships called "Maid of the Mist" have edged up to the chaos at the base of Niagara's mighty falls. After this challenge, they return obediently to their dock 1,000 feet away.

Only once did a Maid of the Mist venture farther — all the way downriver to Lake Ontario, defying the deadly Whirlpool, the currents, rapids and twists, in the Niagara Gorge. It was the most exciting day in that Maid's life.

The ship, second to bear the "Maid of the Mist" name, had been launched in 1854. It was comfortable, steam-driven, paddle-wheeled, about 75 feet in length. A tall smokestack belched wastes from the 100-horsepower engine.

Capt. Joel Robinson guided this vessel proudly into the spume and spray, the thunder and quake of the Niagara River's cascade. He carried many famous passengers such as Queen Victoria's son, later King Edward VII of Britain, who had insisted that the Mist excursion be included on his 1860 American tour.

Despite its world reputation, the tourist spectacular did not thrive. These were years just before the outbreak of America's Civil War, and visitors to Niagara Falls had become few.

Thus, the Maid of the Mist was sold at a public auction in 1861. High bidder was a Montreal shipping company whose offer was conditional: The boat must be delivered into Lake Ontario. This stipulation was a serious one because it meant maneuvering a sizable ship safely through the perils of the lower Niagara River.

Understandably, few sailors were anxious to volunteer for the precarious assignment. At last, for the impressive sum of $500, Capt. Robinson agreed; he hired a crew of two men, an engineer and a mechanic.

Sides of the ship were cushioned with canvas when it left port on June 6, 1861. Within minutes, despite the captain's efforts to control her, the Maid of the Mist was being buffeted and hurled into the Whirlpool.

In one wild toss, the smokestack was knocked loose and fell to the deck. Cutting out of the Whirlpool, Capt. Robinson steered toward the lower rapids. Here the river narrows, and the objective was to avoid being smashed against jagged banks.

Plunging headlong, the ship depended more on luck than on seamanship. Like a toy, it turned, bobbed, strained, in and out of the water. Windows broke, flying glass flew about the deck as the craft struck shores.

Noise, confusion, speed and danger prevented the sailors from being much beside spectators. Once out of the rapids, but not yet out of risk, the captain was able to pick a gingerly course around the swift currents and bends in the river.

When they finally arrived at Queenston, the three crewmen drew into harbor to fill out necessary papers for the clearance of the boat into Canada. Never before had a ship out of Niagara Falls docked at Queenston.

No reports survive about the engineer and mechanic, but Capt. Robinson was said to have aged drastically during his adventure. Furthermore, for the rest of his life, he refused to sail on the Niagara River. ∞

'DISH NIGHT AT THE MOVIES' HAD SHATTERING IMPACT

FIRST PRINTED ☞ 10 – 06 – 91

*M*assively larger than life, the figure of Clark Gable surged across the silver screen. "You belong to me," he thundered in a voice so amplified that walls reverberated.

Words stopped as Gable's arm gathered Joan Crawford to him. The theater was still for the embrace that followed, so still that you jumped when a dinner plate fell crashing to the theater floor.

What was a dinner dish doing among the audience at a polite Shea's neighborhood movie show? You would have to have been around during the Great Depression years to understand a custom like "Dish Night at the Movies."

Like all business during that incredible era, entertainment houses were suffering. To lure customers, banner signs went up under the marquee to advertise a Wednesday evening enticement: "Free Dishes for the Ladies."

Each week, a different piece was distributed: one week, a dinner plate: the next, a saucer; then cups, soup bowls, salad plates, until table settings were completed. Quality was so flimsy that replacements were much in demand.

Thus, housewives were drawn away from their homes to the box offices of community cinemas. As they presented their tickets to an usher, he bestowed on them a thin piece of tableware. Girls were excluded from this bounty unless they paid a full 25 cents admission. This, of course, was a penalty of growing up that everybody ducked as long as possible.

The first problem facing the owner of a complimentary dish was where to stash it safely during the $3^1/_2$ hour double-feature program that ensured. To set a breakable plate on an empty seat or on the floor was to expose the treasure to obvious perils.

The most secure alternative was to sit stiffly, cradling the proud dish in a lap. However. this strategy was never foolproof. Caught up in the drama, a lady might shift position involuntarily; the plate would slip and smash.

Romantic scenes were deadly for newly acquired dishes, and when Fred Astaire danced with Ginger Rogers or Shirley Temple tapped on the Good Ship Lollipop, dishes got lost in the rhythm. Shootouts in cowboy movies evoked enough clatter of glass to scare the horses.

Dish nights were a horror show for ushers, who had to pick up broken plates when the lights went on at evening's end. They far preferred quieter promotions like "Towel Night," "Grocery Giveaway" and "Bank Night."

Even Saturday matinees for kiddies pushed Depression freebies. I can recall cherishing grubby stamp collecting kits or coloring books with scratchy crayons, because I had received them free with my 10-cent ticket to Shea's Seneca.

Yet no other premium had quite the impact of "Dish Night at the Movies." Plates that survived the evening brightened frugal Depression meals. ∞

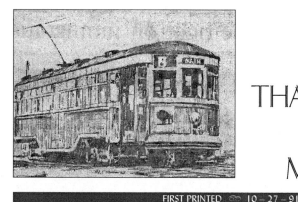

LEGENDARY TROLLEYS THAT RUMBLED ALONG MAIN STREET

FIRST PRINTED ⌒ 10 – 27 – 91

Whenever I go to downtown Buffalo, I ride my bicycle to the South Campus station and board the underground. The subway ride, comfortable and swift, reminds me in a perverse way of those giant No. 8 trolleys that used to ply the same route.

"What time does it leave?" I once asked a conductor who sat smoking a pipe at the front of his trolley at Main City Line Loop.

"When I get ready," he growled back, and I'm still not sure whether he was kidding. At best, schedules back then were unpredictable.

When he was ready, the motorman stood up in his blue serge suit, the back of which was polished to a mirrored gloss. He checked the coin apparatus strapped to his waist.

One last passenger charged up the steep trolley step, just as it was folding. The man's face wore an expression of mad relief. "That was close!" the poor fellow gasped, digging out a coin. Missing a streetcar was serious business, because waits were endless.

The motorman sourly flicked some change from his receptacle. He kicked the pedal of an immense fare-recording machine, mounted overhead. With a grating clang, the figure $8\frac{1}{3}$ cents appeared in the machine window, certifying that a patron had paid by token which sold three for a quarter.

Menacingly, the trolley steps retracted. the doors slammed shut and old No. 8 began another ponderous, protracted grind.

Everybody who rode those dinosaurs before their extinction in 1950 remembers how they rattled, rumbled and swayed over tracks that had long since deteriorated. As the cars rocked, leather straps with porcelain handles clacked noisily against walls. If all the cane seats were full, standees clutched the straps for dear life.

At every busy transfer stop like Delavan or Utica, masses of people shambled off and struggled on. Such an exchange at peak hours might require five minutes.

From the trolley's roof, a pole stretched skyward to draw electric power off overhead wires. Sometimes the pole would jump its wire and hiss a shower of sparks; the effect was spectacular at night, when, like stars, blue and white sparks jabbed the darkness. To remedy this crisis, the conductor had to walk outside the car's rear and tug at a rope guiding the pole back to its wire.

Often mischievous kids would grab the guide rope and snap the trolley pole off its mooring; in winter, the distracted conductor made an irresistible snowball target for those urchins. One more delay for weary passengers.

Riders on the clean, modern Main Street subway don't know how good they have it. The only thing they miss is the fun of telling stories about those legendary trolleys. ∞

HOW THE ICE AGE CAME TO AN END IN SOUTH BUFFALO

FIRST PRINTED ∞ 11 – 17 – 91

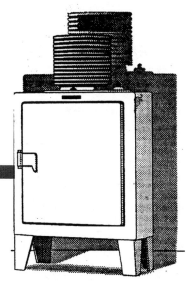

*M*y father used to boast that our family owned the first electric refrigerator in South Buffalo.

If that was so, Dad started a revolution because within a few years, mechanical refrigeration had put an end to the ice age.

I can clearly envision that General Electric refrigerator that Dad was so proud of.

A square, boxy creature, it stood on four legs and had, of all things, a big, circular dome which used to be ridiculed as a "wedding cake."

This strange top identified GE refrigerators of the 1930s. Refrigeration coils were wrapped around a cylinder which re-echoed with peculiar gurgles as the coolant did its work.

Although this early refrigerator was an ungainly looking contrivance, we thought it was modern design carried to an ultimate. The white enamel finish gleamed shiny and sleek.

Often I would catch Dad slipping out to the kitchen just to take another look at his revolutionary wonder.

Every revolution has its victims, and in this case, the old wooden icebox suffered. Ours was pushed unceremoniously to the rear hall where it was demoted to a simple storage of mundane items like household tools and out-of-season footwear.

The door-to-door iceman crossed our house off his route because we did not need his delivery of the regular 50-pound chunk of ice. His livelihood had begun to melt away.

Meanwhile, our family basked in luxury. No longer were we kids dispatched each afternoon to the butcher's or the delicatessen.

Such daily errands were unnecessary when perishables like meat and milk could now be kept indefinitely.

Also, our new refrigerator had a freezing compartment into which steel ice cube trays fitted. If the cube grid was removed, we could freeze our own ice cream in the trays. We learned how to use a special unit to mold Popsicles from a blend of fruit-flavored syrup and water.

Imagine the exciting world where we had a private supply of ice cream and Popsicles.

Actually, our products were filled with ice crystals and never tasted quite right, but we were contented beyond belief.

For 25 years, that same GE refrigerator purred in our kitchen without a service call.

Incalculable are the tons of leftovers it helped to recycle, the thousands of sharp-angled ice cubes which bobbed into glasses of orange pop or the number of times the silver metal door handle was sprung up by a hungry customer.

I have never thought of my father as a radical, but when he brought the electric refrigerator into our house, he started a small revolution. ∞

OLD DOWNTOWN STORES WITH WINNING PERSONALITIES

FIRST PRINTED ☞ 12 – 15 – 91

*E*very store has a personality, and like people they come and go. With Christmas at hand, I can't help remembering some departed downtown stores whose images linger on among Buffalonians.

Take, for example: Flint & Kent's Department Store on Main Street. Specializing in quality and refinement, Flint & Kent kept their cool even in the bustle of holiday shopping.

The dignified salespeople never rushed a customer; and they had a way of letting you know that your doing business at their store was a privilege for them — and for you. Indeed, they were right. All purchases were beautifully packaged in sturdy boxes. Adjustments were politely attended to with philosophical acceptance that life's minor annoyances must be tolerated.

At Eagle, the opposite end of the Main Street business district, was the J.N. Adam store. Founded by a Scottish immigrant and one-time Buffalo mayor, J.N. Adam gave his name and initials to the famous store.

"J.N.'s" climbed to a pinnacle when it occupied a new building in 1937. Escalators were relatively rare then, and shoppers could ride them all the way to the sixth-floor Toyland. Always noted for its Christmas display, J.N.'s toyland was a joy with all the bells, tinkles, chimes, lights, whistles, of fairyland. (AM & A's later has used this structure that J.N. Adam built.)

Denton, Cottier and Daniels' music store on Court Street sang with the delight of Christmas. A pianist was seated at a concert grand in the store's center, and she honored requests.

"Would you play this?" a customer asked, holding out a piece of sheet music. The pianist would glance at the picture of Bing Crosby and Danny Kaye on the cover, smile wearily and crank out, for the 54th time that day, "White Christmas."

Denton's had hundreds of phonograph records on its display shelves and about 20 sound-proof booths for customer listening. Many are the hours I spent in them as a guest at this gracious store.

Buffalo also had its retail clowns — such as Kobacher's, a Main Street transplant from Broadway-Fillmore. Kobacher's each Christmas propped a huge, stuffed Santa Claus in its front window. This Santa rocked and bellowed a half-witted laugh that throbbed up Main Street. The puppet's eyes rolled, and shoppers smiled grimly because the general effect was a little spooky.

Of course, new stores at suburban plazas and malls have had a deep effect on downtown shopping habits.

Yet for many, there will always be magic in names like J.N.'s, E.W. Edwards, Hens & Kelly's, William Hengerer's, Oppenheim Collins and L.L. Berger's. ∽

POPEYE THE SAILOR INTRODUCED WEALTH OF AMERICANA

FIRST PRINTED ∽ 01 – 26 – 92

When I was a boy, I spent Sunday afternoons on the living room floor reading the comics. My favorite was Thimble Theater, starring Popeye.

That great comic strip started to run in Buffalo newspapers 60 years ago. It featured the ridiculous sailor Popeye, one-eyed, forearms like watermelons, always squinting, always biting on a pipe. He owed his strength to consumption of a food rich in iron: spinach.

Popeye's speech smacked of the salt sea: "Blow me down!" he kept saying, and "I yam what I yam..." Hardly a sailor's shore-leave dream, his girlfriend was ungainly Olive Oyl, who had a nasty kid brother called Castor.

Perhaps the greatest of a wonderful cast of characters was J. Wellington Wimpy, a gentle loser, who was consumed with one passion in life: a love for the American hamburger sandwich.

I realized that these Sunday editions of Popeye had something other Sunday strips lacked: a story line completely different from the continuing weekday plot.

Popeye's creator, E.C. Segar, was a man of rare imagination. His signature was always accompanied by a sketch of a smoldering cigar, as a pun on his last name.

Segar used vivid story narrative that used to send me to a strange fantasy world, part adventure, mostly laughs.

While waiting for Sunday dinner, I read, for example, of Popeye's semi-serious expedition to "Plunder Island." On the voyage, he met the Sea Hag and Alice the Goon. Into another sequence waddled a peculiar, ducklike creature called Eugene the Jeep.

Little did I realize then, but I was hooked on authentic, classic Americana. The serviceable military vehicle (and Chrysler's present Jeep line of small trucks) can trace their name to Segar's Thimble Theater. Whenever I hear a weak person characterized as "wimpy," hamburger-loving J. Wellington Wimpy comes tenderly to my recollection. Likewise, modern references to spinach or goon squads.

Popeye, of course, was too popular an invention to be confined to a comics page. He moved to radio (sponsored by Wheatena breakfast food) and to movies (sometimes kids still see the old Max Fleischer cartoons on TV). Various toys and games adopted the one-eyed sailor man like the collectable Lionel handcar, pumped on either side by Popeye and Olive Oyl.

Alas, E.C. Segar died in 1938, too soon to reap the full fun of his creation. The comic strip was continued for years by successors, but none was blessed with that genius that enlivened my boyish Sunday afternoons. ∞

IN THE DAYS WHEN BUFFALO HAD DOUBLE-DECK BUSES

FIRST PRINTED ∞ 02 – 22 – 92

ouble-deck buses are part of London's tradition. Faithfully, they ply their routes to Charing Cross or St. John's Wood, filled top and bottom with cheery Londoners. A few of those shiny red buses even have been exported to Canada's Niagara Frontier, where we see them shuffling summer tourists past scenic glories of this area.

For years in New York City, double-deck buses rolled along Fifth Avenue until their uppity appearance came to symbolize the snobbish elegance of the thoroughfare they traveled.

But double deckers in Buffalo? Yes, the city used them during the 1920s, and they hummed along Delaware Avenue all the way out to Kenmore. It was a period in local history when Delaware coupled natural beauty with a studied charm.

Lined with what were fittingly called "stately elms," Delaware Avenue preened with these huge trees forming almost a Gothic arch over it. This was a street of splendid, dignified mansions bespeaking the wealth and taste of their occupants.

Small, swank shops and stores had sprung up, as well as opulent hotels and apartment houses. The avenue, of course, wound gracefully through that urban jewel, Delaware Park.

Little wonder, then, that city leaders sensed an affinity between New York City's Fifth and Buffalo's Delaware avenues. Just as double-deck buses contributed to New York's ambiance, why not use the same strategy here?

Buffalo's first double deckers lacked an upstairs roof; they also lacked proper springs and inflated tires. Thus, given the occasional tantrums of Western New York weather, it was no surprise that passengers shunned the top deck.

After a few years, improvements were made: Comfortable, padded seats and a convertible roof were installed. However, bus drivers reported continuing resistance to mounting the stairs and taking an upstairs seat.

Since commercial advantage lay in piling up twice the normal capacity of riders, the local transit company raised a big effort. They advertised the fun and vista view of top layer riding; they instructed operators to wait until passengers moved up to provide space for additional patrons.

Nothing worked: Buffalo, it seemed, was not a turf on which double deckers could thrive. As a last resort, the two-story vehicles were run only at rush hours, when passengers were desperate to get home.

Only then did Buffalonians stifle their stubborn reluctance and climb the steps. Gradually, the unpopular double deckers were retired or sold off. No one seemed to regret their passing.

I recall my father describing Buffalo's flirtation with upward mobility. "People here just didn't like them," he always summed up. That was perhaps the best explanation. ☜

ON 'BLUE MONDAY'
THE CELLAR WAS A
WOMAN'S DUNGEON

FIRST PRINTED ∞ 03 – 22 – 92

*H*ousewives of my mother's generation used to refer to "Blue Monday," and not necessarily because it was the start of a new workweek. Blue Monday was washday.

Few mothers held regular paying positions back then, and at least one of the reasons is obvious. Keeping house was a tedious, full-time job. Without machines of modern efficiency, household chores were a ceaseless cycle of drudgery.

But Blue Monday was like no other day. My mother would begin her work even before we kids were packed off for school sorting laundry according to fabric, color, function.

The cellar was a woman's dungeon. Once descended, she prepared to serve her weekly sentence. The washing machine was wheeled into place, its electrical plug jammed into an overhead fixture.

Ponderous and primitive, it stood on wheels rusting from constant dampness. Our family had a drab, boxlike model, containing a perforated, revolving cylinder to jostle clothes. The noise was monotonous, complaining, at times angry.

Mounted on top of the washing machine, its twin rollers forming a kind of idiot grin, was the wringer. I hesitate to contemplate how many pounds of our soggy clothes Mother fed through those jaws.

Washday submerged the housewife. A load proceeded from the wash machine to the stationary tub for rinsing, back to the wash cylinder, back to another tub, and between each operation, all clothes had to pass through the wringer's mouth.

To escape some of the drenching of this ordeal, most housewives stood on wooden duck-boards, rough platforms elevated about an inch off the slippery concrete.

As each load was battled to fairly clean surrender, the housewife faced the problem of drying her products. In summer, this exigency afforded a brief escape from the dungeon when she lugged a wicker basket to the back yard.

With a steady watch for sudden showers that could cause chaos, the laundress fastened each piece with clothespins to a line. The ceiling of every basement in my neighborhood was strung with a web of ropes to take care of drying in winter or bad weather. Heat from the coal furnace helped the cause.

I can recall my mother's frazzled look when she stumbled up from the basement after one of those Blue Mondays. She would remove the net from her hair (worn to prevent accidents at the wringer). "It's done!" she would sigh wearily.

Years would pass before Maytags and Whirlpools spun housewives out of cellar servitude. Yet these emancipating appliances will never purge me of memories of my mother's quiet heroism.

Housewives of that hard-working era, I salute you! You won the Battle of the Basement. ☜

OLD WURLITZER JUKEBOX
HAS LASTING INFLUENCE

FIRST PRINTED ☞ 04 – 19 – 92

*M*anufactured in North Tonawanda, Wurlitzer products brought music to far corners of the world. Of course, the company was famous for its organs, but even more popular were the Wurlitzer jukeboxes.

The classic was Model 1015. It is this massive, reverberating nickelodeon that most of us remember. Forming a Romanesque arch, it was planted at the end of dance floors. Its peripheries were defined with transparent, amber tubes through which bubbles rose in endless ascent.

In far-gone years before my wife and I were married, we used to dance to one of these Wurlitzers at the old Circle Inn on Lake Shore Road at Derby. "Our love is here to stay," the nickelodeon proclaimed.

I slipped a herd of buffalo nickels into the jukebox slot to hear that great Gershwin tune repeated. It was "our song," and my wife used to sing the words while we danced: *"In time the Rockies may crumble/Gibraltar may tumble…but our love is here to stay."*

In a way, I felt like that about the Wurlitzer. It, too, was here to stay. You could feel its vibrations underfoot; it excluded a sense of might, power and endurance.

Between records, the jukebox provided a visual show. In those moments of silence, dancers would cluster around to watch the ceremony of the changing of the records.

Behind a semicircular window, the finished platter would slide back to its nest. Then, robot-like, a tray slipped beneath another record — and more music.

"Won't you tell me when/We may meet again/Sunday, Monday or always?" crooned Bing Crosby, and dancers picked up the rhythm and began their sentimental steps.

That idea of permanence was very big among the Wurlitzer's hits: "The Day After Forever," "Not for Just a Year, But Always," "What Are You Doing the Rest of Your Life?" That's what love was about.

Times have changed. Sentimental waltz melodies have been stilled by louder, stronger beats; Wurlitzer nickelodeons have been replaced by more sophisticated, more strident equipment. Styles in dancing have altered wildly.

Yet an older generation remembers fondly the Model 1015, whose strong heart palpitated with hyperboles of faithful love. Over and over it played "our songs." ∞

RADIO WAS BORN IN BUFFALO IN 1922, AND IT BURPED, SCREECHED AND SPUTTERED

FIRST PRINTED ∞ 05 – 10 – 92

*I*n Buffalo this year, radio celebrates its 70th birthday. It was in May 1922 that signals were broadcast from a local transmitter for the first time.

Until then, the Niagara Frontier had relied on the radio waves from comparatively distant points like WJZ Newark and powerful KDKA in Pittsburgh. Now Buffalo was able to take command of its own skies.

Advertised in newspapers as "The New High Power Federal Buffalo Broadcasting Station," the incipient radio operation chose as its call letters WGR, after the initials of a founder, George Rand. WGR's studio was at 1739 Elmwood Ave.

Local radio pioneers clustered about their sets, sharing earphones to catch that magical gurgling from Buffalo's Baby Radio. Indeed, the newborn made a good share of burps, screeches, and sputters.

Early receivers were the size of a shoebox, their apparatus consisting mainly of a crystal tube to snare the broadcast signal and a series of coils to magnify the sound.

Despite careful nursing, reception was so weak that only by concentrating between tight-fitting earphones could a listener decipher the exciting whispers of the infant.

"Radio Week" in Buffalo began on May 21, 1922. Advertisements promoted sales of sophisticated radio sets. "The Crystal Radio Receiver is *not* an experiment," they insisted. "It is a highly developed instrument." Cost of such a device was about $25, a considerable investment 70 years ago.

Programs on Buffalo's WGR during Radio Week were hardly pulse agitators: a clergyman's lecture on "Six Points to Success," a concert from Victor's

Furniture Showroom, another lecture by Dr. Julian Park of the University of Buffalo on the advantages of college education, a program of Hawaiian singers accompanied by a pianist named W.J. Gomph.

Newspaper sections that described such diverting entertainment were headed "Telephony." One columnist on such a page described Buffalo's premier studio this way: "It is like the living room of some luxurious mansion with heavy, brown, rich, velvet draperies covering the four walls. The floor is encouched with thick rugs of pleasant design."

In my boyhood home, we had several crystal sets, none of which worked very well. I can see my father huddled round-shouldered, maneuvering wires, clasping earphones to his head. Rapt in the marvel of radio, Dad may even have understood a few words among the cracks and squawks.

Some years would elapse before the loudspeaker enabled radio to be enjoyed simultaneously by a roomful of people, before the advent of programs of general family appeal.

It was enough, however, in May 1922, to catch voices magically propelled from a studio on Elmwood Avenue. After all, how much further could science be expected to go? ☜

THE PROLIFERATION OF 'BLUE' WORDS

FIRST PRINTED ∞ 09 – 29 – 92

*N*early everybody has heard of what a shock it caused in the final scene of the 1939 movie "Gone With the Wind" when Clark Gable said the four-letter word "damn."

Before that syllable could be uttered in moving picture theaters, miles of red tape had to be hacked through because strict codes forbade use of strong language. Finally, after persuasive argument that no other word could do the job, Clark Gable was allowed to speak up: "Frankly, my dear, I don't give a damn."

Much water has gone over the dam since that breakthrough, and frankly, even such a cosmopolite as Rhett Butler would be shocked at the four-letter combinations that are now routinely accepted, not only at the movies and on television but in ordinary, daily life.

Signs are held up at football games with rude words for all to see. Dull-witted motorists enjoy pasting vulgar bumper stickers to their cars. You even see men wearing baseball hats bearing four-letter crudities.

Graffiti society has always been low, but the level has steadily dropped below the gutter.

Somewhere in the Hemingway-esque past, may have come the idea that strong men use strong language. As a result, men have groped through the lexicon of foulness in an effort to be strong. In days of equal rights, it is unfortunate that many women rival men's language.

Perhaps hidden somewhere in vulgar speech is also the desire to shock, even to outrage. When many crude words have lost semblance of meaning, they are still used to convey only some vague antisocial resentments.

Consider what is probably the most starkly jagged of the four-letter litany, the F word. I have heard men whose speech is totally reliant on this word although in their articulation, it means nothing.

The F word, depending on inflection or sentence sequence, is employed as verb, noun, expletive, participial adjective, gerund. Having run the grammatical gauntlet, it is naked of meaning and has somewhat the same effect as spitting disgustingly.

221

I suggest that language affects behavior. I suggest that the man who gives vent to explosions of vile words bears a strong risk of blowing up in other directions toward wife, children, associates. I suggest that the person who has stifled his sensitivity to language has stifled also his sensitivity toward life, love, nature. As one speaks, so to a degree, does he behave.

Furthermore, to expose children to rotten language is doubly reprehensible. It is heartbreaking to hear children use gutter words because they learned them at home, on the streets, on television.

Recently, my son competed in the Muny Tennis tournament. A game of frequent frustration, tennis has been known to elicit some vivid imprecations. In one close match, my son's opponent at points of aggravation held up his hands and looked skyward. He smiled to compete a graceful gesture: a refreshing alternative to strong language.

As we grow older, many of us remember our fathers fondly and recollect endearing, admirable traits which we would like to emulate. My dad, at moments of intense stress, would exclaim: "Gol darn it!"

Ridiculous as the expression sounds today, Dad's restraint impresses me. It was the strongest language I heard him utter, and I try to imitate his control. ∽

IN DAYS WHEN CANNING WAS A HOME INDUSTRY

FIRST PRINTED ∞ 10 – 04 – 92

To stroll down our South Buffalo street in autumn was to know what each housewife was doing — not by looking, but by sniffing.

Mrs. Bigelow was busy beside a bubbling kettle of tomatoes; smaller pans held peppers, onions. Stirring, smelling, sampling, I could, imagine industrious Mrs. B. at her massive cauldron because the delicious aroma of chili sauce persistently wafted out to the street.

A few houses farther, Mrs. Carrigg worked on peaches. How could I tell? The unmistakable, peachy fragrance tantalized the nostrils of every passerby.

When I reached home, I found my mother bustling about the stove, pouring a pungent quince jelly into a series of small jars.

Those autumn scenes of my boyhood were unforgettable. It was a season when a woman's place was not only in the home, but in the kitchen.

At our house, neighbors supplied us with apples, grapes and cherries. From the Lancaster farm of relatives, we gathered quinces, crabapples, and tomatoes. Dad would take us on the trolley to Lockport and Olcott Beach where we picked magnificent pears and peaches.

Mother pretended to be happy with our harvest, but in retrospect, I wonder, because her labor was endless. After inspection and washing, the crop had to be processed by arduous peeling, coring, slicing.

Quantities of sugar and pectin were ever on hand as the canning jars were sterilized and then filled with the prepared fruit. Next came the boiling: Those jars were immersed in kettles and cooked for hours.

At a strategic moment, the canner flipped the bail-clamp on the quart Ball jar. With authority, it slapped down, fusing the glass cover and rubber gasket tightly to the jar so that a vacuum would form.

Jams and jellies employed similar techniques, but since the jars were smaller, the housewife would pour a layer of melted paraffin to seal the container top. The procedure was delicate, dangerous and hot.

Mother allowed me to help with final stages. I readied labels to identify each vintage: e.g., Quince, 1936. Finally, we lugged the jars down to the Fruit Cellar, a dark room with shelves on all sides (every respectable house had a fruit cellar.)

Our Fruit Cellar was a thing of beauty with gleaming, glass jars neatly arranged by year and contents. The closest I come to such a splendid room in my house now is the compact, painlessly-stocked freezer. It is not the same. ∞

IN BUFFALO'S GILDED AGE, CITY'S TRANSIT LIFE CENTERED AROUND THE TROLLEY BARN

FIRST PRINTED ᴄᴏ 10 – 18 – 92

*Un*noticed this summer, a Buffalo landmark faded into the past. Undistinguished for any architectural grace, the structure will not be missed except for its affinity to Buffalo in the Gilded Age.

I am writing of Cold Spring Transit Station, a spacious red brick building that stood for nearly a century at the corner of Main Street and Michigan Avenue.

Vintage electric streetcars came and went from this garage in decades when the world moved on rails. The streets around its corner were lined with crossing and intersecting tracks.

To look overhead was to see not the sky, but a web of wires, all charged with electric current that powered the trolley fleet. Like grasping arms, poles reached up from streetcars to clutch the wires.

Early in this century, before arrival of the automobile, the garage at Main and Michigan housed trolleys for all occasions: parties, excursions, freight movement, club or executive meetings, funerals. Life in all its phases was celebrated on the trolley.

Out of Cold Spring Station rattled those tiny cars with cupolas that used to serve small runs like Hoyt Street, No. 7, as well as the massive interurbans that sped to Niagara Falls and Lockport. Then there were the classic Peter Witt cars, the kind still running in Toronto.

In my memory, except for the yellow interurbans, Buffalo trolleys were colored a somber, dark green. In the 1940s, a modern look was sought as the staid cars became light green with a cream trim. It was an indignity.

A "Main and Michigan" sign in the window of an approaching car was a **225** frustration for riders because it meant that ill trolley was traveling only as far as Cold Spring Barns.

Once there, all passengers were discharged, and like tired, ancient dinosaurs, off-duty streetcars crept off for restoration. They were washed, swept, repaired and consoled; they were made ready for the next day's work, hauling people along the tracks that ribboned city streets.

To far reaches of Buffalo the streetcars rumbled: the Main, Parkside and Fillmore lines, respectively Nos. 8, 9, 23; East and West Utica, Nos. 12 and 10; Jefferson, No. 18.

On sidings outside the barn stood plucky snowplows with their sweeping blades that did so much to keep Buffalo streets open in winter storms. Many plow units had originally been open cars that proudly serviced the Great Gorge Route of the Niagara River and now form one of its legends.

With the passing of Cold Spring Station this summer, a vivid reminder of the age of electric streetcar railways vanished. It was a slower time; maybe kinder and gentler, too. ∾

WHEN EVERY PHONE CALL WENT THROUGH CENTRAL

BEFORE THE WORLD WENT DIGITAL, THE OPERATOR WAS THE ARBITER OF ALL

FIRST PRINTED 〜 06 – 21 – 92

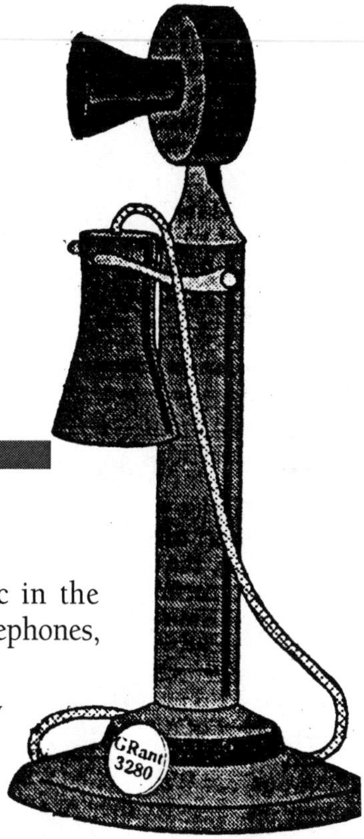

"Number, please!"

Those words still work magic in the memory of anybody who lived with nondial telephones, party lines and dear, old, venerable Central.

It was Central who spoke at the start of any phone call. To pick up the receiver was to catch not a dull dial tone, but a voice human, vibrant, demanding. "Num-ber, plee-az!" she said, savoring each syllable.

This was a more personal world, when even telephone numbers had names. Buffalo numbers, for example, bore presidents' names — Lincoln, Cleveland, Garfield; street names — Tupper, Delaware, Parkside; city districts — Riverside, University.

Thus, a caller would commence: "Central, give me Fillmore-two-seven-three-three." That was it: a euphonious name, followed by four numbers that fell trippingly from the tongue, very different from chewing on today's diet of seven raw digits.

It seems just yesterday that Central and we played the numbers game. Those old combinations spun neatly in our minds' orbits. Even though they have lain buried for years, most folks still recall their old phone numbers and maybe a few others. My home phone was Abbott 1276-J (the letter indicated a party line); my father's store was Triangle 4510. I called my girlfriend at Grant 5658.

227

As soon as you gave the number, Central took over. After she connected appropriate plugs, we either got our party or a terse, succinct explanation why not: "The li-on is busy," or, "Your party does not answer. Shall I keep on ring-ing?"

Central could handle any situation, not only the placement of routine calls. If you were ever hooked on a party line, you may remember Central butting in primly: "You have been talking for 23 minutes. Please terminate your message as other callers are waiting."

With drunks who had trouble enunciating, Central had no patience. "I will place your call when you are sober," she pontificated.

Foreign accents, weak voices, stutterers, pesky kids, callers in distress or emergency: Central's ear was ever alert for the unusual. Never ruffled, never at a loss, she was a practicing psychologist. "Please compose yourself, and I will hel-lup you," she would soothe.

The queenly reign of Central stammered to a close during the 1940s when most large cities automated their telephone service.

No doubt the numbers-only system is here to stay, but I can get sentimental about the personal touch of that woman called Central. ∞

HOME-BREWED ROOT BEER
WAS POWERFUL STUFF FIRST PRINTED ☞ 08 – 02 – 92

*S*even-Up, Orange Crush, Mountain Dew: We didn't have them. On hot summer days there was only root beer. But that Depression root beer was a veritable Vesuvius among beverages.

As was the case with many things in the 1930s, you had to do it yourself. There were no easy-mix packages.

Root beer brewing required yeast, sugar and a small bottle called Hires Root Beer Extract. So potent was this elixir that it would be held at arm's length and measured out like some lethal acid.

Of course, being kids, we needed supervision, and Mother would direct us as we combined ingredients with water in a five-gallon tub. After patient stirring, our brew became heavy, black, inviting. But at its inception, it was not good to the taste. Like any fine liquor, it had to age.

During the depression everybody's cellar was a quarry for old bottle and jars. Some had originally held ketchup; others were beer bottles left from the halcyon days before Prohibition; still others had contained the fiery cough medicines or cod liver oil of legend. We hauled them out.

It was an irony that after an afternoon's work, all we had to show was a messy kitchen with a sticky floor and about 30 neatly sealed bottles of root beer that we couldn't drink. Now we knew how Dad felt when he finished making his home brew, that kitchen-made Prohibition concoction.

We lugged the dark bottles back to the cool, damp cellar, stood them on shelves and waited. And waited. If we

229

held off for three days, the yeast would begin to work, and the root beer pleased drinkers willing to settle for a tame, stagnant potation. If you wanted more kick, it was necessary to abstain for a week. When you snapped off the cap, you knew you had a strong drink because the root beer would sizzle and hiss. You couldn't drink it quickly; it was like taking a spoonful of horseradish.

We always kept a few last bottles; in another week, the aging process took on a new potency. Like shots in the night, bottles would sometimes explode in the basement.

At this stage, root beer could become a weapon. With thumb over bottle lip, we would shake the container until pressure had built up against the finger and we could shoot out a piercing jet at some target, usually a sister.

When I remember the scorching summer days of the 1930s, those batches of feisty Depression root beer are stacked neatly on the shelves of my memory. ∽

TIN LIZZIE WASN'T PERFECT, BUT EVERYBODY LOVED HER

FIRST PRINTED ☞ 08 – 16 – 92

Eighty years ago, in 1912, Henry Ford's Model-T set a world record for automobile production. More than 78,000 of the black, boxy "flivvers"were welcomed into eager American families.

Henry Ford was convinced that people wanted an auto that was inexpensive, durable, easy to repair. He frowned on luxuries and what he called "frills."

With a four-cylinder, 20-horsepower engine, the Model-T could attain a 45 mph speed. Its two transverse springs kept the four wooden, spoked wheels firmly on the ground. Somehow considered feminine, the car was often called the Tin Lizzie.

Henry Ford stubbornly resisted any change to his Lizzie. "No new models, no new motors or bodies," he promised. Ford even had a crusty joke: "You can have your choice of any color as long as it's black."

Ford held out against self-starters. The crank on the front worked fine if the driver set his spark carefully; otherwise, it might kick back hard enough to break an arm.

He also considered a gasoline gauge "a frill." So the only way to check fuel was to take up the front seat and insert a wooden stick into the tank. Because gas drained by gravity, a car with a low supply might have to climb a hill backward.

Headlights were powered by the engine flywheel, a system that could force nighttime drivers to stop and rev their engines when traveling at low speed.

231

There were, of course, no instruments, no speedometer.

Despite such inconveniences, Model-Ts kept selling and by 1914 half the cars in the United States were Fords. Many celebrities drove the Model-T: Charles Lindbergh, Babe Ruth, Pancho Villa, Sinclair Lewis.

Ford cherished testimonial letters from satisfied users. In 1934, Public Enemy No. 1, John Dillinger, wrote a card, "Hello Henry, old Pal. You have a wonderful car. It's a treat to drive one."

Clyde Barrow, the notorious killer of Bonnie-and-Clyde fame, sent his endorsement: "I have drove Fords exculsively (sic) when I could get away with one."

For 20 years, Henry Ford ruled the automobile roost, selling 15.8 million Model-Ts. With mass production, he was able to lower the price from $850 to $290 and to raise workers' salaries to an incredible peak of $5 a day. No wonder Ford felt like a man with a mission.

I have always had a warm spot in my heart for the Model-T. My dad used to take us fishing at a relative's farm in Lancaster. He'd drive down a cow patch to a creek where we parked the car in midstream. Lizzie never complained. ∞

HORSE-AND-BUGGY RAG MAN WAS THE FIRST RECYCLER

FIRST PRINTED ∽ 08 – 30 –92

Although he belonged to the horse-and-buggy era, the neighborhood Rag Man was a practitioner of the future. He was the first recycler.

"Ah-rags…ahh-r-rags," he sang out, a vowel sound always prefixed to the generic word. From his perch on front of a simple, gondola wagon, under a faded umbrella, the Rag Man filed streets with his chant: "Ahrags…ah-bottles."

Relying only on voice to herald his approach, the Rag Man was alert for the sudden rattle of an opening door or window and a housewife's euphonic summons of those days: "Yoo-hoo."

No fevered mount powered his wagon so the Rag Man easily drew the horse to a stop, climbed down several iron cleats to ground and searched for the yoo-hoo-er.

Once in communication, Rag Men always began negotiations without ceremony. "Wotcha-got?" was the conventional starter. This question led to appraisal of accretions of newspapers, battered clothing (i.e., rags), glass bottles and jars, plumbing detritus possibly containing copper or lead, auto batteries, tires, inner tubes.

Such miscellany was haggled over, paid for and hoisted into the Rag Man's wagon. On wet days, he spread a canvas tarpaulin over his wares, then resumed his wagon bench and shook the leather straps, guiding his nag back to the route.

"Ah-rags," the Rag Man continued in that era of hard work. Depending on mood and vocal equipment, he might sound like anything from a tenor at LaScala Opera to a wounded animal.

Syllables would re-echo from trees or houses, and we mischievous kids often picked up the refrain. "Ah-rags, old rags, dish rags, wet rags," we would mock cruelly.

The Rag Man ignored any taunts, adjusted his limp hat and trudged on.

To this day, I can hear that wagon, wooden, spoked wheels with metal edging, crunching over stones along the pavement. The painful, grinding noise was punctuated by the heavy, clip-clop shoes of an arthritic horse.

In my boyhood, neighborhoods relied on Rag Men to clean basements of constant accumulations. However small his payment, the money helped to balance shaky family budgets.

With their creaky wagons and tired horses, recycling neighborhood Rag Men disappeared after the war, but so gradual was their passing that it took time to realize that the species had vanished. ∞

STORY BEHIND THE SCOW
STUCK NEAR BRINK OF FALLS
SINCE 1918

FIRST PRINTED ∞ 11 – 08 – 92

Visitors have often observed the rusting steel barge, settled on rocks in the Niagara River just short of the Horseshoe Falls. It is accepted almost as a whim of nature, so that few people question its origin. Recently, I turned back the calendar and combed old newspapers to learn the barge's story.

At 4 p.m. on Aug. 6, 1918, their workday finished, two Buffalo men were on board a metal scow being towed to their base at Great Lakes Dredging. They had been deepening a channel at an upper-river power station.

Somehow, the cables connecting scow with tugboat came undone, and the older man, Gus Lefberg, realized that he and his companion, James Harris, were floating free downstream. Lefberg, a much traveled seaman, did not dream of any danger; instead he imagined that he and Harris were drifting toward the Canadian shore.

Such a cozy landing never occurred; rather, without power, rudderless, the barge and its two occupants were being lured along a temperamental river.

At first, the men made use of tools on board: Tying lines to empty barrels, they tried to maneuver the barge. Next, they fashioned anchors of heavy, iron pieces — all to no effect.

Soon the steel-bottomed scow was picking up speed with the current, heading inexorably toward the Niagara rapids. In the far distance, Lefberg and Harris could already see spume rising from the cataract and could hear

235
∞

the unmistakable rumble.

By now they fully understood their peril. They would plunge over Niagara Falls. Harris considered lashing himself to the scow while Lefberg sought a cubbyhole in the bulkhead where he could squeeze.

But Lefberg had one final stratagem. Bouncing among huge, jagged rocks, he opened the scow's sea cocks, hoping that the heaving craft would drop on one of the boulders.

Just 900 feet from Horseshoe Falls, the flat barge crashed on a sharp boulder that sliced into the steel bottom. All at once, the mad trip halted. Given that pause, the men had a moment to weigh options: whether to try swimming to safety or to challenge the thundering falls in their scow.

Meanwhile, help was gathering at the Canadian shore. Notes were shot from guns to Lefberg and Harris. Then as darkness fell, stenciled instructions were held in front of powerful searchlights, telling the men to wait.

Sending a rescue boat was impossible, but a breeches buoy was being rushed from the Youngstown Coast Guard Station. While night suspended efforts, the marooned workers spent lonely, terrified hours.

Next morning early, a rope was fired to the barge. Once secured on board, the line supported a basket large enough for one man. Because Harris was a father of a large family, Lefberg insisted that he be the first to leave.

Actually, no one needed to rush, because the scow has been stuck in the same spot for 74 years. In fact, so stable is the barge that weeds, trees and bushes have grown up around it, forming a tiny island. ∞

SMOKE GETS IN YOUR EYES IN RECALLING THE BIG BANDS ON RADIO

FIRST PRINTED ☞ 11 – 22 – 92

*I*t's a challenge to find anything good to say about cigarette manufacturers. However, I have dug deep and come up with one sentimental remembrance.

In days when pop songs glowed with poetic, witty lyrics; in an era when pop performers had talent, Big Tobacco sponsored the big bands on radio.

Airwaves throbbed to the beat: Chesterfields backed Glenn Miller: "Smoke Rings and Shadows/While a cigarette burns" led into Glenn's "Moonlight Serenade" theme. Marian Hutton and Bob Eberle toyed with songs like "Chattanooga Choo-Choo"and "Don't Sit Under the Apple Tree."

Tuesday evenings at 7:30, the Camel Caravan crossed the radio dial. Over the years. Camels featured some of America's biggest bands on its caravan: Benny Goodman ("Let's Dance"); Bob Crosby's Dixieland; Vaughan Monroe ("Racing With the Moon").

Although a lesser brand, Raleigh-Kool cigarettes employed the mighty Tommy Dorsey Band. Known as "the sentimental gentleman" (although he was neither sentimental nor a gentleman), Dorsey had a knack for hiring spectacular vocalists such as Jo Stafford, Frank Sinatra, Dick Haymes and the Pied Pipers.

"Call for Philip Morris," chanted Johnny, the pageboy, as Horace Heidt's orchestra jostled the theme's melody, "On the Trail," from Ferdy Grofe's "Grand Canyon Suite."

Old Gold cigarettes financed the distinguished bands of Artie Shaw and Woody Herman.

237

Lucky Strike gave accreditation to Kay Kyser's Kollege of Musical Knowledge." Between songs, Kay would ask musical questions; if contestants were stumped, he called for an answer from the audience: "Students?" he would shout.

The undisputed leader of pop music radio was "Your Hit Parade," sponsored extravagantly by the American Tobacco Co. With questionable accuracy, the "Lucky Strike Survey" proclaimed the 10 most commonly sung melodies of the previous week.

Saturday night listeners waited in suspense as songs were pealed off, narrowing gradually to the week's top hit: "And now, the No. 1 song that all America has been singing. Lanny Ross, accompanied by Mark Warnow's orchestra, invites you to take a musical journey 'On the Atchison, Topeka and the Santa Fe.'"

It was the heyday of swing music, when everybody listened on radio to the unique sounds of the big bands, and cigarette companies helped to make the fun possible.

My gratitude to these sponsors, however, is grudging as I realize that slick advertising hooked many young new smokers who ultimately paid a steep bill. Regrettably, for years I was one. ∞

BACK IN THE OLD DAYS, NEARLY EVERYTHING HAD TO BE CRANKED

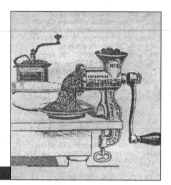

FIRST PRINTED ∽ 12 – 27 – 92

*O*f course there were electric motors when I was a boy, but few were adapted to household uses. Back then, most things had to be cranked.

In the kitchen, for example, when vegetables were prepared for stews or soups, the housewife went to a cabinet and lifted out a ponderous iron apparatus. When its pieces were assembled, they formed a food grinder.

This contrivance clamped onto the side of a kitchen table. Into its wide mouth were forced potatoes, carrots, onions, nuts. Then, grasping a long curved handle, the cook cranked. With a series of fittings we considered sophisticated, foods were shredded into varying degrees of coarseness.

Today's cook would shudder. She turns to the blender or food processor, selects the desired button and with a finger's touch, vegetables are mechanically rendered into interesting spirals, sticks, bits. No cranking necessary.

To beat eggs or cream, in days I recall fondly, we used a knobby-handled instrument with metal whippers at the end. By cranking a small wheel in the center, gears turned.

Pretty soon, responding to the hand's speed, blades were flying fast enough to metamorphose eggs or cream into any thickness. In the basement, Dad kept a similar device that spun drill bits to bore holes. Now the electric mixer and the power drill have sent such tools to the history museum in exhibits called "How People Used to Live."

In my boyhood, science was perfecting a remarkable disk called the phonograph record. This marvel was played on a Victrola, a device that demanded cranking for every five minutes of performance. Dad would turn the handle delicately before he flipped the switch that unleashed the Irish tenor John McCormick singing "Mother McCrea."

Whenever I operate the shiny, chromium machine to grind coffee at the supermarket, my thoughts drift back to the wooden model, whose handle my mother cranked for so many years. After a few turns, the beans had yielded enough coffee to fill the grinder's bottom drawer, plenty for a coffee pot of piquant aroma.

Another household contrivance that required cranking was in the basement — the coal furnace. To shake out dead coal ash, the furnace tender fitted an iron piece to revolving bars at the firebox bottom. He cranked gently, respectfully, knowing that he could stir up dust enough to color a young man's hair prematurely white.

Among the few cranking devices that survive are the can opener and pencil sharpener. Even these are under serious threat of electrocution. ∞

OLD DOWNTOWN LIBRARY SEEMED HAUNTED, SPOOKY – LIKE A GOTHIC ROMANCE

FIRST PRINTED ⌒ 01 – 17 – 93

The original central Buffalo Public Library occupied the same site at Washington and Clinton streets as the current one, but the resemblance halted there.

The old library was brick, gabled, rambling; its successor is sharply rectangled with large window walls. The new building is set back from Washington Street, but the former library hugged the corner.

The old downtown library was many things to many people. To some, for example, it was a station stop in gusty weather.

Library corner has always been a focus for vengeful winds, often accompanied by rain, sleet, snow. To escape such baleful assaults, transfer passengers would trudge up a dozen worn stone steps into a square, slate-floored vestibule.

Here they cowered, prayerfully waiting for an outbound Broadway streetcar. If trolleys were late, as they invariably were, people huddled, clutching shopping bags, bundled in wool coats, poised for the streetcar's approach.

No chance of missing it. The Washington Street tracks were so badly maintained that the building began to tremble and quake when the Broadway behemoth drew near. The conductor rang his bell anyway.

Library doors flew open as riders tumbled from their refuge to struggle up the steep trolley steps; braced for a rocky trip out the No. 4 line.

The library's front reading room was a waiting place of a different sort. Here, at heavy tables and in shaky Windsor chairs, sat a generation of old sailors. Flushed from the Seamen's Home on lower Main Street, every

241

morning they drifted up to the library.

Like characters out of Dickens, they sat reading books about travel, about navigation, about shipping on the Great Lakes, but the dear, lonely old salts were really marking time, waiting for their last long voyage home.

Students worked upstairs in reference rooms which opened like chapters of a Gothic romance. Each chamber was defined in heavy wood and seemed haunted. Small stairways led through oaken arches into tiny rooms with creaking floors.

The air was musty, and old librarians spoke in hushed, mysterious whispers as though in church. These suspicious women resembled bit players in Hollywood suspense movies: "Jane Eyre," "Rebecca," "Dracula." When winter winds gusted, windows rattled spookily; when it rained, networks of drainpipes made the whole place gurgle.

The final time I visited the Downtown BPL was in 1962. The tired building had been emptied, awaiting demolition. I carried my oldest daughter, then a baby, so that one day I could tell her that she had been there.

The present library, built in 1963, is efficient, bright, well-staffed, but it lacks the cast of characters that made its predecessor so intriguing. ∞

GREATEST OF THE MONEY-GRUBBING RAIL BARONS

FIRST PRINTED ⌒ 02 – 07 – 93

*T*he man with the patrician name, Cornelius Vanderbilt, earned the largest share of his wealth and reputation by joining together by rail the extreme ends of the Empire State, New York City and Buffalo.

Perhaps the greatest of the tightfisted, stock-manipulating, salty-talking, money-grubbing railroad barons of his era, Vanderbilt never missed a financial opportunity.

Indeed, such was his devotion to the dollar that Vanderbilt often resorted to spiritualist mediums in an effort to communicate with his dead mother and beloved son. From the afterlife, he enlisted their aid to get information on the stock market, to secure advice for business decisions.

Whatever the source of his counsel, Vanderbilt showed unearthly commercial shrewdness. Always interested in transportation, he had operated ferries and schooners around New York City. When the California Gold Rush erupted in 1848, Vanderbilt seized a chance to get rich — but not by prospecting.

Because there were no transcontinental roads or rails, Vanderbilt hit on the idea of transporting gold seekers on his own fleet. He sailed East Coast passengers to Nicaragua and got them across the isthmus by a combination of ferry and coach.

Once on the Pacific side of Central America, another boat carried prospectors up to California. This cumbersome, but resourceful, itinerary won Vanderbilt a fortune and the spurious title "commodore," a designation he cherished the rest of his life.

The commodore's real genius, however, moved on rails. He had bought up two small railroads along the Hudson River and eventually completed a line from New York City north to Albany. From there, it was natural to look west.

A series of short lines already existed, stretching piecemeal from Albany to Buffalo. With accustomed wizardry for finance, Vanderbilt acquired control of the little companies and joined them to his own.

Soon he had rail lines cutting through central New York State. Thus, the name of Vanderbilt's powerful facility was inevitable: the New York Central Railroad.

This great company became a legend with its crack trains such as the Empire State Express, Wolverine, 20th Century Limited, Hudson River Special and of course, the Commodore Vanderbilt Express. For decades, these glamorous liners were the stuff of dreams, and Buffalo was the epicenter of trains from the great cities of Chicago and New York.

While Amtrak still uses the same famous route for passenger runs from Buffalo to New York City, neither frequency nor luxury suggests what the line once was.

The situation, however, may change with steep air fares and crowded highways. Commodore Vanderbilt's rails offer a practical alternative with a safe, swift, scenic trip across the Empire State. ∞

CHIPPEWA MARKET GAVE FLAVOR TO DOWNTOWN BUFFALO

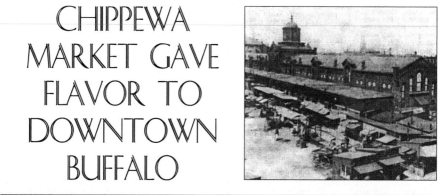

FIRST PRINTED 03 – 21 – 93

*T*he Chippewa Market in downtown Buffalo awakened before sun rise. Shops were opened; stalls were stocked with fresh produce just arriving on wagons and trucks.

By 8 a.m., storekeepers whose business fronted on Washington Street were hosing the sidewalks before morning customers dropped in. The spray diffused the redolence of vegetables and fruits.

Before the Civil War, the Chippewa Market had evolved in Old World tradition, adjoining a church where much daily life began in prayer. From the shadow of venerable St. Michael's Church, Buffalo's downtown market spread over the large block defined by Washington, Ellicott and Chippewa streets.

The famous market became a key distribution point for food to city storekeepers and housewives. Farm produce, meats, bread were all sold daily in mass quantities.

Originally farmers conducted business from their wagons, but gradually permanent structures were built until there were indoor shops that operated year-round.

To follow the inside walkways was to pass vendors of many sorts. Vats of pickles, jams, jellies were everywhere. Barrels and bushel baskets swelled with produce.

Rolls, breads tumbled in the cases of bakery shops; brawny, mustached butchers stalked their corners, wielding knives and cleavers. Occasionally, heavy bells from St. Michael's steeple would bong out the time.

In days of the Chippewa Market, Canisius High School was situated in a

245

mighty, bastille-like structure on Washington Street, just the other side of St. Michael's Church.

When I was a freshman there, my daily errand after dismissal was to stop for fresh vegetables for our family dinner.

"See if the beans look good," Mother would caution me. As winter drew on and pickings grew slim, my instructions changed: "Turnips are usually OK at Rendl's. Get a fair-sized one."

Canisius High was still a bastion of classical study, and carrying my Latin and Greek books, I would wander past the stalls of the Chippewa Market, inspecting cabbage or squash for our evening meal.

At his stand, Mr. Rendl would see my books. "Study hard, young fella, and you won't wind up like me." I was puzzled by his advice because the fat, jolly German always seemed happy, contented and well-fed.

Yet, Mr. Rendl might have known something I did not. Perhaps he had a premonition of giant super groceterias with frozen foods that would render his tiny stand obsolete.

Whatever the case, Chippewa Market was leveled after the war to form a parking lot. Its nearest surviving relative today is Buffalo's Broadway Market, a vigorous veteran and an institution to be cherished. ∞

A SUNDAY AFTERNOON DRIVE
IN THE DAYS WHEN THE AUTO
WAS A GRACIOUS NOVELTY

FIRST PRINTED ∽ 04 – 25 – 93

"*Sunday driver!*" my father would growl irritably, his car trapped in a lane behind a timid motorist, cruising at a daring 20 mph.

Years ago, Dad's reference described the many car operators who took to the roads once a week — on Sunday afternoons. This weekly drive was an American institution when I was a kid, a time when the automobile was a gracious novelty, before it dominated life.

"Let's go to Lockport today!" my Dad would suggest. He liked to have a target for the Sabbath trip. On Sundays in nice weather, I can easily recapture my boyish feelings.

I'd climb up from the running board into the front seat beside my father, because that's where men belonged — near the gauges and controls, concomitant with now departed male supremacy.

The ladies, my mother and assorted aunts, would roost demurely in the Buick's comfortable back seat, which was an experience in Victoriana.

Like a living room, the windows had screens or drapes that pulled for privacy or shade. Fastened to the car's upright stanchions, cut-glass vases held artificial flowers. Although the ladies did not smoke, silverplated ashtrays retracted into every corner.

Tiny shelves folded down from the back of the front seat to form tables. In such elegance, the women often took tea from a thermos. If the afternoon was chilly, the plaid lap robe was spread.

Inspection of the Erie Canal locks at Lockport was a frequent goal of our Sunday motor trip. Many other Buffalonians would also turn up there on their weekly excursion.

Once arrived in the lively canal port, we would leave the Buick carefully parked and stroll along the waterway. It is a comment on the pace of our lives that we found operation of the locks exciting.

I remember one especially eventful Sunday afternoon when we watched the other Crystal Beach boat, the Americana, jousting through the canal locks. It had been sold and was en route to Rye Beach near New York City, via the Erie Canal.

If the day was fine, we would picnic along the stream's shores at Lockport or I would coax Dad to drive on to Olcott Beach. Back then, Olcott jumped with a thriving amusement park where my brother and I could ride little electric cars, a Ferris wheel, a carousel.

Many Sundays we simply drove in the country, stirring up dust and cinders from poorly paved roads. On such aimless drives, nothing more diverting happened than my little brother Joe getting carsick or Dad barking out his window at a scared Sunday driver.

It is difficult to fix an end to the days of the Sunday afternoon drive, because some families still take them. But the car has surrendered the sense of novelty and adventure that came with rutted roads, unmarked highways and unpredictable Sunday drivers. ∞

IN REMEMBRANCE OF THOSE WHO SAT FOR THE FAMILY PHOTOGRAPHER IN DAYS GONE BY

FIRST PRINTED ☞ 05 – 23 – 93

In an attic or closet corner, nearly every home shelters a dusty box of old family photographs. Each picture is mounted on heavy paper stock, often encased in a cardboard frame; each is formally posed.

These brittle reminders of a bygone age were all contrived by a breed that is nearly vanished: the neighborhood photographer.

This artisan, who flourished during the first third of this century, usually operated out of a small store which served as his studio.

Inside, the establishment was at least part theater. Like stage flats, there were painted backgrounds of parklike settings with trees and shrubs, of French doors, scholarly bookshelves, cathedral arches or merely drapes.

Such backgrounds suited special occasions because people of that era came to the neighborhood photographer to memorialize someone's great day: graduation, birthday, wedding, anniversary. Landmark events were sealed at the photographer's, as also were phases in child or family evolution.

One made an appointment after deliberation. The photographer might suggest props: flowers, chairs, toys for kiddies. Large groups required special inventiveness.

At the chosen hour, jubilarians converged, all dressed formally: men in pinching starched collars, slicked hair, dark suits.

Their ladies were supremely corseted, somberly arrayed. Everyone looked uncomfortable and unhappy because an air of destiny hung heavy.

The man who never appears in any picture, the hero of my story, is the neighborhood photographer. Like a stage director, he positioned his group; he exuded ceremony.

He pulled out squeak toys to amuse babies; he dredged up awful jokes to divert adults.

The photographer bent behind his camera and tripod, spread a black tent over his head to close out reflections; he clasped a light flash in one hand and camera release in the other.

"Ready!" he screamed, and everybody looked grim.

In my family's chest of old photos are portraits of long-departed aunts and uncles, their children, forgotten cousins.

My parents grin self-consciously on their wedding day.

My sister and older brother stare soulfully at each other, although in real life, they fought together like panthers.

I appear as a toddler, later in a blue serge suit on my First Communion Day, the year 1931 draped over a potted plant.

In the bottom of each photo, unobtrusive, yet unmistakable, is an embossed signature of the photographer. His work will be scrutinized for generations to come.

Few photographers operate on a neighborhood basis now, their function unsurped by Sears, K-Mart or the easy, amateur camera.

Today's ultimate chronicler of times past is the camcorder which catches all sights and sounds, like the gasp when the best man fainted at my daughter's wedding. Such emergencies were never recorded by the neighborhood photographer. ⌒

IN THE DAYS WHEN THE DRUGSTORES HAD CHARACTER

FIRST PRINTED ❧ 07 – 04 – 93

*L*ost in the enigma of history is the reason old-time pharmacies expanded into ice cream dispensaries. Somehow, most corner drugstores, as we used to call them, installed soda bars with high stools and/or tables and chairs with twisted wire backs.

Remembrance of these operations takes me back to high school days. Then a heavy date consisted of a stop at Parsons and Judd Drug Store's soda fountain, after holding hands through a double feature at Shea's Seneca.

My girlfriend would have a vanilla milkshake, always served with two cellophane packs of crackers or cookies. I was a chocolate-soda man, attacking with an elongated spoon the big scoop of ice cream lounging at the bottom of a tall-stemmed glass.

Our behavior was under the gentle supervision of the pharmacist-owner. Like a figure from a Norman Rockwell painting, this archetype wore a white professional apron and green-tipped sun visor.

On somber occasions, when illness had struck home, I would sometimes be entrusted to negotiate a prescription. Parsons was properly solicitous, making sense out of a physician's scrawl.

Being a neighborhood practitioner, the pharmacist generally knew customers who brought in a prescription. "Oh, I'm sorry Bobby's under the weather," he would hum

251

sympathetically. "Well, this should fix him up."

Symbolic of personal service, most Buffalo pharmacies of my youth bore the name of their proprietor: W.C. Dambach, Zimdahl, James E. Twohey, Van Slyke, Herzog, McDonald, O'Malley, Woldman, Anthony, Morrison, Gorenflo, Roger Smith; partnerships like Harvey and Carey, Smither and Thurstone.

Besides ice cream and prescriptions, drugstores didn't sell much: newspapers, magazines, tobacco, candy and chewing gum. Of course, they all had busy telephone booths tucked into some recess, because many families lacked home phone service.

Pharmacies have gone through the crucible of change. Now, instead of the owner's name, they function under the anonymity of large corporate logos: CVS, Fay's, Rite Aid.

Inside they are really department stores, purveying hardware, auto supplies, food, beer, kitchen utensils.

Other prescription drug operations are relegated to an amorphous island of a massive super grocery market. Characterless, they dispense prescriptions with cold efficiency.

Different from my time, the only indication of customer recognition occurs when the greenish face of the computer lights up on discovery of a programmed number. ∞

NOTHING LIKE A RIDE IN RUMBLE SEAT ON A WARM DAY

FIRST PRINTED 07 – 04 – 93

During the Depression, my cousin Elmer was a lucky fellow. Not only did he hold a steady job, but he was the owner of a gleaming, dark green Chevrolet coupe — with a rumble seat.

Back then, two-door cars were equipped with just a single inside seat, accommodating at most three riders. Any overflow passengers were relegated to a rumble seat. This contrivance folded back from the car's body like another door, and when open, resembled the cockpit of an airplane.

I loved to see Cousin Elmer ease up our driveway, mud guard flaps adorning the wheels, silver parking guides jaunting up from front fenders. When he stepped out of his car, my cousin stood tall, like Charles Lindbergh beside the Spirit of St. Louis.

"Can we sit in the rumble seat?" we kids would wheedle.

"I guess so," came the condescending reply.

Several rubber treads guided a passenger steeply from rear bumper to fender top; then, with a precipitate lurch, the climber dropped into sitting position.

Older folks with stiff knees and rheumatic backs wistfully looked on; the ascent required agility and balance beyond their command. Rumble seats were intended for the young.

Once ensconced on the soft leather of Cousin Elmer's rumble seat, we resorted to longing hints: "Gee, this would be a nice day for a ride, Elmer," or "I'll bet a ride in the rumble seat would cool us off."

Despite such subtlety, often Elmer got the gist. He'd settle behind the steering wheel, back into the street, and we were off for a turn around our South Buffalo neighborhood.

253

No king, crowned and sceptered, sat in his royal coach with more pride and privilege than we kids savored in Cousin Elmer's rumble seat. With deference, we waved to friends along our route; such poor things could never attain our majesty.

Pityingly, we beheld deprived forms of life waiting at trolley stops. Strange to notice how the simple folk live!

Actually a rumble seat ride was bone rattling. Passengers sat just over the car's rear axle and felt every bump with the impact of an electric shock. Of course, being young, we treasured every jolt. It was like Crystal Beach.

Our sweep through familiar streets was always too brief. Elmer would slip into the driveway, and the moment came to descend again to a mundane world.

"Thanks, Cousin Elmer, thanks for the swell ride!" Maybe if we piled on the gratitude extra thick, Elmer would do it again soon.

The rumble seat had a mystique all its own. Never does a summer come but I remember, with gentle regret, that I never owned a car that sported a shiny, red leather rumble seat. ∞

FANTASTIC UNDERWATER VESSEL THAT ROBERT FULTON TRIES TO SELL TO NAPOLEON

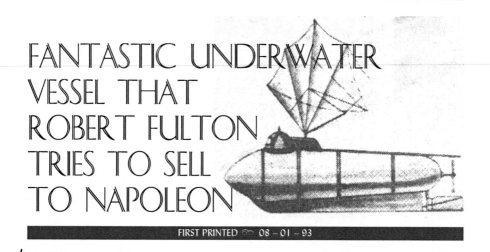

FIRST PRINTED ⌒ 08 – 01 – 93

People know Robert Fulton as a commissioner who helped plot the Erie Canal, or as the inventor of the paddle-wheel steamship. His "Claremont" used to chug placidly along the Hudson River from New York to Albany.

Yet, such gentle facts are only a start to appreciating this remarkable man: part artist, part engineer, part salesman. Born near Lancaster, Pa., before the American Revolution, Fulton first worked in Philadelphia painting miniature portraits on ivory for lockets or rings.

Benjamin Franklin, charmed by his delicate work, secured a grant for Fulton to study painting in England in 1787, a sojourn that was to last almost 20 years.

During that period of turmoil in European history, Robert Fulton changed careers several times, traveled to the courts of Europe, had dealings with some of the era's great men.

When Fulton met Napoleon Bonaparte in 1804, he was trying to sell the Nautilus, a fantastic underwater vessel. This ship, designed by Fulton, was one of the world's first working submarines.

Napoleon was at the height of his rivalry with England, and Fulton explained that the Nautilus could sneak under British naval ships and fasten a timed charge.

Wary of such a crackpot idea, Napoleon requested a demonstration. He agreed to supply an antiquated French battle sloop as target and to have observers present.

It was an exciting show. Fulton and three mechanics boarded the Nautilus at Brest and set sail. About 650 feet from its target, the submarine plunged to a depth of 25 feet.

Manually powered under water, the Nautilus crept beneath the French sloop. From a conning tower, a spike was driven into the boat's bottom; then explosives were fixed to it.

When the submarine had sailed away to safety, a timing device let go and a huge blast tore the empty ship to pieces. Onlookers watched with astonishment.

Despite this dramatic performance, Napoleon remained skeptical and refused to see Fulton, thus losing a chance that might have helped defeat his English foes.

Infuriated, Fulton sailed the Nautilus to England where he performed demonstrations for British Prime Minister William Pitt, who was most concerned to keep the submarine out of French hands.

Continually improving his craft, Fulton hoped to do business with Pitt and the British, but in 1805, events turned against him. At Trafalgar, Adm. Nelson's British Fleet sank the combined navies of France and Spain.

With Britain's absolute control of the sea, nobody had further use for Fulton or his submarine. Discouraged, he returned to America. Although a future as canal planner and steamboat designer lay ahead, nothing was so exciting as his submarine.

Fulton's original ship may have been scrapped in Europe, but at least its name has survived. When the first nuclear submarine was launched in 1954, the U.S. Navy named it Nautilus. ∞

CAN'T BLOT OUT THE MEMORY OF THE FOUNTAIN PEN

FIRST PRINTED ∞ 08 – 29 – 93

*T*he fountain pen, an innovation during my boyhood, solved a century-old problem of calligraphy. Now, the writer was freed from dependence on straight pen and ink pot.

If the owner merely submerged his fountain pen's point into an ink bottle and pumped a lever, he could draw a ration into the pen's rubber cartridge: enough ink to keep an ordinary writer supplied for days.

Early fountain pens were about eight inches long, twice as fat as a pencil, with a barrel top protecting the point. The unit clipped neatly at a pocket edge.

Of course, being a mortal contrivance, the fountain pen was beset with the failings of all gadgetry. It ran dry or, conversely, when overfed, belched out blots of sooty ink.

Sometimes a bladder burst and the owner would find his inside pocket soggy. Investigation revealed that an unsightly glob of ink had soaked right through to an undershirt or into a purse's lining. Such incontinence was typical of cheaper fountain pens.

Associated with adult activity, the fountain pen was a frequent gift for the graduate. Neatly packaged in a long narrow box, it was a token of maturity. To use one was to enter a new, a more responsible phase of life.

Brand names were significant: The phrase "Parker Pen and Pencil Set" fell prestigiously from the tongue. For years, I scribbled proudly with a black Waterman pen my parents gave me for grade school graduation. Later, a smart Esterbrook line appeared on the market.

Varying point sizes were available according to preferred density. Women with dainty script inclined to a fine nib; authority figures generally leaned to a broad point, laying a heavy trail of ink.

A team of auxiliaries surrounded the fountain pen. Bottles of ink had to be readily available; some, like Squib, were popular because they provided a glass cup at bottle top just large enough for the pen's tip. Blotters were in steady use to daub droplets from the pen collar, as well as to prevent smudging of damp ink.

In those years teachers proctoring examinations were harried as they hustled around a testing room, giving drink or first aid to defective or nervous fountain pens. I vividly recollect emergency treatment for students whose pens had suddenly spewed fresh ink on hands, paper and desk, causing crisis in the exam room.

For such situations, experienced teachers maintained a reserve cadre of extra pens for on-the-spot leasing.

There had to be a better way, and of course, there was. Fountain pens dried up abruptly with advent of the ballpoint. Today, only a few stubborn people like me maintain a fountain pen, perhaps because they feel handwriting is improved with it, more probably for nostalgia.

Except for our little band, the death warrant of the fountain pen was signed by the cheap, efficient ballpoint. ∞

GRAVEYARD OF DEPARTED GROCETERIAS GETTING CROWDED

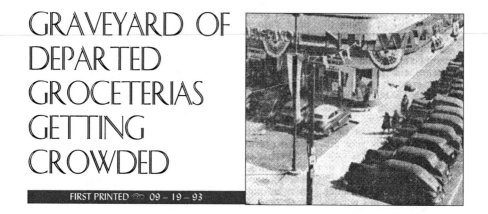

FIRST PRINTED ⌒ 09 – 19 – 93

ven as Bells grocery markets fade into history, Western New Yorkers can hear reverberations.

Shoppers recall Bells private labels such as President's Choice; advertising ploys: the cute colonial kid called Bill Bell; the silhouette of a massive bell.

Passing and replacement of this food chain awaken memories of bygone markets whose logos and promotional verve once livened local bargain hunts.

When I was a boy, the leading grocery distributors in these parts were the A & P, Danahy-Faxon and Loblaw's.

By modern standards, individual stores were definitely dinky: smaller than contemporary 7-Elevens, and generally the store manager helped wait on customers.

Shoppers carried brief lists that they read across the counter.

"Two cans of corn," said the customer.

In response, the clerk turned to the shelves behind him and clunked down the pound cans on the counter.

"A box of Post Toasties."

Since breakfast cereals were light and easily stacked, they were piled toward the ceiling. To snare them, the clerk used a pole with a claw at its end.

After items were assembled on the counter, pencil and note paper came into play for checkout.

A & P developed a whole family of products. Some names hinted at the A & P initials: Ann Page, Jane Parker. Others were orphans with no identifiable affiliations: Iona, Sultan.

Likewise, Loblaw's, whose stores were done out severely in white and

259

black, had produced its private brand lines: Edgebrook, Orchard Park. Danahy-Faxon featured the Red and White label.

Toward the end of the Depression, the self-service concept was catching on, as stores groped to cut costs.

My mother used to dispatch me to a new Mohican Market on Seneca Street (logo naturally was an Indian profile), which I considered great fun.

With a shopping basket, I strolled among rows of cartons (not shelves) picking out Mother's choices, carefully selected from newspaper ads.

"Pork and Beans, 10¢; Wheaties 13 oz. 17¢," read the meticulous, maternal script. "Pound of peanut butter." For this item, I carried my own container to a swelling vat of bulk distribution.

Gradually, regional self-service stores shot up: Sattler's hysterical basement market at 998 Broadway; the Park Edge on Bailey near Abbott.

Other new names surfaced; Nu-Way, Acme, Harvest the Best.

Big discount stores sponsored private grocery market operations: Twin Fair and K-Mart were selling cabbage, hamburger and corn flakes with the rest of the competition.

We learned to "love that Super Duper" and its jolly elephant logo.

The name Bells joins illustrious company in the graveyard of departed local groceterias.

Happily, the new crop of markets, while lacking personalized service, offers a breadth of selection that would have staggered our forebears. ∞

HOLLYWOOD USED BUFFALO'S MAIN STREET TO TEST 3-D WEAPON AGAINST TELEVISION

FIRST PRINTED ⌘ 10 – 10 – 93

efore Hollywood surrendered to TV, it put up a scrap, and one of the battlegrounds was Buffalo's Main Street. This city had been selected to test a new weapon called 3-D.

In the early 1950s, alarmed at dwindling theater audiences, West Coast moviemakers had resurrected an old invention to heighten audience interest. By photographing scenes with twin cameras, a three-dimensional (3-D) aspect could be achieved.

Thus, a pitcher might hurl his baseball at the trick camera; when projected on screen, the missile would seem to be darting straight at a viewer. Shrieks and screams in a theater proved that the illusion was compelling.

Since infant television with its tiny screens could never create this effect, Hollywood studios sensed opportunity to reclaim their diminished crowds.

One inconvenience for viewing: The audience had to wear special glasses, one lens red, the other green, to release the third dimensional image. These eye pieces were distributed with tickets.

Chosen among large cities to pilot 3-D in spring 1953, Buffalo awaited **261** arrival of the first full-length movie using the novel process. "Bwana Devil" opened at the Paramount Theater (a name recently changed from Great Lakes) amid appropriate hype.

A lackluster film, "Bwana" did have some startling effects. Roaring lions seemed to lunge at startled spectators; African tribesmen flung spears which appeared to sail into the theater.

More amusing than these tricks, however, was the audience itself. Hundreds of people sat wearing cardboard-framed, 3-D glasses, all looking like immigrants from some foreign and idiotic planet.

A few weeks after "Bwana Devil", another 3-D special called "House of Wax" was set up downtown. The novelties: huge chandeliers protruded into the theater; yellow smoke wafted out; hot licks of fire bit at the audience.

Soon most of downtown theaters were competing with new 3-D techniques to titillate customers. Screens were enlarged to expand the 3-D illusion; some theaters installed screens of different textures and tints.

For a time, 3-D controlled Main Street. Here are some downtown theater ads that appeared the same week in local newspapers: the Century, "First Time in Buffalo; Giant Magic Mirror Panoramic Screen;" the Paramount, "First Time in America — Dynoptic 3-D;" the Lafayette, "Giant New Magniflow-Astrolite Screen;" the Buffalo, "Cinema Scope — Without Glasses."

Thus briefly, the battle raged on Main Street as the old Hollywood studios struggled for life as they had known it. Gradually, of course, people wearied of 3-D gimmickry and stayed home to watch their new television toy.

Like most battles, the 3-D fight took a few years to show its full results. When the dust cleared it was evident: One, that the era of the big downtown theaters was over; two, that TV was America's victorious entertainment medium. ∽

THE WOODEN MATCHES THAT BROUGHT SPARK INTO OUR LIVES IN THE DAYS GONE BY

FIRST PRINTED ∞ 11 – 14 – 93

With the first chills of autumn, I needed a match to start wood burning in our fireplace. Then I remembered: no more matches. Last Christmas, I had received an automatic lighter: I pulled a trigger, and flame sprang out the end of a 10-inch wand.

I felt a certain regret for perhaps the final purpose matches served in my life — matches that had once sparked many daily functions.

Ohio Blue Tip Matches were a staple in every kitchen when I was a kid. Their rectangular blue box, about 6 inches long, had a sandpaper strike piece on its side. Within, like sentinels wearing bulbous, blue helmets, the matches lay in neat uniformity.

Stoves and ovens back then had no pilot lights: to fire the gas safely required a wooden match. Well do I recall the familiar sequence: Mother would turn the white porcelain jet; a hiss, the sniff of gas, then the scratch of a sulfurous tip.

The gas burner poofed into its fluttering, circular arc, and Mother shook out the spent match. Each day, in short sudden bursts of glory, dozens of Ohio Blue Tips blew their tops over the stove.

Our neighbor, Mrs. Bigelow, had a white receptacle mounted on the wall beside her stove. New matches would drop down to a tray where singles could be easily grasped.

On the metal container was emblazoned the slogan: "Light of My Life."

Family members would reach into the match receptacle regularly. Men went there because only an Ohio Blue Tip burned with enough determination to service the big pipe bowl or fat cigars popular in that hardy age.

263

Through the smoke of years, I can see my Dad or numerous uncles holding the flaming stick, puffing, examining the tobacco judiciously, repeating the operation — all with the same match.

Another routine duty summoned matches to the living room. There, mounted in an ornamental fireplace, sat an auxiliary gas space heater. Difficult to reach through protective grills, the gas jets required cooperation from the long match.

Many a crisp evening was made tolerably cozy when the gas flames licked around imitation logs. However, the ultimate test for any firemaker lay in the basement.

Lurking in a dreary corner waited the coal furnace, devourer of matches and human patience. I would watch my father repeatedly stretch his arm into the cavernous fire pit, fingers clutching a trusty Ohio Blue Tip.

I like to think that the main reason matches have burned out their usefulness is that fewer people smoke today. Other causes are obvious: stoves, furnaces, water tanks are all automatic now, each with its own pilot light.

Ohio Blue Tip Matches still appear in some stores, but their modern role is certainly dimmer. ∞

THE TRUTH ABOUT ORPHAN ANNIE'S UNDERCOVER ORGANIZATION

FIRST PRINTED ∞ 01 – 03 – 94

*T*he only undercover organization to which I ever belonged was Orphan Annie's Secret Society. I became involved when I was a kid: afternoons at 5:30.

Meetings were broadcast over network radio. Secret society members sat in tense silence by their wooden radio cabinets.

Based on the famous Harold Grey comic strip, Orphan Annie lent herself to radio drama in the days of children's serials. Voices were easily identifiable: Daddy Warbucks' venerable baritone contrasted with Annie's perky, pipey falsetto. Sandy spoke in a growl or a happy bark.

Like all mysterious organizations, Orphan Annie's Secret Society was immersed in ceremony. Meetings began with a ritual song: "Who's that little chatterbox? The one with pretty auburn locks? Who do you see? It's Little Orphan Annie."

The syndicate behind Orphan Annie's operation was the Ovaltine gang. In the 1930s, Ovaltine was a product, gravel-like in texture. Mixed with milk, it emitted a taste, part malt and part chocolate — not altogether pleasant.

Of course, any veteran of Orphan Annie's Secret Society remembers that the real reason for drinking Ovaltine was to get possession of the precious inner seal.

This certificate was the key to untold treasure. One inner seal secured a leaky shake-up mug, with a picture of Annie and Sandy, for mixing Ovaltine with milk.

But the plot thickened. For extra inner seals, society members received rings, badges, buttons — and the secret code. This latter enabled the user to unscramble cryptic messages, dictated over the radio.

Here's the way the code worked: even numbers 2, 4, 6 etc. stood for letters A, B, C etc. Odd numbers were given only to confuse the uninitiated.

Thus at a critical point in the radio drama, if, for example, a property deed had been lost, the announcer would breathlessly confide: "Well . . . boys and girls, for members of Orphan Annie's Secret Society, I've got a hint about the lost deed...Got your paper and pencils ready? Here goes..."

Laboriously, conspiratorially, the voice intoned the fateful numbers. When deciphered, they would translate to something like: "Hidden under a rock." Wow! That's what it was like to be in a secret society!

For the fun Orphan Annie gave me, I am grateful. I hope after all these years, that I have not compromised my honor as a club member by divulging arcane information about our secret society. ∞

ALL THE KIDS USED TO READ
BIG-LITTLE BOOKS FIRST PRINTED ⌾ 01 – 30 – 94

Astaple in the library of every kid in my neighborhood was the Big-Little Book.

This novelty item earned the oxymoron in its title because of a peculiar size. Although as thick as a conventional 400-page book, the flat surface measured in inches only $3^1/_2$ by $4^1/_2$. The hard cover of every big-little book featured a colorful illustration.

Authors of these publications collaborated with artists. While the left-hand page contained text, the opposite side bore a cartoon illustration.

Walt Disney Enterprises were deeply involved in Big-Little books at a time when Mickey Mouse trapped the national imagination. I recall being fascinated by a fitful story of Mickey lost in a haunted mansion called Blaggard Castle.

Another book, "Mickey Mouse the Mail Pilot," described an evil character (pictured as a dog) who possessed a giant, magnetic web which attracted pilots (all mice) to their disaster.

Other Big-Little volumes drew inspiration from popular newspaper comics and dealt with the folk heroes of a generation: Dick Tracy, Terry and the Pirates, Flash Gordon, Tailspin Tommy, Smilin' Jack, Buck Rogers.

As relief from such heavy stuff, the Big-Little roster also offered comedy: Harold Teen and Shadow, Reg'lar Fellers, Moon Mullins and K.O., Toonerville Trolley.

Issued in Racine, Wisc., by the Whitman Publishing Co. (which still prints inexpensive children's fare), the Big-Little books had a wide circulation during the 1930s. You could choose from wide selections at any Woolworth, Kresge or W.T. Grant store.

Copies were furiously traded among readers in my neighborhood until book were dirty, battered and worn. Even then, we saved loose pages to color the illustrations with crayons.

So fast and frenzied did new titles hit the sales counters that some of my friends became child bibliophiles, savoring vintage editions. Much envied was the collector who filled a shelf with bright Big-Little tomes.

Occasionally, I spot such books at a flea market, and judging from current prices, the child bibliophile could have turned a big-big profit had he saved his Big-Little Books for later sale. ⌾

THERE'S NO BUSINESS LIKE SHOW BUSINESS

From the Bowery to Broadway
Arnold Fields & L. Marc Fields

Book Review by
George Kunz

FIRST PRINTED ∽ 11 – 21 – 93

The comedy team of Weber and Fields is a part of American vaudeville legend. This book, written by descendants of Lew Fields, is of course about their famous relative, but it concerns more than his life in show business.

Early chapters deal with the period of intense immigration after the Civil War, when America consigned many of its new entrants to New York's Bowery. There are keen insights into these immigrant times, and it is touching to savor the deep dedication to work and success with which huddling masses enriched their adopted country.

For example, in his tailor sweatshop, Solomon Schoenfeld employed all his family for long hours stitching, sewing, pressing, basting. He was slow to forgive one son who escaped such drudgery; that son took the name of Lew Fields and joined with a friend, Joe Weber, to prepare comic acts.

Performing in saloons, dime museums and minstrel shows, Weber and Fields eventually were hired to play Tony Pastor's elite variety house. Audiences a century ago loved ethnic humor, and Weber and Fields did stock spoofs of Irish, Jewish, German immigrants.

With a flair for comedy, the boys developed skits, songs and dances, poking outrageous fun at racial stereotypes. Posing as a German, one would say, "I am delightfulness to meet you"; the other replied, "Der disgust iss all mine." Somehow, all acts climaxed in a fight, as Fields caught Weber's neck in a cane's crook and clouted him mercilessly.

Great names and vignettes continually flash across the stage of this book: Lillian Russell, Eddie Foy and family, John Phillip Sousa. As Weber and Fields organize their own vaudeville touring company, they work with Vesta Tilley, the Cohan family, DeWolf Hopper. They negotiate with Oscar Hammerstein, the Shubert brothers, Abe Erlanger (builder of Buffalo's late, lamented theater). Early admirers of their fun included Grover Cleveland, William Vanderbilt and Stanford White.

Lew Fields was a compulsive gambler, but sometimes this trait advanced his career. Ignoring risks, he bought theaters, developed tour companies, backed burlesque shows with titles like "Roly Poly," "Hurly Burly," "Hanky Panky" and "Quo Vass Iss?" (Quo Vadis).

Moving into legitimate theater, Fields worked closely with other legendary showmen: Victor Herbert, Vernon Castle, Will Rogers, David Belasco, Irving Berlin and Helen Hayes.

Although Lew Fields fell out with his partner, they were noted for their frequent reunions, especially when they needed speedy cash. One such reconciliation drew the pair to Hollywood's Keystone Studios, where they performed in frantic, slapstick chases with the Mack Sennett Keystone Kops.

Hard times struck American theater with World War I and the subsequent Prohibition. In 1921, Lew Fields was forced to declare bankruptcy. Yet, indefatigable, he bounced back, starring again with Joe Weber in a new vaudeville touring company. (In 1925, Fields was paid $5,000 for a one-week stand in Buffalo).

As years exacted their price, the veterans found the vigor of their routine slipping. It was increasingly arduous for Fields to do handsprings at age 57; Weber's old head ached with the repeated knocks of his partner's cane.

More glittering names dance over the pages during this vaudeville revival phase; Eddie Cantor, James Cagney, Fred Astaire, a young Rodgers and Hart.

The tired vaudevillians spent their last years in California. There Fields had retired, supported by his wealthy children. (Herbert was a producer of hit music comedies; as lyricist, Dorothy supplied words for Jerome Kern's best songs.) Joe Weber soon followed, lonely for his old comrade.

A final time, the duo was summoned from retirement for a cameo appearance in "Lillian Russell," a film that featured Alice Faye struggling inadequately in the title role. Happily, two minutes of Weber and Field can still be sampled in an otherwise bleak movie.

It is difficult to catch the sweep of this long book, which aims ambitiously to treat the peregrination from the Bowery to Broadway and from one epoch to another. The work often becomes mired in excessive detail, such as laborious retelling of the plot of each show, famous or forgotten, that affected the era in however a peripheral way.

To wade through it completely (as I did) presumes a fascination with American vaudeville, burlesque, musical comedy and the great vanished stars. For such readers, the rewards and enjoyments of "From the Bowery to Broadway" are bountiful. ∞

THRILLS, CHILLS &
CINNAMON SUCKERS

FIRST PRINTED ⌒ 08 – 17 – 80

*C*rystal Beach Day was summer's high point, and like all great occasions, it had to be provided for. My brother and I would scour the neighborhood collecting Buffalo Evening News coupons for reduced-rate tickets; these we would husband like misers. We made lists of the amusements and rides; we decided which we would go on first, which we would ride most frequently. We studied weather forecasts because nothing could be worse than rain on Crystal Beach Day.

Those were hard times — the Depression days of the 1930s — and there were limits on what families could spend for recreation. But we were among the lucky ones, in this respect, at least. For us there was still that special day — the trip across the water, the picnic, and especially the loops and twists and giddy downhill plunges of the rides.

Each year, as the day grew nearer, our happy memories from past Crystal Beach Days grew sharper, and our impatience for the new one increased.

As I recall, the first boat left from the foot of Commercial Street at 10 a.m. My mother would have packed a lunch the night before, and this we carried in a basket to the South Park streetcar stop. Then came the first of the apparently endless waits: a wait for the streetcar and another for the streetcar ride to end. After we climbed down the trolley steps, there was the walk with many other expectant children and their parents down Commercial Street and through the tunnel to the Crystal Beach Transit office. As we emerged from the tunnel, we saw the Crystal Beach boat waiting. Noble and gleaming in the morning sunshine, the Canadiana seemed to me to represent the ultimate in luxury and pleasure.

After waiting in a long line, we bought our tickets. Then began the next wait. Inside a large, damp enclosure we sat waiting, like immigrants, for a cyclone-fence door to be opened. With maddening leisure, the crewmen laid the gangways and examined the boat before finally opening the gates. Then out lunged screaming children with parents in tow, across the planks and onto the boat.

Once aboard, we began our annual boat-ride ritual. We walked along the first deck to see the engine room. Ever immaculate, hot and smelling of lubricant, the boilers were a masterwork of efficiency. Huge pistons began to move, and we could hear the swish of moving water as the boat pulled away from Buffalo.

My mother, with our lunch basket, by this time would be stationed sedately in a cane-seated chair on the second deck. This was our base; here we would meet if we lost one another.

Meanwhile we wildly explored the boat. We chased one another up flights fore and aft and ran along the extended third deck and down the stairway to an enclosed, wood-paneled second-deck room where the old people gathered. Here a certain decorum prevailed, and we slowed our pace accordingly. Behind this room, music played and a few couples danced.

The boat ride lasted about 45 minutes, and that was enough. We had had our fill of darting around the boat by then. And anyway, once Crystal Beach came into view, everything else lost its luster. We could see the sprawling amusement park and hear the sounds of rides coming to life. The huge Ferris wheel was turning; there were high-pitched whistles and toots from the little train, clanks and roars of wheels from the roller coasters.

Then came more endless waits, now all the more exasperating. There was the tedium of the boat's docking. We watched heavy ropes secured about stanchions and the gangways thrown down. And then there was the rush up the long concrete pier covered with corrugated metal, to the entrance turnstiles.

I could never understand the complications of customs. They were an annoyance at best, and we could barely contain ourselves within view of the old familiar rides that we had been dreaming of since we left them last year.

But to be detained only to be asked some idiot questions like, "Where were you born?" — what a bit of adult foolishness!

Finally we were through the turnstiles and in the park. To the left lay the beach. We could look through the chicken-wire fence separating it from the park and see people swimming or sitting on the beach, reading and soaking up sun. It looked inviting, but our interests were elsewhere.

It was about noon, and though we were practically jumping with expectation, Mother made us have lunch. So into the grove behind the restaurant we went.

By this time the amusements were in full operation. There were the roars of wheels, the ecstatic screams of passengers and the merry-go round music. Familiar, newly remembered smells of waffles, hamburger and onions drifted by.

Poor Mother realized the extent of her unpopularity, and in her defense, she tried to make lunch as quick and painless as possible. When we had finished our sandwiches, we were shouting for tickets for the rides, anxious to be off.

I can remember Mother encouraging us to begin with the merry-go-round or the little train. I was puzzled at the time because I wanted to begin with the roller coaster, but I know now that Mother had a sense of climax — and good common sense as well. "Let them ride the gentler rides first or they never will," she must have thought. I understood her strategy years later when I took my own children to Crystal Beach.

So the merry-go-round, always orderly, well-kept and freshly painted, was first. Mother rode with us. She sat on one of the benches, while each of us mounted a wolf, a lion or llama, or one of the animals in the two inner circles where the carved figures bounded up and down.

After that we went on the little train, pulled by a locomotive that actually was a miniature steam engine, fueled with coal. I can recall getting hot cinders in my eyes, in spite of the grids behind the engine and in front of many cars that were supposed to trap the flying specks. Smiling approvingly, Mother rode the little train with us.

We then graduated to the more dynamic devices. There was the "Hey-

273

Day," where if you rode in the back seat you were swung around on the steel floor at a speed that made your stomach tingle. Its cars were brightly painted, with the names of autos printed on their backs: Ford, Buick and Plymouth.

The "Caterpillar," a rather strange-looking invention that ran on a circular, wave-like track, was nearby. The cars simply followed the track, but at one point a striped canvas umbrella fanned out over the cars. The ride earned its name because it vaguely resembled a caterpillar.

The creators of some of these rides must have been entomologists because next came the "Tumblebug," which was very much like the "Caterpillar." It, too, ran on a circular track, but the waves were much higher and the tickling sensations more delightful. The Tumblebug had about six units in its train, and they did look like ladybugs. Each unit had a name, such as "June Bug" or "Lightning Bug."

We always rode the little autos, too. The original ride operated electrically on the same principle as the subway. Moving between wooden guard rails, each car had an arm that touched an electrical cable on the side. The steering wheel really controlled the vehicle, and the autos resembled 1930 Chevrolets.

When we were thirsty we had lemonade, which Mother had brought from home. Although the big glass jars of green, red and yellow beverages along the midway were enticing, we knew better than to hope, let alone ask, for such luxuries in those hard times.

As a change of pace, we would try the "Old Mill" — which later became "Jungle Land." Heavy, flat-bottomed boats led through endless, airless tunnels. Every so often there was a dioramic scene with a tired, obviously papier-mache animal or specter making a jerky, menacing movement toward the boat.

One year Mother dropped her purse into the water, creating a crisis. She later would tell the story of how kind the operator had been, taking a net and straining through the water until he raised the lost purse, soaked but containing all its valuables.

Sometimes we boys would look into the dance hall with the large crystal ball suspended from the ceiling. Occasionally couples would be dancing to music from a juke box, and we would mimic them in their dreamy shows of affection.

I never liked the "Fun House," but my cousin Bill who sometimes went with us, did. The ever-turning barrel, which we had to creep through along the course, made me vaguely nauseous, and I never enjoyed the little pranks: the wind machine, the electrical shocks, the trap doors. I could appreciate that it was relatively inexpensive, though, lasting some ten minutes and taking only two tickets.

Mother had once gotten sick on the Ferris wheel and never forgot it. She always found an excuse to prevent us from riding it. I didn't really mind because the big wheel seemed so awesome.

My favorite ride was the "Junior Coaster" now called the "Giant Coaster." I still consider this an excellent roller coaster. It has a frightening first hill and some good turns and dips at high speed. It was rather a badge of bravery to have ridden the Junior Coaster. The "Dodgem" was also fun. Located near the coaster, it differed very little from its descendants, the "Auto Scooters," but its cars were old and drab, and the environs always smelled of arcing electricity.

The ride that ruled over all in noise, size and reputation was the huge roller coaster, the "Cyclone." It was unthinkable that we, mere children that we were, could ride it, but we could watch it and listen and cower before its might. The Cyclone stood beside the dance hall and always seemed to me a triumph of engineering. Compressed into a relatively small area, it appeared as a dark monster, brooding, glowering and scolding over everything. Only people older, braver perhaps more foolish, I thought — rode it. (Later in my career, I became an avid Cyclone rider.)

When evening came we had another lunch, this one more welcome than the first. In the same grove as before, we ate out of the basket that Mother had carried with her all day. We could see the gypsies setting up tents on the periphery of the park, lighting candles, putting up their signs. I was uneasy as I watched the strangely dressed people talking among themselves in odd tongues. Like their tents, an air of mystery settled over them. Lights were starting to go on all over the park. The Canadiana could be seen out on the lake as it slowly approached for its final trip back to Buffalo. The day was drawing to a tired close. Sometimes there would be a few unused tickets, which we would spend in prodigal fashion with one last ride on the roller coaster or the Tumblebug.

One final ceremony remained: the buying of waffles and cinnamon suckers. Waffles were eaten either on the midway or on the boat ride home. But the cinnamon suckers were always taken home with us and consumed as the last wistful souvenirs of a great day.

By now we were much different from the children who had arrived ten hours earlier. Weary, subdued and a little sad, we boarded the Canadiana, taking seats quietly beside my Mother on the middle deck. As the boat brought me back to the real world, I watched the wonders of my boyhood fade from view.

A generation later, in the mid-1960s, I returned to Crystal Beach with my own children. Gleefully, I made my toddlers walk the midway with me. "Here," I lectured, "here, children, stood the Cyclone." And the children had to trace the Cyclone's foundations with their mad father.

"And Jungle Land is really the Old Mill. And this was not meant to be a roller rink, but a dance hall."

At that time the little autos still operated, although they had been moved to a new site. As of old, the Hey-Day and the Caterpillar plied their courses. I had long since overcome my Mother's prejudice against the Ferris wheel and now greatly enjoyed riding it with my children.

The little train was new and diesel-powered, the ride attenuated but acceptable, even though I missed the hot cinders. The Fun House had become the Magic Carpet, but what's in a name? As always, a dispassionate man sat unobtrusively masterminding the electric shocks, the jet stream of air.

The Canadiana had, of course, ceased to run. But we walked out on the pier; and I pointed out the piles where the boat used to dock. I also boasted that I could remember riding on its twin ship, the Americana.

In the days since the flat admission fee and the sound of rock music have overtaken the park, I haven't been back often to Crystal Beach.

But last summer I did return once again, this time to collect my children, now mainly of high school age. I arrived about an hour too early, and a kindly guard invited me inside to find them.

To my sorrow, I discovered that many of my favorite rides have been displaced: the Caterpillar, the Hey-Day — both of which I thought in charity too old to be moved — the Old Mill, alias Jungle Land, the Ferris wheel and the old cars, although I spotted a few hulks used as ornaments in a field. And in addition — is nothing sacred? The dance hall now contains something called the "Jolly Roger" that creeps over the respected floors. The foundations of the old Cyclone are long since pasted over with cement or asphalt.

Two things have not changed. The cinnamon suckers, from the Halls' sucker stand, are the same as ever with their old friendly sting. On the way home my generous children produced from a battered bag some Crystal Beach waffles, which they had bought for my wife and me. Whoever concocted that recipe must have sold exclusive world rights to the Crystal Beach waffle makers. The taste is unmistakable; it is subtle and distinctive.

Many things change as time goes on; many gentle customs are replaced by harsher sights and sounds. But not childhood, not fun, not the love of parents for their children — and not Crystal Beach waffles and cinnamon suckers. ∞

DINERS WERE THE FASHIONABLE PLACE TO GO FOR 'EATS' DURING THE GREAT DEPRESSION

FIRST PRINTED ∞ 02 – 20 – 94

*T*he single syllable mounted on a prominent sign board appears in photographs or movies of depression-age, middle America. "EAT," the verb beckons, pointing to a small diner.

Sometimes, by addition of a letter, the word becomes a generic noun: "EATS." Either form advertised an unpretentious neighborhood restaurant.

Urban or rural, little diners blossomed everywhere. Many had begun life as railroad cars, and after being transplanted from main line to Main Street, they were completely refurbished inside.

A longitudinal counter marked the division between stools for customers and the kitchen area with its constantly sizzling griddle. A few tiny tables or booths paralleled front windows.

"What'll you have?" was the common greeting as a counterman confronted a hungry face.

Food in diners varied from very good to simply putrid, depending on the skills and dedication of the owner. All meals were served from china cups and plates; cutlery was heavy metal, eclectic from dozens of liquidation sales. Tables were covered with traditional red-checkered cloth which, except for emergencies, was changed weekly.

Location, of course, was vital to the prosperity of any diner. To be situated at the end of a streetcar route ensured a regular flow of passengers and motormen. Lavatory facilities provided an additional lure for these transients.

A dining car near a factory or warehouse determined a steady clientele during work breaks, lunch hours and shift changes. It also dictated the spin of the menu.

In college days, I worked part-time as a freight handler at the DL & W Railroad Terminal at the end of the Main streetcar line, where Metrorail cars are serviced now. Across South Park from my workplace was a dining car to which hundreds of us railroad workers crowded daily.

Called "Hank's Diner," this modest establishment specialized in a chili that was so hot we were glad to return to the wintry blasts off Lake Erie for relief. Hank also featured a respectable roast beef dinner. Other entrees were unpredictable and entailed long waits.

From diner's end, a nickelodeon droned a popular song: "They call it the Jersey Bounce/The rhythm that really counts..."

While I dined, I used to study two pictures hung behind the counter. Calvin Coolidge looked sourly from one frame; out of the other, Franklin Roosevelt examined my intake with detached curiosity.

A few such diners still operate, particularly in small town centers, but the steam has been taken out of their business by fast-food operations like McDonald's or Burger King.

These franchised restaurants are all identical in quality. Their hamburgers and milk shakes taste the same, served from disposable plates and cups.

Decor is likewise bland and monotonous. Nowhere worldwide, could a customer attack a Big Mac while contemplating the cold stare of Calvin Coolidge. ⚭

SPRING CLEANING IN THE OLD-FASHIONED WAY

FIRST PRINTED 05 – 08 – 94

*S*pring cleaning was a common phrase in my boyhood. It was an annual event which, in practice, closely resembled a tornado. True, no roofs were swept off, but in its wake, household furnishings were scattered wildly across the ground outside.

After a long lingering winter, a few lovely, mild days carried the suggestion that better weather had arrived, that the furnace could burn out. For the first time in months, windows were thrown open, and fresh air blessedly spun through the house.

"I think it's time for spring cleaning," housewives would proclaim fatefully.

On a pleasant morning, the ordeal began. Stuffed furniture, pianos, cabinets were pushed around so that carpets could be freed. Beds were stripped of sheets, pillows, blankets. Curtains and drapes were slid off their rods. Once loose, everything was lugged systematically to the yard.

Bedding was propped up to luxuriate in the sunshine. Over a network of rope lines, blankets and drapes were suspended to flutter in spring breezes.

Carpets demanded special attention. Recipients of incalculable winter crud, carpets were stretched over a double (for strength) line. From a basement arsenal emerged several carpet beaters.

Resembling medieval instruments of torture, carpet beaters sprouted a pattern of heavy wire growing from a wooden handle. Bashing the wire web against a worn rug produced massive clouds of smut.

281

"Hit it hard! It's really dirty!" came the repeated exhortation. No matter how dedicated the carpet's punishment was, continued whacking evoked additional gasps of soot.

Wielders of the beater, often overcome by spasms of coughing, worked in relays.

Inside the house, meanwhile, with pails and scrub rags, a crew labored at floors, chairs, windows, shelves. Endless boxes of Spic and Span cycled from package to pail, from mop to drain. We were like souls possessed in this furious ceremony of the season.

What was the reason for such mad disruptions? Why this insane compulsion to spring clean? Basically, there were two factors: first, vacuum cleaners were ineffective weaklings. Although massive in size and noise, their suction power was puny.

Then, there was that fuming monster lurking in the basement: the coal furnace. Whatever that brute did not give in the way of heat, he assuredly belched up in mighty expulsions of grime, gas, dirt, ash, into living quarters. These demons had to be exorcised in the annual rite of spring.

All day, the orgy continued: finally toward evening, life returned to the expunged house. Rugs were relaid; furniture repositioned; chattels restored to their former places.

After the day's devastation, the house did smell good with a combination of soap and fresh air. Spring cleaning, like some ancient magic, had cast its spell. ∞

J.P. MORGAN TRIED IN VAIN TO ESCAPE FROM HIS RIDICULOUS NOSE

FIRST PRINTED 🙟 06 – 05 – 94

Although legendary financier J.P. Morgan could sniff out multi-million dollar investment profits, his nose was of no help.

In fact, except for Cyrano, no man suffered more for a nose.

Morgan's proboscis, butt of endless editorial cartoons, was no laughing matter to its owner. Of huge, flamboyant dimension, it extended bulbous and livid red. When he was a young man, the Wall Street tycoon was afflicted with acne rosacea, a skin condition that left his nose the color and texture of a strawberry.

A constant traveler, Morgan had sought medical help in every section of the world. Doctors were unable to offer any comfort other than the advice that he alter personal habits. J.P. Morgan was accustomed to smoking about 30 fine Havana cigars each day. He loved generous bumpers of brandy after heavy, rich meals. Doctors shook their heads disapprovingly.

Each spring, Morgan sailed to Europe on his private yacht, the Corvair, along with a 69-man crew; frequently his peregrinations drew him across the Mediterranean to Egypt. On these jaunts, Morgan denied himself none of the pleasures that contributed to the nasal problem.

J.P. was also renowned for the beauty and style of his many mistresses, including stunning showgirls like Lillian Russell and Maxine Elliott. His lavish generosity helped such companions to forget the ridiculous nose.

Because of his disfigurement, Morgan shunned photographers and declined to have any artist do his portrait. Toward the end of his life, however, he submitted to a three-minute session with photographer Edward Steichen.

The famous portraitist would always recall Morgan's "blazing dark eyes" and "huge, deformed, sick, bulbous nose."

To hide this, Steichen used shadow skillfully and retouched his negatives, thereby obscuring "the monstrous organ."

283

Morgan grudgingly approved the result, leaving a $300 tip.

Wielder of fabulous corporate power, friend of kaisers and kings, collector of exquisite rare books and paintings, J. Pierpont Morgan was tall and imperial. Yet all these attributes could not conceal that clownish nose. ∞

THE SPIRIT OF CHRISTMAS PRESENTS

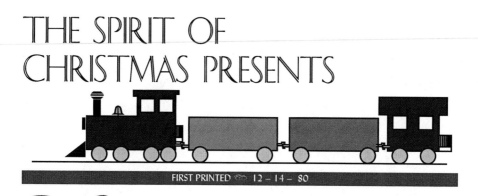

FIRST PRINTED ∞ 12 – 14 – 80

When I was a boy, Christmas of course meant presents to me, but the actual opening of the gifts was only a part of a wonderful season. Before the great day there were the weeks of mounting excitement, always heightened by the trip downtown to wander the toylands of Hengerer's and AM&A's and all the others, to listen to the Christmas bells and Kobacker's monotonously laughing Santa, and to hope. After the holiday, there were the days of delighted play with the new possessions.

And usually my fondest hopes in those early December days of the 1930s — and my greatest pride in each succeeding January — had something to do with an electric train.

The brightly decorated stores of the Christmas season were full of alluring playthings for my younger brother and me to gaze at, but there was always something special about electric trains. They were like no other toys, not only because they offered, in miniature, some of the glamour of the great trains that were so much a part of Buffalo life in those days, but also because they extended the range of play.

An electric train, if you had the right one, was a toy of great possibility. It could be the center of infinitely variable scenes and fantasies and plots. And it extended and expanded the versatility of other toys as well. Toy soldiers could ride in the cars; big building blocks could be stacked into tunnels and bridges; Lincoln logs and miniature building sets made perfect freight.

All of this was possible, that is, if you had the right train. For several years, unfortunately, I did not.

In my early boyhood, I had inherited from an older relative a massive red, large-standard-gauge Lionel engine, with a train of several red Pullman cars. However, the engine was a source of fury to me; it never worked. One Christmas I was presented with a shiny green observation car to add to this old

285

train. The car was manufactured by the Ives Toy Company, and on its side it bore the lie: "Ives Toys Make Happy Boys." It did not make me happy; rather it added to my frustration, because to move, it needed a working engine. Mine would only sputter, struggle a few inches forward and smoke ominously. Furthermore, in trying to remedy its ailment, I received a series of electrical shocks.

As the Christmas after the year of the Ives car drew closer, my desire for a new train grew fierce. I knew my parents realized my unhappiness at having to push my cars manually around the tracks, and even though it was then the heart of the Great Depression, I dared to hope their sympathy would overcome the financial difficulties and I would find the train of my dreams under the Christmas tree.

That year, like every other, eventually brought the pre-Christmas trip downtown.

Main Street was designated "Santa Claus Lane" for the season, and the electric street lamps were colorfully decorated to heighten the festive atmosphere. I remember make-believe lamplighters making rounds at twilight, dressed colorfully in Colonial costumes, moving with lighted poles from one street lamp to the next. The lamplighters, really students hired for the season, pretended to go earnestly about their duties despite the obvious absence of real flame, and they mightily impressed my brother and me.

Every department store had its own distinctive personality. J.N. Adam, in the present AM&A's building, held one definite attraction: its sixth-floor toyland. As soon as I emerged from the elevator, I could hear (I can hear it still, in my imagination) the dings, chimes, chugs and hums of toys. Festooned with tinsel, the room was a whirl of activity. Early versions of Fisher-Price toys were mounted counter-high over an endlessly moving circular belt. This arrangement caused the toys' wheels to turn and to emit the festive dings from their tiny mechanisms. It was clear even then that those primitive Snoopy Sniffers and other push toys were destined to make a mark in the toy world.

But on a platform in one corner, I saw the display most magnetic to me. I watched the sleek, serious-looking electric engines pulling their trains through tunnels, across bridges, up hills.

Outside again on "Santa Claus Lane," we passed Lafayette Square and the old Buffalo Public Library on our way to Hengerer's, where each door was richly ornamented with wreaths. In my eyes, Hengerer's most important specialty was toy soldiers. On the first floor there were extravagant displays of W.H. Britain lead soldiers. Set inside heavy oak counters, they represented many eras. There were French soldiers of the time of Napoleon; American fighting men from the War of 1812; British grenadiers, relics of the years of empire. All would have ridden beautifully, I knew, in miniature gondola cars.

Adam, Meldrum and Anderson's, situated then on the west side of Main Street across from its present location (on a site from which Abraham Lincoln once spoke), was renowned for its Christmas window displays. This time the imaginatively conceived display was on a "Santa's Workshop" theme, with elves working spiritedly in front of an approving Santa. Several windows showed toys only, and my brother and I gazed inside these long and intently, making countless mental notes of Christmas requests.

AM&A's had a cafeteria in its basement with swiveling chairs mounted on posts, and this was an important stop on our itinerary. I selected a chocolate soda and reached with a long spoon into the tall glass, all the while keeping a watch on yet another toy-train layout, this one in the AM&A basement toyland.

My favorite store, though, was S.O. Barnum's, which was on the east side of Main between Swan and Seneca. For many years before he opened his own business, my father had worked for Barnum's as a buyer, and now he was always our tour guide there. To Barnum's we came that Christmas — with the implied arrangement, as usual, that by making hints, we children would be selecting our own Christmas gifts. In the past, what we most admired had often had a happy way of turning up under our tree on Christmas morning.

With much ceremony, Dad opened Barnum's heavy door, ornamented with holiday decor. "Come on in, boys," he said loudly to my brother and me.

Splendid for Christmas, Barnum's had counters on the left with toy soldiers made of plaster-of-paris. Lifelike, they stood in various groupings, the price of each on a gummed label before him.

Nearby were Western-style models, and discreetly, my brother said to Dad, "I like the covered wagon set with the mules, but it's so expensive."

Dad gave a pointed "Uh-huh," and we knew Joe's preference had been recorded.

"Do you want to go downstairs to look at the electric trains?" Dad asked.

Down the creaky wooden steps we walked. All around us, bullet-like capsules shot through pneumatic tubes, carrying money and records of business transactions. Then, on a wooden shelf in the basement, I saw a Union Pacific Streamliner, canary yellow with brown. This Lionel train was 0-Gauge in size and consisted of just three elongated units. I gasped in wonder and knew that my father noted my pleasure. This was the train of my dreams.

That Christmas my parents, who could ill afford it, presented me with the yellow streamline train.

This should, perhaps, be the end of the story. The train, satisfyingly different from its predecessor, ran flawlessly. My dream was realized, and perfect happiness could be expected to ensue.

But alas, the truth is that things didn't quite work out that way. Very quickly, there were two important objections to the streamliner, one my mother's and the other mine.

My mother had been led to believe that this train could be compressed into a small section of the living room, perhaps (an old dream) that it could even run cozily around the Christmas tree. Actually the span of the Union Pacific model suggested the broad West over which its prototype ran. To mother's chagrin, the entire room was dominated. The train ran in and out, among and under chairs. It seemed to be everywhere.

The other objection, my own, arose from the disappointment of my hopes for switches or cars that would adapt to different imagined situations, carrying toy soldiers or cargo of some sort. The streamliner was beautiful but did not lend itself to my patterns of play. What I wanted was a freight train like the ones I used to see when we went out driving in the country — the kind from which engineers waved to us. This streamliner was too impersonal, with no sign of people.

My childhood friend, Charlie Bigelow, had an American Flyer freight train with which he and I played tirelessly. I wanted something like that.

Another year passed, and soon there was other ceremonial trip to Barnum's where Dad renewed annual Christmas greetings to his friends and took us on our tour. By this time my younger brother Joe was ready to point out the toy that, in the old tradition of older brothers, I had prepared him to signify his deep desire for. The train I wanted. In Barnum's basement that year, there was a big table covered with electric trains and their accessories. One train, which was purring through tunnels, activating crossing rails and showing evidence of great purpose, was a freight train of five pieces: engine and tender, tank car bearing the Sunoco logo, a flat car carrying timber and shining red caboose.

Brother Joe and I gasped our delight together. Dad got the message, and when Christmas came, there was the new Lionel freight train set for us. The beautiful but joyless Union Pacific streamliner hummed off into oblivion.

And now the story does wind happily toward its end, because we had fun beyond measure with this new train. The set fit neatly into a small oval of our dining-room floor, and each Christmas we were given additional cars for our new engine to pull or new accessories to complement it. One year we received a boxcar painted a brilliant yellow (so immaculate a boxcar never rolled on the rails); another year, a gondola, especially welcome because in it we could transport soldiers or tiny barrels, suitcases or steamer trunks.

There was also the year we received the automatic gateman. Whenever the train approached his shanty, the door sprang open, and the gateman, perfectly groomed always in his dark blue suit, popped out, waving his warning flag.

The Lincoln Logs Company used to sell a set of sturdy figures to fit a railroad situation, and eventually we had those, too: a conductor consulting his watch, a passenger carrying a Gladstone bag with whom my brother Joe always identified in play. (Perhaps it was a harbinger, since Joe is now a Buffalo physician who bears his medical instruments in a small Gladstone bag.)

Though we often had the train out at other times, it was always set up for Christmas, and I will always think of it primarily as a Christmas toy. New Christmases brought new additions to it and for a while after each Christmas it would still be set up, its new refinements still novel and exciting.

And then, at the melancholy end of every Christmas season, my brother and I would take our electric train apart, wrap each car affectionately in newspaper and return it for storage to its box. In a way, taking the train apart was like taking down the Christmas tree — a sign that the magic season was past.

I am glad we packaged our railroad cars so carefully because I still have some of them, and they still gleam. When my first child, a son, was born, I was overjoyed at having an excuse to get out my old toys and to bring my rare stock back to operational strength. This I did with dedication, and by the time my son was old enough to appreciate it, we had miles of track, new engines pulling the old cars and switches sending trains off in all directions. On his second birthday we even had a freight train chugging around our Christmas tree.

My brother Joe and I, ever the best of friends, often chuckle over recollections of our childhood playthings. Our wives have grown accustomed to this, and they wait tolerantly until the fits pass. I suppose they realize that we are just middle-aged boys and that as such, we are entitled to think sometimes about toys, especially toy trains, and especially at Christmas. ∽

DRY DAYS & THE ORLEANS

FIRST PRINTED ∞ 08 – 29 – 82

*T*his most dismal ferry brightened a sober period of history in Buffalo.

In the days of passenger steamers, Buffalo was host to many graceful ships. During the summer, the North West and its sister ship, the Northland, used to stop here on lake cruises; another pair of beautiful sisters, the North and South America, sailed from Buffalo to Great Lakes ports. There were the "D & C" boats, their initials standing for their destinations, Detroit and Cleveland. There was the beloved Canadiana, which sailed to Crystal Beach.

Then there was the Orleans. For more than 30 years, this passenger ferry returned to its pier at the foot of Ferry Street each April after a winter hiatus, ready to cross the Niagara River between Buffalo and Fort Erie, back and forth. Its range was as limited as its beauty.

The Orleans always listed lopsidedly. Rather than sailing, it staggered like a drunkard. The engines clanked and wheezed unhealthily, as though the ship's superstructure were in danger of shaking apart. The very idea of this tub challenging the rapid currents of the mighty Niagara was laughable. But the Orleans was always something of a clown. In the days before great bridges like the Peace Bridge or the Grand Island bridges, Western New York had an insatiable need for ferry boats to connect it with Canada.

In the 1920s, Buffalo had special need for international ferries. Right after World War I, the American Congress had passed a new law, called the Volstead Act, which quickly became the 18th Amendment to the Constitution.

Buffalonians, like other Americans, suddenly realized the extent of what Congress had wrought. It had become illegal to buy or sell any intoxicating beverage. In plainer words, no longer could there be champagne toasts at weddings or cocktails before dinner in restaurants. Worse still, on hot summer days, after slow, stifling hours at the office or factory, there was no longer any cold beer to drink. It was Prohibition.

The most obvious haven for Buffalonians in such an emergency was its international next-door neighbor, Canada. The "noble experiment" in enforced abstinence from alcoholic drinks drove many Americans to nearby Fort Erie, where beer still flowed cool and abundant.

How handy the proximity to Canada! How downright pleasant, on sizzling August days, simply to take a short ferry ride across the Niagara River to Canada — if only a ferry were large and spacious enough to accommodate the increasing number of travelers! Enter the Orleans to fulfill this palpable American need.

Like its whole career, the entrance of the Orleans on the Buffalo scene was comical. Imagine thirsty Buffalo beer addicts waiting at the pier in sweltering midsummer heat. Then imagine a rattling tub puffing to the rescue.

Something like that happened. The Orleans had served on the St. Lawrence River and been purchased by the Erie Beach Co. in the Prohibition era. Built in the Gay Nineties, the Orleans had a capacity of fifteen automobiles and 360 passengers. Cars fit on the first deck, lining the sides of the ship. The second deck accommodated pedestrians; there were stationary benches along the walls and movable, wooden ones in the center. From a third-deck cabin, the captain presided. Both ends of the ship were snub-nosed.

For each trip, the ferry departed with high drama: Horns bellowed, shrill bells rang from some unseen corner; platforms slammed, waters churned and swished. Then the old boat snorted off on its ten-minute voyage.

During the 1920s, the Orleans did a brisk, near-capacity business. It began service at 8 a.m. and made two round trips across the river every hour. Its final crossing to Buffalo for the day was around 11 p.m., when it carried the last group of beery Buffalonians to home port. The passengers, like the ship, leaned unsteadily.

The demise of the Orleans began with the opening of the Peace Bridge in 1927 and the end of Prohibition in 1933. Cars became more abundant, and most people opted for speed and convenience, rather than leisure, for their crossing.

Patronage declined through the '40s, except in the weeks when the Fort Erie race track was open. Even then, there were few pedestrians, on whom the boat depended for a profit. The Orleans suspended service in 1952 and was docked on Grand Island, near the Bedell House.

There was a trace of the jester even about the old ship's death. In March 1955 a huge ice build-up in the Niagara River raised up the Orleans and jammed it against the porch of the Riverside Bedell House. There it rested, like one old lady sitting wearily in the lap of another.

Crippled and useless as it was, the Orleans was not permitted a noble retirement. It was owned then by Clarence Fix of Grand Island, who turned the ship's carcass over to John Nelson of West River Road for ultimate disposition.

Torches cut up the 200 tons of iron work that made up the Orleans. This was sold for scrap metal. What remained — the benches, floor planking, and captain's cabin were hauled to the beach and burned.

Grim though the ending had been, there was occasion for an ironic smile. For, like an ancient Greek warrior, the old Prohibition tub had been accorded the dignity of a formal immolation. ∞

REMEMBERING THE ERLANGER

FIRST PRINTED ☜ 10 – 18 – 81

*B*efore its final curtain 25 years ago, an elegant theater brought the country's brightest stars to Buffalo.

At the corner of Delaware and Mohawk, inside the very walls now enclosing offices of investment brokers, attorneys and insurance companies, there stood the Erlanger Theater. The Georgian style of its facade is still handsome, like something sketched in England by Sir Christopher Wren, and for many Buffalonians who pass it

daily and enter through its aluminum and glass doors, it has become the 120 Building.

For others, it will always be the Erlanger.

When its curtain fell for the last time, 25 years ago, the theater was not demolished. Instead, its seats, boxes, its splendid mezzanine and its stage were removed. It became an office building. The Erlanger's life had been short, less than 30 years. Like a meteor, it had blazed brilliantly, briefly, and then slipped into darkness.

Seats in the Erlanger were not luxurious; leg room was not spacious. There were posts in the orchestra section that partially blocked the view. But the Erlanger had a majestic dignity, a responsible pride in its classic tradition.

It had obviously been designed for only one purpose: professional, live theater. Whenever it was used for some other medium — films, for example — things were not quite right. It was like hearing a banjo played in church or sipping white wine by candlelight at Burger King; somehow the two did not mix.

In its prime, there was about the Erlanger just a suggestion of the shabbiness that characterizes some great theaters. The mirrors could have used a **293** little more polishing; carpeting soon showed signs of wear. When you walked in, the Erlanger seemed to be a little of the Broadway theater spirit transported to Buffalo.

Construction of the Erlanger was undertaken by Hotels Statler Inc., and it was designed by Warran and Witmore, the New York City architects who had also planned the Statler Hotel in Buffalo and Grand Central Station and the Biltmore and Commodore hotels in New York City.

If you can still observe a harmony in appearance between the Erlanger building and its hotel cousin across Delaware Avenue, this is no mere coincidence; theater and hotel were intended to complement one another.

After its construction, the theater was leased to Abraham Lincoln Erlanger, the somewhat reticent owner of a theater chain. Erlanger gave his name to the theater but otherwise shunned publicity, wishing to have attention focused instead on his stage personalities. He insisted, with an insouciance that now seems quaint, that in his theaters there would be "purity at any price." He was, he said, willing to sacrifice profit in the interest of moral standards.

The Erlanger Theater opened Sept. 4, 1927, with Fred Stone in a musical called "Criss Cross," featuring songs by Jerome Kern. The city's popular mayor, Francis X. Schwab, had been given complimentary, bronze-plated tickets for Box No. 1 to take his wife and seven children.

It promised to be a great opening. And it was. Both marquees, the main one on Delaware and the one on the Mohawk side, were festively lighted. Through the heavy, brown mahogany doors passed Buffalo theater-goers, anxious for a first look at their new 1,500-seat theater.

No one was disappointed. The lobby walls made generous use of Alabama cream marble; the ceiling was a soft green.

In the theater proper, a huge chandelier, gleaming with 486 lights and clusters of crystal, was suspended from the dome. There were three boxes on either side.

Before the stage was a tapestry curtain of gold and old rose.

In the orchestra pit a permanent house group of eighteen musicians, led by Max Joseffer, was playing.

Stairways to the mezzanine were lined with more Alabama marble; the walls bore crests of America's original thirteen states. The steps were of marble, covered with rubber matting. The mezzanine was like a drawing room of an English estate home, paneled in walnut with cove lighting.

This was the shell of the Erlanger. Inside was the realization of great, professional theater. If you think of the names of legendary players on the American stage, you are thinking of actors who performed at Buffalo's Erlanger.

The grand ladies of the American stage, Helen Hayes and Lillian Gish, played there frequently. Miss Hayes was the beloved old queen in "Victoria Regina" and the unlucky Mary Stuart in "Mary of Scotland."

Miss Gish played in "The Star Wagon" with Burgess Meredith.

On television, we still see the endearing Irish actor Barry Fitzgerald simpering with Bing Crosby in "Going My Way." At the Erlanger, Fitzgerald appeared in sterner stuff: "Juno and the Paycock" and "Playboy of the Western World."

Also at the Erlanger, Basil Rathbone recreated Romeo's ill-fated love for Juliet — Buffalo's great Katharine Cornell. In the same 1933 cast was a remarkable Mercutio, a young actor with an unusual voice. His name was Orson Welles.

Tallulah Bankhead was Cleopatra here. Beatrice Lillie played in Shaw's "Too True to be Good." George M. Cohan starred in "Ah, Wilderness." Eva LeGallienne did repertory: "Rosmersholm" and "Camille." Ed Wynn got laughs in a 1932 vehicle called "The Laugh Parade." Walter Huston sang "September Song" in "Knickerbocker Holiday."

There were others, too: Alfred Lunt and Lynn Fontanne, Cedric Hardwicke, Gloria Swanson, Ethel Waters, Brian Aherne, Fay Bainter, Katherine Hepburn, and naturally all the Barrymores.

For several decades, the Statler and the Erlanger provided that ambiance that made evenings unforgettable: dinner before, or supper after the theater. College boys like myself went to the Statler bar after a 1941 performance of "Macbeth" with Maurice Evans and Judith Anderson. Overwhelmed, we discussed learnedly and endlessly the spectacle we had just witnessed. Another time we stood about the Statler lobby to get a glimpse of Jose Ferrer and Paul Robeson after "Othello."

The Erlanger survived the war years and limped into the 1950s with severely shrinking audiences. Television, because of its novelty, was having serious effects on the size of all entertainment audiences. Traveling theater companies were very quick to remove the weak stop from their touring schedule, and Buffalo increasingly lost shows. The deadly cycle of dwindling audiences and lackluster productions caught up with the Erlanger. Soon the once-glamorous theater had stopped to spurious, non-theatrical uses. My own farewell to it came when, for some forgotten reason, I saw a hypnotist performing to an audience of about 100. I have tried to erase this ghastly, ghostly spectacle from my recollection.

The theater changed owners several times. In September 1941, it was sold to Nikitas Dipson of Batavia, owner of a string of moving-picture houses. In 1956 it was acquired by a Rochester purchaser and scheduled for complete demolition.

There were the usual last-minute struggles to save the theater, which was not yet 30 years old. Groups formed, lovers of theater united, but it was too late; it was the wrong year for saving theaters. Never before in its modern history had Buffalo been without a professional theater, and perhaps no one realized what a serious blow was being struck at the city's cultural lifeline.

Eventually the Erlanger fell into the hands of its present owner who, instead of demolishing it completely, converted the building into office space.

Paradoxically, the Erlanger was betrayed partly by its good location, a factor that made it expensive for any owner to maintain in idleness. Perhaps, too, Buffalo's civic pride was close to its low point in 1956. Landmarks were falling all around us, and with the growth of television, theaters seemed particularly expendable.

The Erlanger was in the wrong place at the wrong time. It was like one of the doomed, tragic characters who used to stalk its own stage, grappling for survival against impossible odds.

The 120 Building lives on, useful and still graceful; live theater in Buffalo is again ascendent — in other locations. But the Erlanger now survives only for an increasingly small group that remembers it in its days of grandeur. Like the passing of a grand lady, its death is a sad loss, and one that merits regret. ∞

COAL DUST MEMORIES

FIRST PRINTED ∞ 11 – 28 – 82

inter is the season for remembering when troublesome King Coal ruled our homes and our lives.

Like an invading army gathering its forces, about to storm a city's defense, winter lurked ready to pounce. Ominous were the scowling, gray skies and then, all its weapons ready, winter would strike. Propelled by the strength of the wind which was its advance artillery, a cannonade of snow began.

The coal furnace in our house had already been started, usually in October. It was our first and foremost defense against the onslaught of winter, and to light it — and then keep it going — was an annual ordeal.

Coal and its attendant inconveniences, in those days a generation or two ago, was as much a part of a Buffalo winter as the snow itself. When some social historian of the future studies changes in American life, I am sure he will record the influence of the coal furnace and its passing, because it had a mighty effect on all of us who tended it.

When my daughter was little, I cautioned her that if she didn't behave, Santa Claus would leave coal, instead of goodies, in her Christmas stocking.

"What's coal?" my daughter asked in full flower of her innocence.

It suddenly occurred to me: Gone are the rail locomotives of my era which devoured coal and belched out steam; gone, too, are the coal furnaces that used to heat nearly every American home. What, she might well ask, is coal?

Coal is getting a lot of publicity again now, in these days of dwindling and expensive oil and gas. Coal is available; coal is patriotic. But for those of us who lived through the era of the coal furnace, the prospect of a full-scale coal revival is not exactly inviting.

Coal season started early in the fall — or even in summer, on the day of the coal delivery. A heavy truck would back into the driveway, and a coal man, black with soot, would fix a chute to the rear of his truck. A terrible racket ensued as a ton of black anthracite slid from the coal truck down the steel chute, through the basement window and into a storage bin. It was both frightening and exciting.

Once inside our house, the coal gathered dust, except for forbidden times when we children played on it, scampering like kittens, mindless of the effect on our clothes.

Nearly every basement held a coal furnace. Because I lived in a two-family house, we had two. Squat and formidable, they reminded me of a fat husband and wife who were feuding and, in their petulance, never turned to face one another. Near the pair were twin coal-bins, black and grimy.

To start the fat, round coal furnace into operation, my father would chop up jagged pieces of wood, saved from various household projects, while I shredded newspaper and picked up wood chips from the floor. Dad, always a careless and over-hasty worker, would usually cut his hand in the course of his work. Indeed, lighting the furnace always seemed to involve bleeding fingers and wood slivers.

Dad would layer a fire bed in the furnace: newspaper shreds first, then twigs and wood chips, finally sizable pieces of two-inch lumber. There was a bucket protruding from the back of the furnace, and this had to be filled with water — the idea being to give the hot air, coming from the furnace, a measure of humidity. A system of chains connected the cast-iron draft door in front and the damper in the rear to a primitive control center upstairs. By manipulating these chains, so legend went, one could keep the house comfortable in all weather.

I doubt that anyone in our household ever mastered this technique. Upstairs we would pull these chains, eliciting clanks and growls far off in the reaches of the house, but our furnace fire was generally roaring out of control when a moderate spell came and sinking in sub-zero snaps.

When all was ready for the lighting, dad would put a match to the bottom level of our fire-bed. Up would come the bright flames, as first newspaper, then the wood caught fire. When the conflagration was at its highest, in would go the first shovel of coal. We would see sharp, blue tongues of flames licking through the coal pieces, and we could smell the familiar odors of igniting coal dust. Henceforth, until spring, it would be someone's duty each day to "tend the furnace."

The consequences of forgetting the furnace were stark. That meant that winter's frosty soldiers would be free to enter the house and creep into every corner so that the home was uninhabitable. So serious was the situation that I can recall once getting permission at South Park High school to go home because I had forgotten to tend the furnace.

Each day, the coal furnace had to be emptied and fed. To empty it, we would take an iron handle and fit it to a rod which formed part of the firebed. By turning the rod, ashes would be deposited dustily on the furnace floor. This operation was called "shaking the furnace," and it often left the shaker covered from the hair down with a uniform dusting of fine, white ash.

Then, taking the heavy, deep-bellied shovel, the furnace-tender would noisily scoop up coal, open the fire-box door and let fly. In went the shiny coal — one, two shovels. A long, appraising examination followed. Was there flame licking through the fresh injection of coal? Had the fire been choked with too much fuel? Many considerations filled the mind of the furnace tender.

Later in the day, when the dust had somewhat settled, I can recall going to the cellar to take out the ashes. Opening the big, bottom door, I would sur-vey the morning's deposit, then take the coal shovel and dig. Into corrugated steel buckets went the weighty ashes; again the entire scene was attended by clouds of dust. Sometimes great clusters of carbon waste called "clunkers" would stick between the rods and have to be pried loose.

This was the era of the Great Depression; we would frequently pick out from the ashes any unburned pieces of coal and consign them to the fire box for a second effort at their combustion. (Some neighbors routinely sifted their ashes, reclaiming bits of unconsumed coal.)

That night, last thing before bedtime, the furnace-tender made his final trip. Again, the practiced examination of the state of the fire; again the coal shovel and "banking" the furnace for the night; A check to see that the water level in rear was adequate and that the appropriate aperture, damper or draft, was open.

Once each week, there was, of course, a garbage collection. Sturdy, wooden wagons pulled by horses took accumulated refuse away. Usually the next day would bring ashes collection. All the corrugated steel buckets were resurrected from all the basements and lugged laboriously to the curbs.

The ashes were heavy. My brother and I would take a handle and so drag the containers through snow to the street side. Another wooden wagon would come by, pulled by another pair of patient horses. A team of patient men, usually recent immigrants who would joke or complain among themselves in a foreign language, trudged house to house emptying the buckets. Of course, both the men and the horses engaged in this project were incredibly caked with coal ashes so that, as a boy, I wondered if they could ever be clean.

Coal was a bother, but it did have its uses, of course. One, as I've hinted earlier, was threatening children at Christmastime. (In my day, they knew exactly how exciting coal would be in their stocking.)

It was also handy, of course, for snowmen. The facial features were usually fashioned by sticking lumps of coal into the snowman's head.

Coal ashes were useful in summer for enriching the soil of the garden. And in the winter, they were customarily sprinkled on people's driveways for traction when the ground was covered with snow and ice.

The storms that brought the ashes to the driveway were not, of course, much different from storms today. Even as weariness with the furnace and the gray skies and the cold beset us, General Winter would group his forces for a grand offensive. The assault would begin softly with a gently falling snow; then, overnight a wind would whip the peaceful flakes into a fury and the winter offensive was on.

For a day or more there would be snowy chaos. Windows were pasted with blobs of snow; school would be closed. While the wind blasted, we would be prisoners, happily separated from the world. Then, gradually, the enemy forces would withdraw, the sun would shine, and facing us would be the task of making life normal again.

We had a long narrow driveway with hedges on one side and a cyclone fence on the other. To dig it out presented considerable snow removal problems, but my father's impatient and hasty character made things even worse than they might have been. He assumed that he could break through nearly any snow build up. Maybe his car would be momentarily stopped, but with a little "rocking," as he called it, he would be free.

Rarely did things turn out so simply. Impatient with waiting, Dad would try to back his car out, and the consequences were always the same.

"Can you guys give me a little shove?" he would call. Dad had a propensity for guiding his rear wheel into the hedges. By now, a bit of rocking usually had ground that wheel through the snow and into the frozen ground. It was odd to find ourselves dealing with mud instead of snow, but there the wheel would be in the midst of hedge-roots, a few dead leaves and earth.

Our first rescue measure never changed: We ran to the cellar and got ashes from the furnace. These would supply grit for traction. The next problem was to keep Dad calm; he always wanted to get into his car and try "rocking" again.

"I think I could get out if you'd give me a push," he would exhort.

A whole army of us would gather. Women, children — the strength of all would be joined to get Dad's wheels out of the snow and mud. "Let's rock her." Dad would holler. "One-TWO; one-TWO."

Like galley-slaves, we pushed for the down beat. The car might lurch a little, and our hopes would rise, only to have them slip as the vehicle slid even deeper.

"One-TWO. I think we're getting her!" Dad would shout.

A cold wind carried the smell of carbon monoxide and a burning clutch as Dad continued rocking his car, shifting excitedly from first gear to reverse. Neighbors and passing strangers, attracted by the spectacle, would help us. Soon it was hard to find a place on the car at which an additional pair of hands might fit.

It was inevitable that with our brigade of soldiers pushing, we must get the car free eventually. And we always did. I can remember Dad's smug look as he finally broke through. "There, I knew we could do it with a little shoving!"

Once Dad managed the apparently impossible: He got a curved rear bumper hooked around the upright steel post of a cyclone fence like a horseshoe around a stake. I thought in my boyish way that we would have to remove the car's bumper in order to free it. But with Dad's directions and the usual human army, we somehow got the car off the fence.

These days, whenever I catch myself lavishing too much sentiment on the past, I try to think of winter. Better snow-fighting equipment has largely removed the desperate ruts which used to torment our cars, I remind myself, and traction mats have reduced the need for coal ashes that we applied to skidding wheels.

To make myself further contented with the present, I bring back this scenario: Waking early on a winter morning, I am surprised to find steam coming from my mouth. Even in bed, I feel cold. Gradually rousing to another day's reality, I hear voices from another room.

"Dad, did you tend the furnace last night?" Mother is asking.

A sleepy voice from my father: "What?"

The insistent question is repeated.

"Oh, my gosh," replies Dad, (who never swore). "I forgot. It must have gone out."

Mother would go to the kitchen to light the oven so that we could have one warm room to dress in. My father would creep off in disgrace toward the cellar to look into the vastness of the exhausted coal fire.

"What's coal?" my daughter had had the temerity to ask me. Coal, daughter, was such stuff as nightmares are made of. It once governed our lives, it seems. And just maybe, it will again. ∞

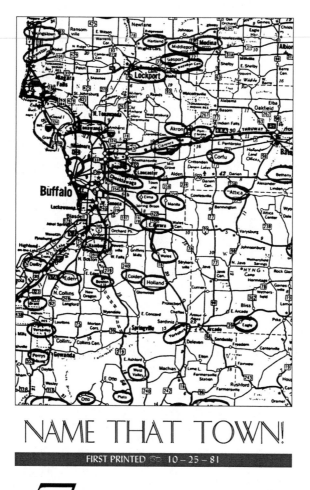

NAME THAT TOWN!

FIRST PRINTED ∞ 10 – 25 – 81

*I*n honor of Founding Fathers, philosophers and faraway places, the settlers of Western New York gave their communities some interesting names.

"Poems with a noble music," Robert Louis Stevenson called the place names of America. "There is no part of the world," he wrote, "where nomenclature is so rich, poetical, humorous and picturesque as in the United States."

The towns and villages of Western New York reflect those qualities so admired by the much-traveled author of "Treasure Island." Their names not only indicate a national and international past, but also refer to the roots of our civilization.

The most obvious source of place names is in the surnames of famous people. Thus, Amherst took its name from Lord Jeffrey Amherst, a British general in the French and Indian War; Depew, from railroad executive and U.S. senator Chauncey M. Depew; Perrysburg, from Commodore Oliver Hazard Perry; Bolivar, from Simon Bolivar, the soldier-adventurer who led South Americans in revolt against Spanish rule.

Sheridan took its identity from the dashing, witty British playwright, Richard Brinsley Sheridan. The villages of Plato and Aristotle pay honor to the great Greek philosophers.

Locally prominent or revered personalities lent their names to other towns: Colden, so called for Cadwallider D. Colden, a state senator; Lewiston, for New York Governor Morgan Lewis; Youngstown, for merchant John Young; Porter, for Judge Augustus Porter. Williamsville, Ransomville and Sinclairville memorialize early settlers Jonas Williams, Clark Ransom and Samuel Sinclair.

Reuben Wilson was the first supervisor of the town on Lake Ontario that bears his surname. Myron Holley of Holley, N.Y., was an early Erie Canal commissioner. The surname of Colonel Joseph Brant, a Mohawk chief, and the first name of Marilla Rogers were appropriated by Brant and Marilla. ∞

"NUMBER PLEE – AZ"

Like Lily Tomlin's Ernestine, Buffalo's "Central" had power she sometimes seemed to wield with joy.

FIRST PRINTED ∞ 08 – 28 – 83

There was once a time when you would take the telephone off its hook and hear not the dull, lifeless hum of the dial tone, but instead a human voice, filled with vigor and insistence. "Number please," this voice would say. (And "Hurry up about it," the same voice would imply.)

You always had your number ready because all telephone calls used to be placed verbally. There was no dial system.

The telephone voice (always female) was referred to as "Operator" or simply "Central." She dominated the telephone system, and although there were many operators, they all sounded the same.

Placing a call went something like this:

Central: Number please. (Pronounced "Number plee-az")

Caller: Fillmore 0749.

Central: Fill-more oh-sev-en-fo-ar-ni-yun?

Caller: Yes.

Central: Thank you.

Little, muffled, burping sounds followed as the operator made her connections. Then it was either the "Hello" on the other end of the line or Central again, saying, "I'm sor-ry. The line is bus-y" or "There's no answer. Shall I keep on ring-ing?"

No one ever saw Central. Like a character in a book or a fairy tale, she had to be imagined, and probably everyone's mental image of her appearance was a little different from everyone else's. I imagined her in an office somewhere, staid and mysterious, listening censoriously to the trials and errors of the members of the human race who incidentally happened to be her customers. Central could, in fact, "listen in" on any call that went through her switchboard. This fact added to the aura of god-like omniscience that surrounded her. It seemed she had an ability to size up any situation and all its implications. Many victims had stories to tell about her powers. I had an uncle who stammered when he got excited. One time, the "number plee-az" situation got to him, and he had trouble spitting out his number. He tried a couple of times unsuccessfully. "Make your call when you've sobered up," Central cautioned — and cut him off while he was still sputtering.

When I was growing up during the Depression, my friend Charley Bigelow and I went through a phase of making phone calls just for fun. We would phone the local movie-picture shows and ask what features would be playing the coming week. We weren't really thinking of going to the movies; there was simply a fascination about using the telephone — speaking to unseen strangers and having them speak back. Everything began with the operator's "Number plee-az," and after a few of our theater calls, she would say: "That's enough of these calls. Find something else to do." One time Charley worked up his courage to tell her it was his telephone to use as he wished. "Listen, kid," said Central. "Don't get snotty. I'll call your parents and talk to them when they get home." That ended our fun for that day.

It would have been hard to get an obscene call by Central. In fact, it was hard even to play a telephone prank. Charley and I once heard from our schoolmates of a terrific joke to play. You phoned someone and pretended to be a telephone company representative. Then you said: "We're testing your telephone. Would you please stand five feet from the telephone and whistle?'

People must have been more naive back then, because when we tried it we actually got some to cooperate.

The payoff came when the victim returned to the phone after the whistling performance. It was then that you sprang the punch line on him: "Use French's Bird Seed," you said cruelly.

After we completed one such sequence, the phone at the Bigelows' rang harshly. It was Central. She had overheard us, and she had one succinct message: She was sending the police immediately to arrest us. Happily, they never came, but Central had thrown the fear of prison bars into us, and we never again dared try the French's Bird Seed routine.

Such lively telephone banter, of course, could only happen when one could get through to Central at all — not always easy if the family was on party line. This arrangement cut costs for the subscriber by enabling him to share service with other families, a practical idea but one that often tried the fiber of human charity.

A 1933 New York Telephone Directory has this advice: "If, when you are phoning, you hear either party come in on your, line or hear successive clicks, it indicates that another party is trying to call. Politely inform the other party that the line is in use and request him to hang up..." The telephone company's instructions go on to describe telephone etiquette and the measures that would promote party-line harmony.

In practice, patience and politeness often broke down on the party lines. Growls like "Get off the line!" " You still talking?" and "Why don't you marry him and save a telephone bill?" were, alas, common. In rural and semi-rural areas, telephone party lines might accommodate as many as twenty families. The telephone would ring all day long, but the rings — in a sort of simple Morse code — were patterned so you could listen for your special combination. You might have a directory listing like 801-R2. The "R2" would indicate that you were to answer only the two-ring signal. Or the last two digits of a four-digit number might indicate your signal.

Your signal was usually a combination of long and short rings (a la Morse). You would listen for two longs and a short, four shorts, three shorts and a long, or whatever your particular combination was.

Unless you were just plain curious, you would ignore all other rings; however, a yen for news and a lively interest in community affairs often prompted rural party-liners to tap in on interesting calls of their neighbors.

Imagine Central's role in all this: She had to have rhythm to knock out the various rings. And she was even called upon to arbitrate party-line disputes that sometimes approached open warfare.

In the city, your party-line status (and the corollary fact that you had to cut costs) was revealed by a letter after your telephone combination. My Aunt Barbara's phone number was Jefferson 4999-J; Uncle Charlie and Aunt Anna were Fillmore 8606-W. When we finally had a home phone toward the close of the Depression, we were Abbott 1276-J. The final letter was the mark of the plebeian, too underprivileged to be able to afford a private line.

I could see Central savoring in a number like that; "Abbott won-too-sev-en-six-jay-a?" she would say, but a sniff was implicit in the "jay-a", showing that she knew who belonged to the unwashed masses.

There was more character still to the telephone numbers that we Buffalonians used to speak out loudly and clearly to Central. In those far-off days, telephone numbers had spark; they were not merely the modern, bare seven digits, broken with one pause. Central demanded telephone combinations that were, in fact, a combination of name and number.

Buffalo had telephone exchange names derived principally from presidents' names or from the names of the city's geographical districts. Way back in the '30s, the names Delaware, Parkside and Crescent in telephone numbers denoted those districts near Delaware Park. University numbers were in North Buffalo near the University of Buffalo. Lovely old streets in the Kleinhans Music Hall area carried the Lincoln exchange. (The Buffalo Philharmonic number used to be Lincoln 5000.)

On Buffalo's West Side there were the Grant, Garfield and Riverside exchanges. East Side numbers were prefaced by the names Jefferson and Fillmore. South Buffalo of the 1930s was all Abbott. In Downtown Buffalo was the domain of Washington and Cleveland. Thus AM&A's department store used to be Washington 4050; The Buffalo Evening News was Washington 4000; Buffalo City Hall, Washington 4200.

Tom Hochwarter, a New York Telephone engineer, says telephone exchange names were not rigid in their geographical designations and that many exchanges overlapped. To us, who spoke them, however — and certainly to Central who listened to them — the association of exchange and geographical area was immediate.

When you flirted successfully with a pretty girl and she surrendered her phone number, you drew conclusions automatically. "University 3613," she might reveal pleasantly, and you inferred that she was from North Buffalo, maybe a prestige address on North Park.

With the rise of the dial telephone, Central's role in bringing speakers together began to decline. Customers could dial directly a local number. Central's role was to make long-distance connections.

Hochwarter remembers that with the gradual extension of the dial system, telephone exchanges had to be dropped, changed and added to conform to requirements of the automated dial system.

Imagine how Central felt when new magic names hit her in the late 1930s and early '40s. Humboldt, Bailey and Taylor were added to the East Side. Bedford and Victoria joined the West Side lineup. North Buffalo assimilated Circle, Amherst and Windsor. South Buffalo replaced Abbott with Triangle, Woodlawn and Fairview.

Suburban Buffalo telephones were another story. Until the '50s, suburban numbers were brief: 145-R, 62-W, 330-W-13, 7-J and the like. Then, gradually, the suburbs developed their own family names: All Williamsville numbers were prefixed by Plaza; Orchard Park became Idlewood; Hamburg was Emerson; Grand Island, Bridge; Lancaster-Depew, Regent; Wanakah, Frontier; the Tonawandas, Jackson and Ludlow; West Seneca, Hobart.

Poor Central! With all these changes coming thick and fast, she must have known that, so to speak, her number was up. The old telephone order was passing; the machines were changing her job.

The final blow came with long-distance direct dialing in the 50's and '60s. Automated switching equipment replaced the human hand that had connected and disconnected voices to one another across the city and the nation.

There's a new generation of phone customers who don't remember Central at all. For some of us, though, she lives on in memory, omniscient as ever and still uttering her all-occasion opening phrase: "Number plee-az." ∽

MY PRIVATE CENTRAL TERMINAL

PUBLISHED IN BUFFALO SPREE ∞ SPRING 1987

*T*he tower of the New York Central Railroad Terminal still dominates Buffalo's East Side. At its base are the vaulted passenger concourses once the gigantic stage, as radio used to say, on which are acted a thousand dramas daily.

When I read recently that this cavernous, but deserted, building had been sold to a private investor, I was jealous: From long habit, I felt that the terminal belonged to me, and no realtor had consulted me about its sale.

My ownership, I confess, was based rather flimsily only on long intimacy. In my youth, I had spent much of my time in the Central Terminal. Like Quasimodo at Notre Dame in Paris, I had grown familiar with the pulsations of the New York Central in Buffalo because I worked there.

It would be a pleasure for me if I could write next that I had been employed as a locomotive engineer, a conductor, a train dispatcher, even a uniformed guard. But I was none of these. Again like Victor Hugo's Quasimodo, mine was a modest position: I was a freight handler.

During my college days, part-time jobs were hard to find, so I jumped at the chance to earn 88 cents an hour. Railway Express Agency was willing to pay this desirable wage to workers who would empty the contents of trailer-trucks onto wagons, drag the wagons to freight cars and there reload the cargo.

Perhaps the gentle past is weaving its magical web, but I cannot recall being unhappy with my lot. Dull though the job was, sooty though the environment and freezing, the winter days, I enjoyed my fellow employees, and most of all, I loved the railroad station and the action that revolved around it.

At the Central Terminal, I serviced baggage cars that became part of the great trains of legend. Through Buffalo's Central Terminal passed the Washington and Philadelphia Express, the 20th Century Limited, the Empire State Express. In a tiny way, I was part of them.

Readily can I conjure remembrances of those redoubtable trains. After I had pulled shut the door on my express car, just before train departure I would stand aside to view the spectacle.

With an enormous whoosh, the great, steam locomotive would make its first exhalation. Wheels turned, cars began to rattle by: tender, baggage cars, coaches, Pullmans. I watched passengers lounging in the club car, sampling desserts in the diner.

When a train had chuffed and whistled away, routine drew us expressmen to the terminal's coffee shop. Once in the concourse, caught in the maelstrom of itinerant life, we rubbed elbows with the sophisticated travelers of the time: lovely women bound for New York City; well-dressed businessmen waiting to leave for the Midwest.

As I walked toward the restaurant, I passed the huge, high-ceilinged waiting room with its murals of early Niagara Frontier history. Nearby stretched the 12-foot-high blackboard, listing train arrivals on one side, departures on the other. To keep this huge board current, clerks were constantly climbing a scaffold, scratching away with chalk.

Crossing the soaring main concourse, two foci fought for everybody's attention. One was the stuffed bison whose glass eyes scrutinized each passer-by. (Difficult to clean, this mighty beast was later moved to Buffalo's Museum of Science and replaced by a metal facsimile of similar size.)

The other attention getter was the massive clock mounted in the middle of the area's largest collection of periodicals. In addition to newspaper dailies from around the country, there were the slick national issues of *Look* and *Life*, *Liberty*, *Collier's*, the *Saturday Evening Post*.

On a separate section lay the pulp magazines: *Weird Tales*, *True Love*, *Thrilling Detective*, *Flaming Western*. Each lurid cover illustration was almost a parody of the publication's contents.

Those were the days of railroad bustle and activity. Interesting or functional shops fringed the terminal's periphery: barber shops, clothes-service stations where waiting travelers could have their hats blocked, shoes shined, suits pressed; toy and souvenir stores, boutiques.

I cannot begin to number the times my brigade of expressmen invaded the terminal restaurant. Sitting on stools at the circular counters, we listened for PA announcements of train delays and planned our strategy for the coming hours.

Although I frequently had coffee with my colleagues, my visits to the Central Terminal's restaurant were not limited to these occasions. After college dances, the Central Terminal was a popular spot for a late snack.

Specific incidents at the Central swell my long familiarity. Late one hot August night, while I was on duty, a crowd began to assemble in the concourse. Spirited people waved pennants, signs, banners.

That night, the Buffalo Bisons had clinched the International League Baseball Championship by winning a game in Rochester. Fans had spontaneously assembled to welcome home the conquering heroes.

Cheers reverberated as the athletes entered the terminal concourse. Somebody had the idea, in view of the large turnout, of bringing the team up to the railing of the mezzanine balcony and introducing the players one by one.

Straight and tall those Baseball Bisons stand in the concourse of my memory: brawny farm boys, overcome with the ceremony, coughing self-consciously as their names were called, trying to say something and having their voices choke.

Last summer, I ventured back to a Central Terminal, now locked and lonely; peeking in windows, I walked all round the outside. In the solitary splendor within, I spotted the brass railing where the ball players had stood. I saw the proud bison, dwarfed by the classically arched ceiling.

By circuitous turnings that I knew from a long acquaintance, surreptitiously I entered the building. Disturbing roosting pigeons, I made my way to the main concourse. All was quiet desolation, only my footsteps resounding along the halls which once throbbed to the cadence of thousands.

On that lovely June morning, despite the neglect about me, I was certain that my Central Terminal would somehow survive. New roles have been found for once-gracious structures, which have fallen on bad times. If the walls of Troy were built with music, Buffalo's Central Terminal is sustained with memories.

Thus, after my initial envy had subsided, I was relieved, even happy, to learn that the New York Central Terminal had been bought by a rival admirer, a man with ambitious, affectionate plans for the building's future.

Such elegance cries out for a renaissance. ∽

THE SHIRT MENAGERIE
FIGHTS IT OUT

FIRST PRINTED ⟨⟩ 02 – 05 – 84

*T*he alligator: Supremely slothful and slimy. Ridiculous with jaws that open like a pair of scissors and eyes half-crossed like a drunkard's. Who would want the likeness of such a creature crawling on the breast of a gleaming new shirt?

Millions of polo-shirt wearers respond, "We would!" because, incredible as it seems when you really stop to think about the nature of the beast, the alligator label is, of course, the symbol of affluent sophistication, the acknowledged badge of prep.

Teen-agers have been known to shear it off worn shirts and transfer it with painstaking stitches to another model. Counterfeiters have tried to pass off fakes in the marketplace. Status-conscious adults also are hooked by the alligator jaws. President Reagan himself appeared at a news conference flashing an alligator on his shirt. In one suburban West Seneca street, there's even a Scottie dog that's been seen wearing an Izod.

But who is this alligator, anyway, that started the whole animal emblem, snob-appeal, cutesy-label craze? Actually he's a French crocodile now nearly 50 years old.

Rene Lacoste was a tennis star during the 1920s, and he bore the nickname "Le Crocodile." At the height of his popularity, he wore a shirt with a crocodile emblem neatly sewn on it. Later, after his tennis career waned, Lacoste started selling crocodile-labeled shirts in France. Still later, in 1951, the Izod division of the David Crystal Apparel Co. imported the crocodile line from France and secured the franchise to peddle Lacoste shirts on the North American continent. It was only a small switch from crocodile to alligator, and voila!

The final step in Americanizing Lacoste's crocodile came in 1969, when General Mills, maker of Wheaties and a raft of other 100-percent American breakfast foods, climbed into the alligator pit. General Mills bought up David Crystal Apparel, including the Izod-Lacoste operation, and put its longtime sales skills to work. The result: mass croc-mania.

So much for the alligator. Now let's consider the horse. On the farm, it was once a trudging, hard-worked beast. But get a sleek model, brushed and gleaming, with wraps on its ankles, put a rider on its back and a mallet in

313

that rider's hand, and you have a symbol of elegance: the Ralph Lauren polo player label.

The horse-with-polo-player is the alligator's main rival. In fact, in many areas, it has outrun its claw-footed competitor.

Anything but swank in his beginnings, its designer, Ralph Lauren, whose real name is Ralph Lifshitz, grew up in a grubby section of the Bronx. As a boy in the early 1950s, he dreamed of climbing out of the squalor and into an exciting, sophisticated world.

"My friends were hoods wearing motorcycle jackets, but I was wearing tweed bermudas and button-down shirts," Lauren says. His first job as a designer was with Beau Brummel Ties Inc. There in 1967, he designed wider ties, and when the style caught on, he formed his own tie company.

What to name his own line? Lauren looked for an insignia that would embody the class and elegance that he aspired to. He happened on polo, that game so long identified with the vigorous, patrician British gentleman. He named his company Polo and devised that player-on-horseback label.

On shelves and counters of many stores, the horse and the alligator come face-to-face in mercantile combat. Sibley's Amherst branch carries both lines, and Mary Berger, manager of the men's department, finds the Lauren line the hotter seller. Although Lauren's basic polo shirt starts in price at $31.50 versus a comparable Izod at $26, Berger believes that the polo horse has more appeal to the status-conscious.

Jenss, which also has both leading names, notices private labels increasing in popularity recently. Also, after featuring the Lauren line for five years, the store is putting the horse out to pasture. It will retain the Izod.

Although J.C. Penney stores do not market horse or alligator, they have spawned an animal all their own. In fact, in its catalog Penney's meets the alligator power head-on and with defiance. "See You Later, Alligator," it taunts. "Here's our Fox."

Pictured in the catalog is "Their Emblem," the well-known alligator, hotly pursued by "Our Emblem," a blue-and-white, full-tailed fox, which embodies the J.C. Penney challenge.

The ad goes on to claim that the Penney fox decorates clothes of "the same quality, fit, comfort, good looks and easy-care fabrics as the well-known brand...and at dollars less."

Representatives at Western New York Penney stores decline to be quoted by name, but one buyer estimates that the fox had been chasing around Penney country for about ten years. "Of course," he concedes, "the fox may be something of a copycat."

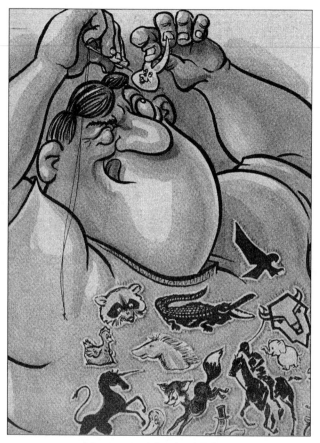

A management trainee at Penney's Seneca Mall store has noticed among his customers "as much interest as ever in labels" but a willingness to compromise for the fox label in view of his more manageable price. On sale, a basic fox shirt will sell for about $10 less than the basic alligator.

Alligator appeal has also shaken staid Sears Roebuck into an animal confrontation. In 1980 the Sears dragon entered the clothing arena. This dragon, not at all forbidding, is a cute green or blue jagged-backed fellow belching two red jets of flame. "You see why the dragon is our symbol for quality at low prices," boasts the Sears catalog. Like Penney's fox shirts, dragon shirts cost $5 to $10 less than Izod's alligator.

To Al Thornton, a salesman at Sears' Eastern Hills men's store, there is nothing unusual about Sears' adoption of the dragon. "It's natural to want a symbol to represent the maker's individuality," Al says. From the sales standpoint, he finds it helpful to assert the store's identity.

Imitation is, of course, a form of praise, and traipsing behind the successful alligator, horse, fox and dragon comes a menagerie of tiny animal emblems: penguin, bear, rabbit, seal, tiger, turtle, unicorn, lamb. Each one signifies a weaver's effort to keep up with the pace.

There are also those who satirize the label appeal and hope to make a profit from poking fun at the whole phenomenon.

There's the "Pig Shirt," purveyed by Hog Wild! of Boston. "What's a fat, pink pig doing on a classic polo shirt?" its advertisement asks. The answer: "Causing alligator tears, for one thing." Hog Wild! carries its joke a step further by offering a new line — the Pork Avenue Collection, with designs by Calvin Swine.

Then there are Rat Shirts, marketed by Rat D'Egout (French for sewer rat) of Cincinnati. Available in five colors, these shirts carry the emblem of a scruffy, long-tailed rat.

Another bit of whimsy, discontinued recently at Jenss, had a polo player riding an alligator. "A conversation piece," commented a Jenss buyer, "which never really caught on."

Perhaps the zoo parade in shirts will have a limited life span, but, like badges of honor, they're still being flaunted now proudly or sarcastically — and firmly led by that king of bestiary, Rene Lacoste's cunning little croc. ∞

A GERMAN NAMED QUINN

The only foreigner in a classroom full of young Irishmen finds embarrassment, confusion — and finally acceptance.

FIRST PRINTED ⌇ 03 – 18 – 84

he Buffalo of my boyhood had no wall like the one that cuts through Berlin, no checkpoints for travelers from one section to another. Yet there were clear divisions, mostly ethnic. Italians lived on the West Side, Germans and Poles in separate areas on the East Side; in the north district dwelled the earlier immigrant families of several origins who had accumulated money to buy better homes.

On the South Side of Buffalo lived the Irish. Proud of their redoubt in the shadows of the steel plant, the Irish supported big parishes like Holy Family. Papal and American flags decorated church and school. But also there hung a green flag with a golden harp, a symbol of national identity dear to the emotions of the South Buffalonians.

By a series of accidents too complicated to bear explaining, my family emigrated from German East Buffalo to Irish South Buffalo. We bought a big two-family house so that Aunt Jenny and her family could live upstairs while we occupied the lower flat.

The year was 1928, and I was ready in the fall to enter Holy Family Parochial School. Once there, I realized from the start that something was differ-

317

ent about me, and it wasn't only the fact that my mother stubbornly dressed me in a shirt and tie.

The ultimate difference was brought out pointedly at the daily calling of the attendance roll. The nun-teacher would read students' names: Kathleen Buckley, Francis Cunningham, Maureen Doyle, Mary Fallon, Robert Murphy, William O'Brien, Patrick Tully...and in the midst of such plain, straightforward names would come mine — George Kunz.

I can still remember Sister Agnes struggling with the accident of my German name. Like their students, all the school's Mercy nun-teachers were Irish, and their pink, sweet, little faces receded into the white, starched wimples.

George ... Kunz. Why did teachers always pause between my first and last names, I wondered? Why did the other boys and girls snicker? At first I was not certain, but I blushed in embarrassment. Sister would smile in her puzzlement at my name and emit a syllable that sounded like "Quinn." George...Quinn. Gradually I came to understand my problem. I was a foreigner among the Irishmen.

Through some form of attrition, I became known as "George Quinn." The other kids referred to me as "Quinn," and I was too confused to put the matter right.

Talk about identity crisis. By day, I appeared just another son of a South Buffalo Irishman: I was George Quinn. By night, I was scion of second-generation German immigrants: George Kunz.

The confusion became too much for me, and I explained my problem to my mother. Who was I, George Kunz or George Quinn? Mother took the course that seemed most reasonable. I was to go to Sister Agnes and explain the difficulties of my situation.

This I did the next day. Sister listened to my peculiar problem, which no doubt I garbled in the telling. Sister Agnes, who spoke with a charming but heavy Irish brogue, decided on a sensible course of action.

After morning class began, she made a general announcement: "Boys and girls, we have been making a mistake about George's last name, and hereafter, we all want to pronounce it correctly...uh...ah..." Confused, she began to stammer. "How do you say your last name, George?"

In front of a large group of 35 grinning, young Irishmen, confusion was contagious. I said something like "Quinn," and I remained George Quinn indefinitely.

My parents were able to speak and understand German, but in those years they retained fresh memories of anti-German prejudice in World War I. They did not want their children to learn the old language, and except when our elders were exchanging secrets, we never heard German spoken around the house. Consequently, and unfortunately for us, my brothers and I learned no German until many years later, and then the hard way — in school.

Our pastor at Holy Family, Monsignor Nash, was a man of great intelligence and scholarship. In his years as a seminarian, he had studied at Innsbruck, Austria, and he spoke German fluently.

Each week Monsignor Nash would visit a different class at Holy Family to question students about catechism, to reminisce about his travels or simply to get acquainted.

Before speaking, he would scan the class roster for familiar names. "Bridget Cleary. Where are you, Bridget?" Bridget would stand up. "I know your father. Is your father still at the rolling mill?"

"Yes, he is, Monsignor," Bridget would reply brightly. "Convey my greetings to him," Monsignor would say with courtly dignity.

Once, our pastor's eye lit on my name. "George Kunz!" he called, giving my name its full German inflection. When I stood up, he continued, "Wie geht alles in deinem Vaterland?"

I was dumbfounded. All eyes were turned on this spectacle. I knew he was speaking German, but I had no notion of the meaning of his words.

"Ich spreche auf Deutsch mit deinem vater. Sprichst du nicht Deutsch mit einem namen wie Kunz?" he said.

Sister Agnes smiled; a few students snickered; I felt foolish and ridiculous. I suppose the monsignor assumed that any second-generation European family in America held onto its mother language.

That afternoon, walking home from school, my classmate Jerry Shea asked me seriously, "What does it feel like to be a German?"

Somehow, Sister Agnes discovered that my father kept a men's furnishings store. Immediately she sensed an important connection; the classrooms at Holy Family School were in constant need of empty boxes to hold chalk, ink wells, dust cloths and the like.

My father was most gracious and prompt to respond when I relayed the request for empty boxes, but somehow I never thought he would make the delivery personally.

One day there was a loud knock at my schoolroom door, and there were Sister Anna, the principal, and my dad. They were all smiles, and Sister Anna led Dad in to meet Sister Agnes. There they were in front of the whole class, exchanging introductions. In either hand, my father was holding a selection of about 50 miscellaneous empty boxes, all tied together with twine.

"Boys and girls," Sister Anna said, "this is George's father. I want you to stand and say, 'Good morning, Mr. ...ah ... Quince.'" She made a real effort because the most I ever rated was Quinn.

Obediently, we stood and chanted, good morning Mis-ter Quince." Dad was beaming, his bald head aglow in the overhead light.

I was especially embarrassed because on a sock box he held there was a picture of a man standing in his underwear, one foot rakishly on a chair. Pipe in mouth, the fellow was adjusting a garter attached to one sock.

A few of the Irish kids noticed this jaunty pose. "That's the way Germans dress," somebody said.

In my years at Holy Family School, I grew accustomed to the humor and relaxed sense of fun so typical of the Irish. I began to love this national group; I still do. Many are the freezing March days when I have considered myself an honorary Irishman and shivered through the St. Patrick's Day Parade, always watching for the contingent from my old South Buffalo parish.

Years after I had graduated from Holy Family School, after the Second World War, I became a teacher myself and was taking some graduate courses on Saturday mornings at Canisius College.

There were nuns in some of my classes, and through the veils I recognized my old teacher, Sister Agnes. Much older now and suffering from arthritis, she turned as I approached her to reveal the same pink face, recessed in the wimple.

"Sister, do you remember me?" I asked foolishly, because I had been a boy when Sister Agnes knew me.

The face, alert as ever, sharpened; the eyes squinted at my thinning hair and tried to remove the changes of years from my face.

"I used to be a boy in your class at Holy Family. My name is George..."

She interrupted me. "Yes," she said crisply. Her expression relaxed as she smiled in the triumph of her memory. "I remember you now, George ... Your name is George...ah...Quinn."

There must be a moral in all this. Maybe it's as simple as the old saying: Once an Irishman, always an Irishman. ☜

MARY JO, SAM SCHUMAN AND THE HOTEL STATLER BALLROOM

PUBLISHED IN BUFFALO SPREE ∞ SPRING 1988

*C*he Statler is no longer Buffalo's finest hotel — in fact, it is not a hotel at all. Several years ago, extensive changes metamorphosed the grand old matriarch into "Statler Towers," a dignified office building.

One day, during the Statler's transformation, an errand brought me to the former hotel. There I found a foyer busy with reconstruction. Carpenters and painters were bustling about as I walked past the once elegant Statler Ballroom.

Although the room was deserted, the ballroom's lights were on, and the doors were unlocked. With a native penchant to snoop, I walked inside. That morning in late winter, the grand ballroom looked much as I remembered it — except that it was completely empty. In fact, all I found in the gold-leafed, Georgian room were Mary Jo McConnell, Sam Schuman and memories of my first summer formal.

Dates — especially to school dances — were rigidly structured in the 1940s. A girl would never, never phone a boy — except to ask him to escort her to her school dance. An act of feminine surrender, such an invitation carried profound excitement.

"Hello. This is Mary Jo McConnell," the telephone voice told me. "Are you busy on June twenty-third?"

I could have answered that no, I wasn't, because my social life as a high school senior was a wasteland, but I did not. Somehow, I conveyed the idea that I was happily available.

"I was wondering if you'd like to go to the St. Mary's Sem dance with me — at the Hotel Statler Ballroom," she added, as if this last fillip were necessary to entice me. Poor Mary Jo, her social life could not have been exactly thriving either, if she was asking me. We had only met at Sullivan's Ice Cream Parlor, and here I was scoring my first big social success.

Quickly I expressed my willingness because mention of the Hotel Statler Ballroom, like visions of sugar-plums for the younger set, brought dreams to me of indescribable glamour. The Statler was storied; it was Hollywood splendor come to Buffalo.

Mary Jo explained her invitation: summer formal; I should appear at her

321
∞

house at 9 p.m., we would double-date with some friends in their car.

Of what "summer formal" meant, I had no idea, but my researches led me to Fifth Avenue Clothes, a business that once thrived at the corner of Main Street and West Eagle.

West Eagle Street has now been covered by Main Place Mall, but if you can, recall the corner with me: Schulte's Tobacco Store on one side, Regal Shoes across Eagle on the other. Suspended, above the door to Regal's was a seven-foot high golden boot, such as cavaliers wore at the time of Charles II.

In the second floor window overlooking the elegant boot was a sign: "Fifth Avenue Clothes — Suits to Rent, Sam Schuman, Prop." It was here that Mary Jo McConnell's invitation had led me.

"Bing!" a loud, grating noise assaulted as soon as the door opened, and I was face-to-face with the proprietor, Sam Schuman. He looked up at me with blinking, myopic eyes, several tape measures hanging from around his neck. Out of every pocket and cranny of his vest, marking pieces of chalk and soap protruded. Automatically, with habit bred of years, Sam seemed to size me up: callow kid, first dance, 40 long, very flat seat on his pants.

"I need a summer formal for a dance on June twenty-third ...at the Statler Ballroom," I added, thinking, I suppose, that an old hand like Sam could be impressed by a drop of the Statler name.

The tape measures began to fly around my waist, under my arms, in my crotch. With each calculation, Sam made a note on his pad with the care of a medical research scientist.

Then I tried on a white coat for fit. I must have been a simple case because immediately Sam grunted with a combination of satisfaction and world-weariness. We made financial arrangements, and Sam explained that a $5 deposit was required to insure safe return of his clothes.

"You vant a shoit too?" the proprietor asked. No, I said, I had a shirt. But did I have a shirt for a summer formal, a shirt with studs? "Vun shoit!" Sam summed up, making a final note.

Walking down the steps, I found myself again under the golden boot of the Regal Shoe Store. My first steps toward an evening of glamour and excitement at the Hotel Statler had been taken.

To tell the truth, I had never danced with a girl to this point in my career. However, I had seen Fred Astaire, and dancing was obviously very easy, but to reassure myself, I had practiced a bit at home privately, holding a broom stick as a partner and listening to the radio in our kitchen.

Nor had I ever had a formal date — although this was not from lack of interest in girls. To put together an evening's entertainment, I felt that I needed a car, and this was outside my reach. No, until now, the extent of my female contact was tablehopping at Sullivan's Ice Cream palace on Abbott Road. It was at Sullivan's that I had met Mary Jo McConnell of St. Mary's Seminary.

Mary Jo was a pretty girl, possessed of a fresh, all-American charm. Her father was a supervisor at Bethlehem Steel and thus, could afford to send his daughter to St. Mary's Seminary. To a public high school senior like me, this affiliation carried untold snob appeal.

St. Mary's Seminary, some will recall, was a preppy finishing school located in graceful, old Victorian buildings at Franklin and North Streets. Their dances were important enough to be written about in the daily papers.

The intervening weeks after my preliminary visit to Sam Schuman dragged on with increasing anticipation until I found myself again under the Regal golden boot to pick up my summer formal.

"Bing!" sang the bell, and Sam Schuman, enmeshed in tape measures, was walking to meet me.

"Summer formal for the Statler," I said, trying to seem knowledgeable.

"We're all ready for you,' Sam said, producing a clothing box with my name taped to it. On all sides was printed, "Fifth Avenue Rental Clothes." On the top was a picture of a young man done out in tails dancing with a beautiful girl whose head was tilted back rapturously.

"Now you get back your deposit when you bring back the suit on Monday," Sam explained again. I paid over some gift money I had been hoarding since Christmas.

A short walk took me to Swan and Washington Streets where the three South Buffalo trolleys used to grind up to their stations. All the way home on the Number 16 South Park streetcar (and those streetcars used to give you a long ride for your $8\frac{1}{3}$ cents), I contemplated the romantic picture on the Fifth Avenue Clothes box. Debonair, charming... that was my idea of me.

A few last practices with the kitchen radio, and I was ready for the real thing. Carefully I removed the summer formal and laid it out on my bed. Tenderly, I opened the starched shirt and practiced inserting the tiny studs where I was accustomed in my rude past only to buttons. Respectfully, I tore the cellophane bag enclosing the pre-tied bow tie.

No one was at home to admire me as I fitted these items of grand apparel to my person, but when I finished, I examined myself in the mirror: hair plastered with Wildroot greasy kid stuff, a double-breasted white jacket with huge padded shoulders, black trousers with a shiny stripe up the side. Elegant, a combination of Fred Astaire and Cary Grant. In fact, on that summer night as I emerged on the street, it seemed wrong not to have a limousine waiting at curbside.

Instead I had to walk to the McConnells' house. Several dogs barked at me as I crossed the street. Mrs. Riley, who never missed anything in the neighborhood, clicked her lips and said, "My, ain't we ritzy tonight!" As I walked through Cazenovia Park, some small boys, unaccustomed to such grandeur, whistled and threw stones.

No matter. I arrived at McConnells', and Mary Jo answered the doorbell. Breathlessly lovely in a gown that showed off her tanned shoulders, she ushered me into the front room. Pretty soon, her parents came in to meet me. They seemed as self-conscious as I was.

"Suit pretty hot on a warm night like this?" asked Mr. McConnell, examining my gleaming white coat. "Oh, it's not bad;" I answered as if in my social stratum I had grown used to such minor discomforts.

"Well, you have a warm night for the dance," Mrs. McConnell said.

"Better than rain," her husband shot back.

After about ten minutes of such sparkling talk, our double-dating couple arrived: Meg Cudahy, Mary Jo's school friend, and her date, a suave college freshman named Ken Darcy. We piled into a big Oldsmobile that Ken supplied. It was one of those big, boxy models with the sneering front grill, elongated, bullet-shaped headlights and hydromatic shift. Meg was kidding Ken about his sunburn, which they all referred to as a "tay-on."

Ken drew up snappily at the marquee of the Statler's Delaware entrance, and the girls and I unloaded while he parked the car. On first acquaintance with the inside of the Statler Hotel, my self-confidence began to erode. Inside the brass, revolving doors, the magnificence stunned me. Never, outside the movies, had I beheld such luxury.

Other girls, no doubt also St. Mary's Sem students, were swishing airily through the lobby on the arms of young men wearing summer formals, but looking much more poised about it than I felt.

Mary Jo and Meg spotted some classmate friends and hustled over to say hello. I was left alone in an alien and unfriendly Statler Hotel, outside the main ballroom. Gawkily self-conscious, I wondered desperately what Fred Astaire would do.

Ken Darcy bounded up the steps. "The Olds is safe asleep at the Vendome," he said breezily to me. "Where are the girls?" He sauntered over to join their group.

Youth is thoughtless, youth is cruel, but most of all, youth is inexperienced. Mary Jo and company had left me standing, and I was too stupid to tag along so I lingered, getting more rattled by the minute.

The conversation broke up, and Mary Jo rejoined me. As if to apologize for leaving me stranded, she took my arm, and we entered the ballroom. I was overwhelmed by the splendor, the mirrors, the cushioned red carpet. A band inside was imitating Artie Shaw's "Begin the Beguine."

Ken and Meg floated off on the dance floor so I took the cue. "Care to dance?" I asked uncertainly. Mary Jo smiled, and wet with the perspiration of inadequacy, I tried.

I tried, God knows, but it was nothing like Fred Astaire; it wasn't even like our kitchen. I was taking sudden, mincing, unpredictable steps. Something was going all wrong. Mary Jo was stumbling and falling. I had the feeling that people were looking at us.

The only cure was boldness. Holding with sudden firmness to my partner, I tried a flashy turn such as I had admired from Fred Astaire, and next thing I knew, Mary Jo was down on one knee.

Unable to follow such fast footwork as mine, she had tripped and half fallen. Blushing and overcome with humiliation, Mary Jo marched to one of the tables set up at the sides of the ballroom.

What a moment! An utterly crestfallen Fred Astaire, I followed. There we sat watching the passing scene, all kinds of dreams crumbled on the floor. I tried to recover the situation later, but Mary Jo refused to give my dancing a second chance. However, Ken Darcy asked her to dance, and she readily accepted his invitation. Left alone at the table with Meg Cudahy, I chewed the ashes of humiliation.

After dancing with Mary Jo, Ken returned to the ballroom table, where I had been struggling some minuscule conversion with Meg. He made the suggestion, "Let's go to the bar!"

It was all new to me, but I followed the group from the ballroom, down the foyer to the Statler bar. Dimly lit, the old Statler bar used to be a station stop several times during a dance.

Ken took orders. The girls were having something called a Pink Lady. "Bud?" Ken asked me, and only later, did I discover that I had ordered a big, round glass of Budweiser beer. We sat around a small, round table, the top fastened to a single stem leg.

Ken drank his beer with astounding haste, and I tried to keep pace. However, it was no time at all until Ken was asking "Refill?" Another big glass was placed before me.

I recall the sensation first of being very full with the quantity of beer; then I started feeling dizzy. Ken Darcy offered me a cigarette, and soon I was puffing frantically, drinking beer and trying again to feel up to the situation.

Tobacco and beer! Which contributed more to my accident, I do not know. I was puffing so eagerly that a long, fiery peak had developed on my cigarette. Then, all at once, the flaming point broke off and fell on the front on my double-breasted white coat.

Everything was happening: I was standing and trying to brush away the sparks; the white coat was glowing like an ember, and Ken got up to help me. He bumped the round table which tipped on me spilling the contents of ashes and glasses into my lap. There were Pink Ladies sloshing their cherries and orange peels all over my black pants. It was ridiculous.

After the commotion subsided and the fire had been put out, Ken showed me to the men's room and even helped to clean me off. But when we finished, there was no concealing that I was a mess. I had pants, not only wet, but sticky. My starched shirt was smudged and limp, but worst of all, a big, round, jagged burn gaped through the front of my rented, white jacket.

There are some scars, some experiences so vividly horrid that forgetfulness mercifully erases then from the memory. So thoroughly have I put away the conclusion of that first formal dance that I cannot remember the remainder of the evening. Somehow it ended.

The following Monday, I was back on the South Park streetcar with my Fifth Avenue Clothes box in my lap and one thought uppermost in my mind. With the jagged, charred hole in his white coat, Sam Schuman would vent his wrath on me. My deposit would be only a start toward the paying for the ruin I had caused.

I lugged the box heavily up Main Street, past Shelton square. Wearily I looked at the old Palace Burlesque with its animated sign of chorus girls kicking their legs skyward. I crossed Main Street at Harvey and Carey's Drug Store, and already the big golden boot of the Regal Shoe Store came into view.

Even the "Bing" sounded glum as I entered Fifth Avenue Clothes. A woman stood behind a mountain of crumbled evening clothes — coats, pants, shirts, — all in a heap.

"I damaged my summer formal." I confessed.

"Oh-oh," was all she said as she held up the scarred jacket. Then she crowed out, "Oh, Sam!"

Enter Sam in his vest and tape measures. In a glance, he grasped the extent of my crime. "Vot happened?"

SPLENDOR AT THE END OF THE LINE

FRIST PRINTED ⌒ 04 – 11 – 82

N THE 1940s, people spent a lot of time on the rails. Those were the glory days of the trains, when locomotive whistles echoed through city and countryside many times a day and night, and when every child wanted to grow up to be an engineer.

In those days, when a long trip usually meant taking the train, Buffalo's rail terminals were bustling places, filled with travelers and humming with activity. Ornate and lavishly built, they were the city's palaces.

Nowhere was the rail era's glory more apparent than in Buffalo's terminals.

I, too, spent a lot of time then on the rails and in the terminals — in fact, probably a lot more than most people. But my perspective was a bit different from the traveler's. And a good deal of my rail time was on the Buffalo trolleys.

Each day I would finish my last class at Canisius College about noon and catch a Main Street trolley to the Delaware, Lackawanna and Western Terminal at the foot of Main Street.

My job at the DL&W was to empty trucks and load their contents onto a wagon that measured 4 feet by 9 feet. After pulling the wagon to a railroad baggage car, I transferred my cargo from the wheels to the rails. I was employed by the Railway Express Agency, and by title I was a freight handler. For about two years, I worked in Buffalo's three great railroad terminals.

I was stationed for most of the time at the DL&W, and while I was there, I used to look forward to going upstairs, to the terminal's second level. The foundations were so secure that the second floor could support the massive steam engines and the trains they pulled. I often saw as many as three trains sitting "upstairs" — on the second level — at one time.

Downstairs, I worked in the grit like Cinderella. And when I pulled my loaded wagon to the creaking elevator, I knew I was ascending to a better world. After unloading, I would park my wagon and steal into the terminal. Wearing my dirty rags, I would try to forget how out-of-place I was. To step into the DL&W Terminal was to go from the scullery to the ballroom. The high ceilings soared, tiled in brown and gold. An ancient Roman would have been comfortable in that place. The lobby reminded me of some extravagant Roman effort — the Baths of Caracalla, perhaps. Even the drinking fountain, recessed in the wall, followed the classical-arch motif.

Sipping a Coke, I would watch the busy, prosperous people making their travel arrangements or taking hasty refreshments before they left for what I imagined to be exciting destinations.

When the DL&W was demolished three years ago, I read of extensive vandalism that had preceded its destruction. Someone had even systematically removed the water fountain, piece by piece. Whoever that ambitious vandal was, I congratulate him on his discriminating taste, if not on his methods of acquisition.

When times were slack at the DL&W or when there was an emergency at the Railway Express office at the Lehigh Valley, I would be sent there to help

out. The Lehigh Valley Terminal was located only a block from the DL&W, just across Main Street from Memorial Auditorium.

Like the DL&W — and so many other railroad stations built during the days of the rail barons — the Lehigh Terminal owed much to classical architecture. A gleaming white marble building, it had eight majestic columns three stories high. The Lehigh was smaller than the DL&W, but its white marble created a striking effect. Trains left from the south side of Washington Street and a broad tunnel under Washington connected the terminal with the tracks.

Crises frequently occurred at the Lehigh about 10 p.m., when the Black Diamond was ready to leave for New York City. The trouble often would involve something so crucial as a load of baked goods that had just arrived by truck and needed quick loading so the Black Diamond could leave punctually. I would trudge over with a sense of importance to the Lehigh — because the Diamond needed me. There were times, however, when I was just as needed at the DL&W.

Once, at the DL&W, a bull was being transported in a wooden crate. Animals often were shipped this way, but this bull became so upset it almost kicked its way out of its box. Several of us shoved the crate into a corner of a freight car, in effect reinforcing the collapsing sides with the walls of the steel car.

But the beast wasn't ready to quit. It continued to kick. There were two coffins nearby containing mortal remains. We irreverently shoved these against the bull's crate, trying to buttress it. Still, he kicked and raged. With unconcealed cowardice, we shut the car doors, content to leave well enough alone. Let the boys at Central Terminal, where the car was being sent, worry about the bull.

I had only one mission to the New York Central Terminal, which still stands on Paderewski Drive on Buffalo's East Side. But I often rode on baggage cars being shunted cross-city; the ride was half the fun because I had all kinds of unfamiliar views of the city as I traveled under bridges, into industrial sidings, through people's back yards.

Central Terminal dwarfed its downtown sisters. DL&W and Lehigh had eight or ten tracks each, but the Central had a tubular concourse with access to 26 tracks. Its walkway led to a square waiting room filled with long, oak benches. The sides were of a brown, shaded tile; on the ceiling were paintings of historical events on the Niagara Frontier.

What splendor lay in store for a passenger arriving in Buffalo! Passing from the waiting room to the grand concourse was unforgettable. The vaulted ceiling was vast, reminding one of a basilica. Windows near the top admitted a shadowy light. Directly below was a newsstand packed with periodicals and surrounded by people. Nearby were all kinds of stores and shops, all neat, all prosperous.

It is difficult in these days of air travel to realize that not very long ago, Buffalo's Central Terminal was the place where sophisticated travel began. It was here that beautiful people gathered, struck poses, had drinks, waved farewells. Through the Central passed the trains of railroad legend: the 20th Century Limited, the Empire State Express, the Commodore Vanderbilt.

Haughty at one of the entrances was a magnificent stuffed bison, his eyes wild, his nostrils snorting. The bison was a symbol to the traveler that Buffalo was a proud city, independent, on the move. (It now stands in the city's Museum of Science. An acceptable bronze substitute is in the Central Terminal.)

I always look back on my days as an expressman with pleasure. The era of rail travel was civilized; it was gracious. I mourn the passing of the Lehigh Valley Terminal and wish that I had snatched some shards of marble to remember it by. I had hoped a scheme might be successful to save the DL&W.

I realize that chances are faint for the Central Terminal ever again to be used for its original purpose. Yet, I heartily wish that somehow it may be spared to serve an honorable function, perhaps as the retail and banquet center its present owner envisions.

Like many Buffalonians, I regret the passing of all our city's rail transit — all except the rails and trolleys on Main Street, and these I do not need to regret because, in a way, they are returning.

We are building a new light-rail transit line, and so bringing back what was lost. The glory days of the trains are over, but once again, at least, there will be some of the romance of the rails. ∞

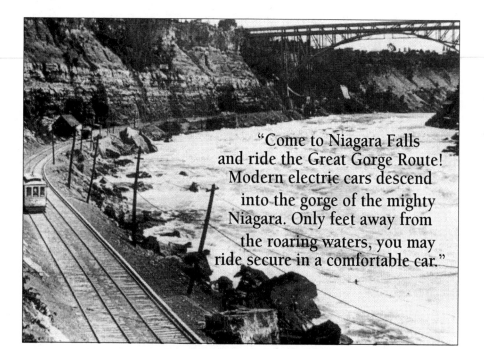

"Come to Niagara Falls and ride the Great Gorge Route! Modern electric cars descend into the gorge of the mighty Niagara. Only feet away from the roaring waters, you may ride secure in a comfortable car."

THE TROLLEY IN THE GORGE

FRIST PRINTED ∞ 02 – 17 – 86

*U*nfortunately, you can't really take this ride. The above ad ran in newspapers more than half a century ago, and the Great Gorge Route has faded into memory and fable and the archives of historians. But once people could ride in comfortable cars — open in summer, closed in winter, all the way from the American side of the Falls to Lewiston, within feet of the tumbling river.

The dream of laying trolley tracks at the foot of the Niagara Gorge was an old one long before the feat was actually accomplished. Planners had noticed a natural path paralleling the teeming Niagara as it rushed north toward Lewiston.

It was about a century ago that the Niagara Falls and Whirlpool Co. was formed based on the idea of a one-track installation from the base of Prospect Park to a point 400 feet north of the Whirlpool. There were complications over terminal locations and rights-of-way, and the company dropped the project. But great ideas do not die easily. In 1889, a Buffalonian, Capt. J.M. Brinker, bought up the franchise rights of the Whirlpool company. He hired engineers and geologists to study the feasibility of getting an electric car into the Niagara Gorge. Brinker envisioned a route from the Falls to Lewiston.

For months, engineers explored the gorge. Often they had to be lowered on ropes to test the sides of the chasm. They reported that the proposed railroad was possible but that there would be great difficulties. First, tons of rock would have to be cut or blasted to provide a descent for tracks from the city of Niagara Falls to the river's edge. Then workers would begin a long battle with nature. After all, the river's banks were filled with the results of centuries of erosion. Some rocks of immense size squatted in the center of what was to be a right-of-way.

Brinker was undaunted, and in 1890 construction began. About 800 men worked the roadbed. To save commuting time, they lived in camp sheds along the route.

Gradually, they carved out a path wide enough for two trolley tracks and strung electric wires on poles.

After five years of work, Brinker's company made the first trial runs in the late spring of 1895. Incredibly, the whole system functioned.

On July 18, 1895, amid music and ceremony, the Great Gorge Route officially opened. Two trolley cars pulling four trailers left Lewiston at 11:20 a.m. carrying 300 guests, reporters and an Italian band from Buffalo. Cameras clicked, music blared and then — maybe in an omen of troubles that would dog the gorge line — part of the forward trailer jumped the track only a short distance out of Lewiston.

A near-panic ensued. There were cries and screams as passengers struggled to get off the cars. Although the mishap was a minor one, many passengers refused to reboard, preferring to go back to Lewiston. The hardier stayed with the ride and continued to a picturesque spot near Devil's Hole where Brinker's company provided a picnic lunch.

The rest of the run went without a hitch, and passengers gave glowing descriptions of the dramatic ride they had taken.

For some reason, perhaps because of the opening-day mishap, the spectacular route did not catch on commercially for some years. The original sponsors of the Gorge Route, including Brinker, sold out their interests. The new owners, the Niagara Gorge Railway Co., had a new dream: to run a trolley-belt line on the Canadian side of the Niagara River as near to the gorge's edge as safety allowed.

They made good on the plan, and the new line crossed some superlative Canadian Parklands, affording panoramic views. On the American side, the ride was at the foot of the gorge; on the Canadian side, the ride was at the gorge's pinnacle.

The next step was obvious. What if the two routes were combined? What an unforgettable experience for anyone!

In 1899, the suspension bridge at Lewiston was reconstructed with trolley tracks in its center. The Gorge Route on the American side merged with the Canadian belt line, forming perhaps the most dramatic two-hour trolley ride in the annals of electric railroading.

After reaching the Gen. Brock monument at Queenston, cars carefully descended to the low-level suspension bridge and recrossed the lower Niagara.

The trip soon had exciting extensions, too. A passenger could transfer to a trolley to Youngstown and Fort Niagara or make a connection at Queenston for a steamer to Toronto.

There were stopover privileges so that riders could dismount, pause, picnic, observe; many honeymooners would fondly remember tender moments along the river as they waited to catch the next trolley along the world-famous Gorge Route.

Rockfalls on the tracks were a constant problem, but after the first five years of operation, the cliffs became more stable. On busy days, as many as 38 cars were operating on the line at the same time. In addition to its regular rolling stock, the Gorge Route maintained a special car to accommodate the rich, the royal and the famous. Named "the Rapids," this private car had carpeting, drapes and wicker armchairs.

The Gorge Route ran from May 1 to March 1. During the wet spring months, the trolleys had to stop because too much rock, jarred loose from thaws and refreezings, fell on the rails. It is a commentary on the Gorge Route's engineering that during 40 years of operation, no passenger was injured by falling rocks.

There were accidents, though. In 1905, an avalanche of ice tumbled onto a car, killing the motorman and injuring five passengers. Five years later, after a collision, one trolley vaulted the embankment and tumbled into the river, killing twelve.

In July 1917, after heavy rains, a length of the roadbed gave way, and a large open car carrying about 60 riders toppled down into the river. No accurate accounting of deaths from this tragedy was made since the fare register was never recovered from the turbulent riverbed.

An accident of a different nature occurred in 1913. The Niagara Falls garbage disposal plant then stood above the gorge. On one unfortunate summer day, a garbage chute broke, dumping a mighty load downward into the gorge just as — you guessed it — an open-sided trolley car loaded with tourists was grinding along. No deaths were reported, but there was considerable unhappiness.

In its heyday, about 300,000 passengers rode the sensational route every year. The round-trip fare was about a dollar.

Among the famous people who traveled the Gorge Route were the Prince of Wales, later to be King Edward VIII of England; Prince Henry of Germany, son of the ill-fated Kaiser Wilhelm II; a Spanish king and queen; and renowned actress Sarah Bernhardt.

On Sept. 6, 1901, President William McKinley climbed aboard a trolley with his wife to tour the Niagara Gorge. He got through that ride safely, but hours later he was shot at Buffalo's Pan American Exposition.

Despite its glory and worldwide reputation, the Niagara Gorge Route was expensive to maintain. Rock slid onto the tracks in spring. There were always hazards of operation and dangers to passengers. In the fall of 1935, a sudden slide deposited about 5,000 tons of rock on the roadbed. Beset by maintenance problems and overwhelmed by the expense of this latest catastrophe, the Great Gorge Route closed down forever.

Many of its famous yellow cars were ignominiously burned, and the tracks were torn up. Nature took over again in the Niagara Gorge.

After about half a century of abandonment, little remains now of the Great Gorge Route. There is still a definite pathway — wide enough in some places for a double track. But trees and vegetation have overgrown it. At Devil's Hole, you can still spot wooden ties, studded with rusting spikes. At Artpark, if you walk down the path toward the river and keep your eyes open, you can see two tracks of the Gorge Route — stretching about 10 feet.

Also at Artpark are the two pyramid-shaped pylons that used to support cables of the old Lewiston-Queenston Bridge; the bridge that carried the Gorge Route trolleys.

Those remains are not much for this exciting ride that drew presidents and kings, honeymooners and tourists speaking scores of languages. Not much to serve as reminders of "the Great Gorge Route — the Most Magnificent Route in the World." ∽

DOO-DOO-BE-DOO
IN BUFF-A-LOE

Remember the days when simple,
catchy tunes were local advertisers'
favorite medium?

FRIST PRINTED ∞ 01 – 20 – 85

*I*t's hard to pinpoint when melody was first coupled with the pitchmen's message to create the singing commercial. The huckster's singsong goes a long way back.

But it is clear that in the 1940s and '50s the art form known as the advertising jingle had a kind of heyday of cheery, naive charm. The jingles of today, slick and smoothly professional, almost deserve another name; they're often true songs, hardly distinguishable (if you're not listening carefully to the words) from the easylistening light pop they often interrupt.

But the jingles of the days of radio's golden era and the early days of television were jingles worthy of the name. They were simple ditties that assaulted the senses in a direct hard sell. They may have grated on the ears of listeners at the time, but they have a particular nostalgic charm today.

There are scores of memorable national jingles from that era, but local businesses had them, too. And the old Buffalo jingles have a special nostalgic tug now because some of them recall businesses long lost to the city.

Take department stores. Is there a Buffalonian over 40 who cannot sing the melody that went with these words?

Shop and save at Sattler's

Nine-nine-eight Broadway...

There was a far-off time when Sattler's, now gone forever after years of sad decline, was more than a simple department store. It was a gigantic bargain table to which customers battled their way for another big sale. Every week, newspapers would carry pages of screaming advertising messages like this: SATTLER'S BUYS COMPLETE INVENTORY OF HUGE MIAMI CLOTHING STORE!

337

Tables and counters down at 998 Broadway would be piled high with shoes, gloves, underwear — anything, and customers were infected with hysteria buying. There was only one Sattler's, and everybody knew where that store was because radio reverberated with the singing commercial whose words arrived at this climax:

Shop and save at Sattler's
Nine-nine-eight Broadway...In Buff-a-loe-oe,
Nine-nine-eight Broadway...Go there today!
(On Thursdays, the last line became "Open tonight!")

Back then, people didn't talk about sexy voices, but if they had, they would nave noted that the feminine Sattler's singer had one. The "in Buff-a-loe" was extended as sensuously as a long look across a singles bar.

The Sattler's music campaign was largely the work of the store's flamboyant advertising manager, Bob Cornelius. The jingles were performed by a couple from central New York named Lanny and Ginger Gray.

Another local store, Victor's, soon got into the jingles act. After all, if it worked for Sattler's, why not?

Shop at Victor's furniture department store,
With lots of bargains on every floor.
Thrifty Buffalo shoppers know,
Victor's is the place to go.
Everything for the home and everything to wear,
Are priced at terms beyond compare.
The place to shop, you'll soon agree
Is Victor's — Pearl and Genesee.

Victor's purveyed its message with a straightforward, masculine approach. Tiny Schwartz, a towering baritone who used to sing at college dances during the 1940s, put spark into the lyrics. Victor's address never attained the fame of "998," but the singing did help.

Advertising for the Big E, the old Erie County Savings Bank (now Empire of America FSA) produced a memorable singing commercial in the 1950s. Frank Loesser's hit musical *Most Happy Fella*, playing at that time in New York City, contained a song called "The Big D" (for Dallas). It was a natural for conversion to "The Big E."

Big E, little r, little i - e, Big E, Erie County Savings Bank.

In its middle section, the jingle really came alive:

So, bank at the Big E;
It's safer than a pig-gie,

And it pays you a great, big three percent.
So, bank at Big E, my, oh yes... (reprise)

Peter King, of Levy, King and White advertising, remembers making the Big E commercial. After writing the words, King approached Loesser, who made the music arrangements and directed the recording. The Big E bought performance rights from Loesser along with his services.

Subsequent versions of the "Big E" song, King says, were arranged by Skitch Henderson, bandleader of the old Steve Allen show, and were recorded in New York City.

One of the cheeriest-sounding Buffalo singing commercials hit the airwaves in the early days of television. It was the Kaufman's Rye Bread song:

I'm a jolly, little baker,
And you'll find me on the label
Of Kaufman's rye bread.

The fat, jolly baker who animated the TV screen was also a creature of Peter King. Music for this jingle was written and sung by Chuck Goldstein in New York City. Goldstein, a Buffalo native, had been a Modernaire with Glenn Miller's orchestra before he took to the jingle business, at which he was highly successful.

Beer is not brewed in Buffalo any more, but one of the last local breweries left its music behind it:

One little, two little, three little Indians
Let's relax with the Iroquois Indians.

The second line was later adapted for an early television weather show:

Let's check the weather with the Iroquois Indians.

So went the song with aggressive tom-tom accents. Iroquois had taken up the American Indian motif and plugged it hard in its ads. Its music was written by Bobby Nicholson of Channel 4 and recorded at local studios. Nicholson later went to network television in New York City, to become Clarabelle the clown on the *Howdy Doody* show.

Iroquois used to wrap up its song-commercial with a crescendo of poetic exhaltation proclaiming, "It's Iroquois Time!" An Iroquois competitor, the George F. Stein Brewery, had an equally dynamic end to its singing commercial:

With Stein's on the table, and a good song ringing clear!

For this rhapsody, male voices sounded like the Yale Glee Club pouring out their hearts in the introduction to the Whiffenpoof Song about the tables down at Morey's and the place where Louis dwells. Actually, the melody and lyrics came right from Sigmund Romberg's "The Student Prince."

Stein's Brewery also marketed a beer called Canandaigua. Herewith its singing tribute:

Canandaigua,
Canandaigua, It's better beer for you. Canandaigua,
Canandaigua, It's liquid cheer for you ...

Such claims were accompanied by a boogie-woogie beat, concluding with the invitation:

So order Canandaigua, boy,
And make mine the same!

True jingle-lovers' pulses quicken at remembrance of Wildroot Cream Oil. Wildroot was Buffalo's own hair cream, and it had a memorable singing commercial. Wildroot was a client of Batten, Barton, Durstine and Osborne Advertising Agency, and arranged to have Nat King Cole record its anthem:

You want to get Wildroot
    Cream Oil, Charlie,
It keeps your hair in trim.
It is non-al-kee-holic, Charlie, Made from soothing
Lan-o-lin.
You want to get Wildroot
    Cream Oil, Charlie,
Start usin' it today-ay...
You will have a tough time,
Charlie,
Keepin' all the girls away...(Hi ya, Baldy!)
Get Wildroot right away-ay!

The comic voice that inserted "Hi-ya, Baldy!" near the end was irresistible. Even if Wildroot made greasy kid stuff, the business should have survived just on the merits of Nat King Cole's commercial.

On River Road in Tonawanda, there was a Buffalo-owned gasoline refinery named Frontier Gas and Oil. For a time, Frontier had a chain of gas stations whose colors were light blue and white. They used to advertise on radio and on early television with music and these words:

If it's Frontier, it's the finest;
Step on the gas and see!

Gasoline turns the mind to taxicabs. This was the jingle that City Service Taxi sponsored:

For the finest taxi service in
Buffalo, Cleveland Four-Oh-Oh-Oh.

The rising "Ohs" indicated the telephone number.

The food stores have tried music. The Loblaws chain borrowed the melody of the "Arkansas Traveler" for its commercial:

Going on a Loblaws saving spree,
Lots more food for every
dime and dollar...

(In more recent times, Super Duper relied on harmony with the exhortation to: "Love that Sooo-per Duper!")

A Buffalo beverage company made a syrup in the 1930s called Queen-O. When mixed with water, it produced a sweet, chemical-tasting drink that vaguely suggested various fruit flavors. We children of the Depression thought it was wonderful. Some poet in a forgotten advertising office must have tortured his sense of the erotic to fantasize Queen-O with a singing jingle that finished up:

And here's the way to make
love stay,
Give your girl a sip of
Queen-O every day.

Community moving-picture houses were once thriving businesses. There were three major movie networks operating in the Buffalo area: Shea's, Dipson's and Basil Brothers. Aside from the Lafayette Theater downtown, Basil Brothers operated neighborhood shows like the Genesee, the Apollo and the Maxine.

So lyrical were the Basils about their successful movie empire that they had lovely female voices singing of it:

There's a Basil movie show
around the corner.
B — A — S — I — L ...
Bay — ay — azil!

It's a long way from the old-time singing commercials to those of the 1980s, but the trip back in memory can be fun.

Gentle or brash, appealing or obnoxious, singing commercials have added flavor to life in Buffalo. And in the process, they've become a part of its history. ∽

CHANCE
ENCOUNTERS

FRIST PRINTED ∞ 02 – 12 – 95

*T*he first words we spoke on the day my wife and I met were not whispered, not romantic. We exchanged no flirtatious glances; in fact, that opening dialogue assumed the form of a stilted question and answer.

"Did you look for work last week?" my bride-to-be asked demandingly of the stranger before her.

"Yes," was my humble response.

As if not content with this abjectness, my future life partner pursued the matter aggressively: "Did you refuse any jobs?"

Without realizing that this was a defining moment, I shook my head. "No," I said truthfully.

Years later, when our children — especially the girls — were little, they made me repeat this tale endlessly. "Tell us about how you and Mom met," they pleaded.

I would resist because I felt that the story had grown stale and because it required explanations that were distracting to the plot line. I had to use terms beyond children's ken: laid off, bankruptcy, receivership, unemployment insurance, reporting time. I feared that I might raise a family haunted by ghosts of labor law.

"Please tell us again," Mary begged, and what father could refuse her big, tender eyes?

I began the familiar narrative. "Many years ago, I worked for a company called the International Railway Company..." And I was off.

The IRC, as we called the predecessor to Metro Transit, operated all city bus and streetcar lines. My job, as a service representative, was to write and circulate news releases involving route or schedule changes; I also answered letters of complaint, of which I received an abundance.

During the era I worked there, the IRC, with impossibly tangled finances, sank into bankruptcy. Legally appointed receivers set about company reorganization and, in the process, eliminated many jobs, my own among them.

Here I explained to my children that I was paid $26 per week, the going

343

stipend then for the unemployed. I had to report to the insurance office on Franklin Street every Tuesday at 8:30 a.m.

"I would wait in a long line to be interviewed and to sign for my next insurance check. One week, I noticed a very pretty, dark-haired girl at the line's end taking charge of us claimants."

"That was Mama!" middle daughter Katie piped in.

I nodded and detailed our initial conversation. I told of signing the voucher and leaving the office. At this point, my audience looked distressed: Was this the end? Might I never again see the pretty woman? What would become of them?

Several weeks passed, and early winter saw the breakout of a nationwide steel strike. Local unemployment insurance stations swelled with claimants from Bethlehem Steel, one of the area's largest employers. Swamped with applicants, the state insurance office needed help.

In the midst of this crisis, I reported one morning to sign for my check — only to discover that I was no longer unemployed. I had been drafted to process new claims, and during my training, I was placed under the supervision of the pretty, dark-haired woman who had recently interviewed me. We remembered each other.

The children's faces perked up; perhaps it gave them a satisfaction to infer how circumstances were converging to give them identity. Thus, indeed, we are all strangely products of the small whims and chances that brought our parents together.

"Is that the end?" little daughter Margie asked.

I sighed. "Not quite. Your mother and I would talk on our breaks and one day, I asked her to have lunch with me." At Coffee Shop Corner, corner of Franklin and Eagle, we sat opposite one another over an excellent luncheon. I looked across the tiny table at my companion, and I had a curious thought: "This might be the girl for me."

She was — still is.

Only recently New York State has closed its office at 200 Franklin St., where my wife and I met. The building has since been razed and the site cleared for a parking lot. Whether the site will hold a new structure or remain a parking lot, the corner will always maintain a special significance for us — and our children. ∞